Limited Company Accounts

Tutorial

NVQ Accounting Unit 11

David Cox

Douglas Meikle

Derek Street

osborne
BOOKS

Published by Osborne Books Limited
Unit 1B Everoak Estate
Bromyard Road
Worcester WR2 5HP
Tel 01905 748071
Email books@osbornebooks.co.uk
Website www.osbornebooks.co.uk

Cover and page design by Richard Holt

Printed by the Bath Press, Bath

British Library Cataloguing in Publication Data
A catalogue record for this book is available from the British Library

ISBN 1 872962 96 3

Contents

Acknowledgements

The authors wish to thank the following for their help with the editing and production of the book: Jean Cox, Michael Fardon, Michael Gilbert, Rosemarie Griffiths, Claire McCarthy, Jon Moore and Liz Smith. Particular thanks go to Roger Petheram of Worcester College of Technology for reading the text, commenting upon it, checking answers, and always being prepared to discuss any aspect of the book.

Thanks are also due to the Association of Accounting Technicians for their generous help and advice and permission to reproduce extracts from past examination questions and the Standards of Competence. Thanks also go to Interbrew SA and to Tesco PLC for permission to reproduce extracts from their Report and Accounts, and to the Accounting Standards Board for permission to reproduce extracts from their accounting standards.

Authors

David Cox, the lead author of this text, has had more than twenty years' experience teaching accountancy students over a wide range of levels. Formerly with the Management and Professional Studies Department at Worcester College of Technology, he now lectures on a freelance basis and carries out educational consultancy work in accountancy studies. He is author and joint author of a number of textbooks in the areas of accounting, finance and banking.

Douglas Meikle, who has contributed the chapter on International Accounting Standards, is a Chartered Management Accountant with over twelve years experience as an Accounting lecturer at York College, where he is the AAT course leader. He has also taught accounting and finance on a wide range of professional, management and business studies courses.

Derek Street, who has compiled a number of the Student Activities, has had over fifteen years' experience of teaching accountancy students, including the AAT qualification at all three levels. His lecturing experience has been gained at Evesham College of FE, Gloucester College of Arts and Technology (GLOSCAT) and North East Worcestershire College where he is currently Head of Department, Professional Studies.

Introduction

Limited Company Accounts Tutorial has been written to provide a study resource for students taking courses based on the NVQ Level 4 Accounting Unit 11 'Drafting Financial Statements (Accounting Practice, Industry and Commerce)'.

Limited Company Accounts Tutorial commences with the purpose of financial statements (including a study of key aspects of 'Statement of principles for financial reporting'). It then develops the preparation and presentation of final accounts of limited companies – including the use of cash flow statements. The impact of accounting standards on financial statements is considered in detail. The text includes the interpretation of accounts using accounting ratios, and the preparation of consolidated accounts for groups of companies.

An important development in accounting is the European Union regulation that requires all EU companies listed on a regulated market (eg stock market) to prepare their consolidated accounts in accordance with International Accounting Standards from 1 January 2005 at the latest. Chapter 9 gives an overview of the principal International Accounting Standards and shows an example of accounts prepared using these standards.

using the tutorial

Limited Company Accounts Tutorial provides the student with the theoretical background to the subject while at the same time including plenty of opportunity to put theory into practice. The chapters of *Limited Company Accounts Tutorial* contain:

- a clear text with worked examples and case studies
- a chapter summary and key terms to help with revision
- student activities – with answers at the end of the book

The tutorial text – with questions and answers – is therefore useful for classroom use and also for distance learning students.

the workbook and tutor pack

Limited Company Accounts Workbook, the companion volume to this text, contains extended student activities and practice examination tasks. The answers to these tasks are included in a separate Tutor Pack.

If you would like a copy of any of our texts, please telephone Osborne Books Sales Office on 01905 748071 for details of how to order, or visit the Osborne online 24 hour shop on www.osbornebooks.co.uk where you can purchase the workbook and obtain an order form for the Tutor Pack.

Web directory

There are a number of websites which will help to supplement your studies for Unit 11, *Drafting Financial Statements.*

information and accountancy news

www.accountancyage.com
- news and information service
- regular newsletter

www.accountingtechnician.co.uk
- website of AAT's magazine
- a Study Zone with articles written exclusively for the web
- question and answer surgery
- past AAT questions
- archive of magazine articles

www.accountingweb.co.uk
- news and information
- includes a students' discussion forum

www.asb.org.uk
- the Accounting Standards Board
- gives details of accounting standards and current projects
- includes a student section
- links to related sites, including the Financial Reporting Council and the Financial Reporting Review Panel

www.companieshouse.gov.uk
- gives information about forming and running companies
- provides details of how to obtain copies of company accounts and other statutory information

www.dti.gov.uk
- Department of Trade and Industry
- a large webside with links to various sections of the Department

www.hmso.gov.uk
- access to statutory instruments affecting the preparation of company accounts

www.iasb.org.uk
- the International Accounting Standards Board
- gives a summary of international accounting standards

accountancy associations

A selection of accountancy bodies and associations is given below, with their website addresses. As well as details of members' and students' services, they give information on assessment and examination schemes. Some sites also provide a news and information service.

www.aat.co.uk   – The Association of Accounting Technicians
                            (see also www.aatstudent.co.uk)

www.acca.org.uk   – The Association of Chartered Certified Accountants

www.cima.org.uk   – The Chartered Institute of Management Accountants

www.cipfa.org.uk   – The Chartered Institute of Public Finance Accountants

www.icaew.co.uk   – The Institute of Chartered Accountants in England and
                            Wales

www.icas.org.uk   – The Institute of Chartered Accountants of Scotland

firms of accountants

A selection of accountancy firms is given below. As well as advertising the firms and their services, a number of sites include technical information and notes on recent developments in accounting.

www.deloitte.co.uk   – Deloitte & Touche

www.ey.com   – Ernst & Young

www.grant-thornton.co.uk – Grant Thornton

www.kpmg.co.uk   – KPMG

www.pwcglobal.com   – PricewaterhouseCoopers

www.osbornebooks.co.uk – additional study material

The Osborne Books website www.osbornebooks.co.uk will be used to give information about changes and updating of the topics covered in this book.

Please note that if you have not studied the financial statements of sole traders and partnerships, or would like to revise them, explanatory material and questions may be downloaded from the Student Resources section of www.osbornebooks.co.uk

this chapter covers . . .

Technician Level Unit 11 'Drafting Financial Statements (Accounting Practice, Industry and Commerce)' builds on earlier studies of financial accounting at Intermediate Level. Unit 11 comprises two elements:

- *draft limited company financial statements*
- *interpret limited company financial statements*

In this chapter we begin our studies by considering the

- *general purpose of financial statements*
- *elements of financial statements*
- *accounting equation*
- *development of the regulatory framework of accounting*
- *Statement of Principles for Financial Reporting*
- *accounting concepts*

Note

If you have not studied the financial statements of sole traders and partnerships, or would like to revise them, explanatory material and questions may be downloaded from the Student Resources section of www.osbornebooks.co.uk

NVQ PERFORMANCE CRITERIA COVERED

unit 11: DRAFTING FINANCIAL STATEMENTS

element 11.2

interpret limited company financial statements

A   *identify the general purpose of financial statements used in limited companies*

B   *identify the elements of financial statements used in limited companies*

INTRODUCTION TO *DRAFTING FINANCIAL STATEMENTS*

Technician level Unit 11 of NVQ Accounting *Drafting Financial Statements* is concerned solely with the financial statements of limited companies. It comprises two elements:

- Element 11.1 Draft limited company financial statements
- Element 11.2 Interpret limited company financial statements

For most students, this is the first time that you will have studied the accounts of limited companies. It is appropriate, therefore, to put limited companies in context. In previous studies you will have prepared the financial statements of sole traders and will then have moved on to the accounts of partnerships. The transition from sole trader to partnership financial statements is not too big a step with, instead of one person owning the business, two or more owners. The step from sole traders/partnerships to limited companies is rather greater as we deal with incorporated – ie formed into a corporation (company) – businesses, where the owners are members (shareholders) of the company.

private sector organisations

Companies – together with sole traders and partnerships – are private sector (as compared with public sector organisations – such as local authorities, central government, the National Health Service – and other not-for-profit organisations – such as societies and charities). The following diagram illustrates the types of private sector organisations:

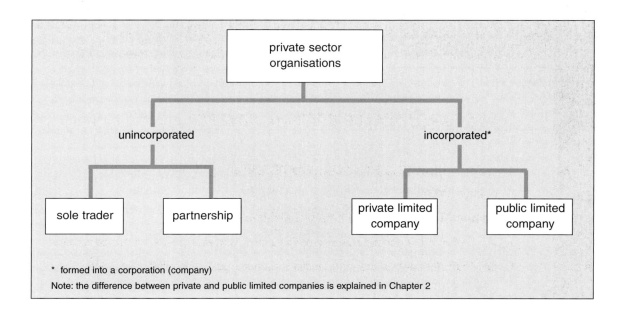

* formed into a corporation (company)

Note: the difference between private and public limited companies is explained in Chapter 2

sole traders, partnerships and limited companies

Limited companies are more complex businesses to set up and to run. Chapter 2 explains the advantages of forming a company, the difference between private and public limited companies, and the types of shares issued. Chapter 3 covers limited company published accounts – which are available to shareholders and are filed at Companies House. The following diagram illustrates the key differences between sole traders, partnerships and limited companies:

	sole trader	*partnership*	*limited company*
ownership	• owned by the sole trader	• owned by the partners	• owned by the shareholders
legal status	• the sole trader is the business	• the partners are the business	• separate legal entity from its owners
members	• one	• between 2 and 20 (normal maximum)	• minimum of one shareholder; no maximum
liability	• unlimited liability, for debts of business	• partners normally liable for entire partnership debt	• shareholders can only lose their investment
legislation	• none	• Partnership Act 1890	• Companies Act 1985, 1989
regulation	• none	• written or oral partnership agreement	• Memorandum and Articles of Association
management	• owner takes all decisions	• all partners normally take an active part	• directors and authorised employees
financial statements	• private – not available to the public	• private – not available to the public	• must be filed at Companies House where available to the public

In particular, note from the diagram that:

- the Companies Act 1985, as amended by the Companies Act 1989, regulates the setting up and running of limited companies
- a company is a separate legal entity from its shareholder owners
- companies are managed by directors who are themselves shareholders
- companies – unlike sole traders and partnerships – must file their annual financial statements with Companies House, where they are available for public inspection

LIMITED COMPANIES

A walk or a drive around any medium-sized town will reveal evidence of a wide variety of businesses formed as limited companies – banks, shops, restaurants, hotels, bus and train operators, delivery firms. Many of their names will be well-known – HSBC Bank plc, Tesco PLC, Marks and Spencer plc, etc – and to be found in most towns and cities; others will be known only in their own area – Wyvern Wool Shop Limited, Don's DIY Limited, etc. The letters 'plc' stand for public limited company – this can be a large company whose shares might (but not always) be traded on the stock markets. The word 'limited' refers to a private limited company – often a smaller company than a plc, but whose shares are not quoted on the stock markets. In fact there are far more private limited companies than there are plcs. In Chapter 2, we will look further into the differences between the types of companies.

Virtually all limited companies can be described as being in the *private sector* where they are owned by shareholders who are looking for the company to make profits. A small number of limited companies are set up by not-for-profit organisations – such as societies and charities – to provide mutual services for their members and the community.

objectives of companies

For most limited companies the profit motive is commonly the most important objective. Profit is measured as the excess of income over expenditure; sufficient profit needs to be generated each year to enable the owners (shareholders) to be paid dividends. Often there is a conflict within business between short-term profit and long-term profit: for example, a major investment in training will reduce this year's profit, but may well help to increase profit in future years. Once the profit motive has been satisfied, and particularly as a company increases in size, a range of other objectives is developed: examples include environmental issues – taking initiatives to improve the environment through becoming more energy efficient and reducing waste – and being a good employer – adding value to the output by providing better facilities and better training for the workforce.

FINANCIAL STATEMENTS AND THEIR PURPOSES

financial statements

The two main financial statements used by limited companies are:

- an **income statement** (for example: profit and loss account), which measures the financial performance of the company for a particular time period (the accounting period)
- a **balance sheet**, which provides a statement of the financial position of the company at a particular date

Income statements usually cover a twelve-month time period (but do not necessarily run to 31 December – the end of the calendar year); the balance sheet shows the financial position of the company at the end of the accounting period.

objective of financial statements

What is the principal objective of financial statements?

'The objective of financial statements is to provide information about the reporting entity's financial performance and financial position that is useful to a wide range of users for assessing the stewardship of the entity's management and for making economic decisions'

This quotation is taken from *Statement of principles for financial reporting* issued by the Accounting Standards Board (see page 21).

Note the following from this definition:

- **entity** – an organisation, eg a limited company, whose activities and resources are kept separate from those of the owner(s)
- **financial performance** – is reported through an income statement
- **financial position** – is reported through a balance sheet
- **wide range of users** – financial statements are used by a number of interested parties (see below), from existing and potential shareholders through to lenders, employees and government agencies
- **stewardship** – the entity's management is accountable for the safe-keeping of the organisation's resources and for their proper, efficient and profitable use; the financial statements enable users to assess the effectiveness of management in this role
- **economic decisions** – information from the financial statements is used to help in making decisions about investment or potential investment in the entity, eg to buy or sell a company's shares, to make a loan to the company, or to help in deciding whether to supply goods or services

users of financial statements

There is a wide variety of users – both internal and external – of financial statements of limited companies, as shown by the table on page 14.

Internal users include company directors and managers, employees.

External users include existing and potential shareholders, lenders, government agencies, the public, etc.

Each user is interested in a number of different aspects, as the diagram on the next page shows.

contents of the financial statements

As financial statements are the principal means of communicating accounting information to users they must provide details of:

financial performance

- they assess the stewardship of management
- they make possible an assessment of the effectiveness of the use of the company's resources in achieving its objectives, eg in profitability
- they allow comparison to be made with the financial performance from previous accounting periods

financial position

- they provide information about the economic resources used by the company
- they provide information about the liquidity, efficient use of resources, and financial position of the company

ELEMENTS OF FINANCIAL STATEMENTS

Elements of financial statements are the building blocks from which financial statements are constructed – that is, they are the classes of items which comprise financial statements.

The elements of financial statements are as follows:
- assets
- liabilities
- ownership interest
- income
- expenditure
- contributions from owners
- distributions to owners
- gains
- losses

FINANCIAL STATEMENTS: LIMITED COMPANIES

Who is interested?	What are they interested in?	Why are they interested?
Existing and potential investors in a business	• Is the company making a profit? • Can the company pay its way? • What was the sales (turnover) figure?	• To assess the performance of management • To see how much money can be paid in dividends • To see if the company will continue in the foreseeable future • To see if the company is expanding or declining
Lenders	• Has the company made a profit? • What amount is currently loaned? • What is the value of the assets?	• To check if the company will be able to pay interest and make loan repayments • To assess how far the lender is financing the company • To assess the value of security available to the lender
Suppliers and creditors	• Can the company pay its way? • What is the value of the assets?	• To decide whether to supply goods and services to the company • To assess if the company is able to pay its debts
Employees and trade unions	• Has the company made a profit? • Can the company pay its way?	• To assess whether the company is able to pay wages and salaries • To consider the stability of the company in offering employment opportunities in the future
Customers	• Is the company profitable? • What is the value of the assets? • Can the company pay its way?	• To see if the company will continue to supply its products or services • To assess the ability of the company to meet warranty liabilities, and provision of spare parts
Governments and government agencies	• Has the company made a profit? • What was the sales (turnover) figure?	• To calculate the tax due • To ensure that the company is registered for VAT and completes VAT returns on time • To provide a basis for government regulation and statistics • To see how grants provided have been spent
The public	• Is the company profitable? • Can the company pay its way?	• To assess employment prospects • To assess the contribution to the economy
Managers	• Is the company making a profit? • Can the company pay its way? • How efficiently is the company using its resources?	• To see if the company is expanding or declining • To see if the company will continue in the foreseeable future • To examine the efficiency of the company and to make comparisons with other, similar, companies

The way in which the elements link together in the financial statements of income statement and balance sheet, together with definitions, are shown in the diagrams on the next page.

importance of elements of financial statements

The importance of the elements of financial statements is that they define the items which can be included in financial statements. The elements are appropriate for the financial statements of limited companies:

- a profit and loss account to show gains or losses for the accounting period
- a balance sheet to show assets, liabilities and ownership interest at a particular date

THE ACCOUNTING EQUATION

The accounting equation underlies the balance sheet of a limited company and relates to the following elements:

$$\text{assets } minus \text{ liabilities } equals \text{ ownership interest}$$

Ownership interest increases with

- gains from the income statement
- gains from non-revenue items, eg upwards revaluation of assets
- contributions from the owners (shareholders)

Ownership interest decreases with

- losses from the income statement
- loss from non-revenue items, eg downwards revaluation of assets
- distributions to owners (shareholders)

In the balance sheet of a limited company, the ownership interest is represented by the share capital and reserves of the company. The profit and loss account links directly to the balance sheet where profits are added to, or losses are deducted from, the capital – thus the profit and loss account explains how the change in capital came about, together with any changes in capital made by the owners – capital introduced or repaid. Some non-revenue gains or losses are reported separately from profit and loss account – a statement of total recognised gains and losses (see page 61) is used.

To summarise, ownership interest is represented by:

- capital from owners (shareholders)
- profit or loss from profit and loss account
- other gains or losses

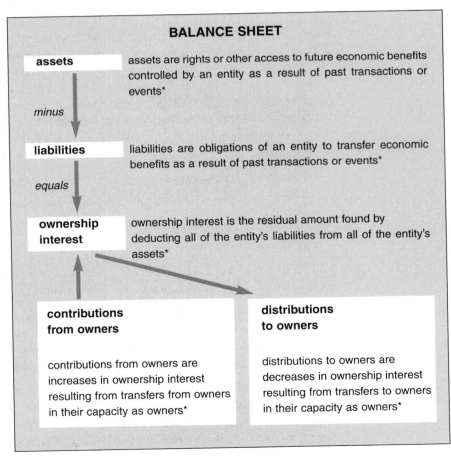

INCOME STATEMENT

income

minus

expenditure

equals

gains or losses

income incorporates all forms of income and revenues

expenditure incorporates all forms of expenses, sometimes referred to as revenue expenditure

gains are increases in ownership interest not resulting from contributions from owners*

losses are decreases in ownership interest not resulting from contributions from owners*

Note: gains and losses also incorporate gains and losses arising from non-revenue items, such as the disposal of fixed assets and the revaluation of assets and liabilities

BALANCE SHEET

assets

minus

liabilities

equals

ownership interest

assets are rights or other access to future economic benefits controlled by an entity as a result of past transactions or events*

liabilities are obligations of an entity to transfer economic benefits as a result of past transactions or events*

ownership interest is the residual amount found by deducting all of the entity's liabilities from all of the entity's assets*

contributions from owners

contributions from owners are increases in ownership interest resulting from transfers from owners in their capacity as owners*

distributions to owners

distributions to owners are decreases in ownership interest resulting from transfers to owners in their capacity as owners*

* definitions taken from *Statement of principles for financial reporting* – see page 21.

THE REGULATORY FRAMEWORK OF ACCOUNTING

The regulatory framework forms the 'rules' of accounting. When drafting company financial statements, accountants seek to follow the same set of rules – thus enabling broad comparisons to be made between the financial results of different companies.

The regulatory framework comprises

* accounting standards (in the form of Statements of Standard Accounting Practice, and Financial Reporting Standards)

* company law

* Statement of principles for financial reporting

Collectively, this regulatory framework is often referred to as 'UK GAAP', ie the United Kingdom's Generally Accepted Accounting Practice. For companies quoted on the Stock Exchange, UK GAAP will also include the Stock Exchange's *Listing Regulations*.

An important development over the next few years is the European Union (EU) regulation that requires all companies listed on a regulated market (eg stock market) to prepare their consolidated accounts in accordance with International Accounting Standards from 1 January 2005 at the latest. Member states of the EU have the option of extending this regulation to apply to all company accounts – listed and unlisted companies, unitary and consolidated accounts. Chapter 9 (page 276) gives more information on international accounting standards.

The diagram on the next page shows how the UK regulatory framework has developed during the last thirty or forty years.

accounting standards

Since 1971 a number of accounting standards have been produced to provide a framework for accounting and to reduce the variety of accounting treatments which companies may use in their financial statements.

Statements of Standard Accounting Practice (SSAPs) were issued by the Accounting Standards Committee (replaced by the Accounting Standards Board in 1990) between 1971 and 1990. Twenty-five standards were issued – over half of these have now been withdrawn and replaced by Financial Reporting Standards.

Financial Reporting Standards (FRSs) have been issued by the Accounting Standards Board (ASB) since 1991. A list of current FRSs, at the time of writing, is shown on pages 95-96. The ASB's aim has been to develop standards that are consistent with one another and to reduce the number of options allowed in the preparation of financial statements.

International Financial Reporting Standards (IFRSs) have been developed by the International Accounting Standards Board (formerly the International Accounting Standards Committee) with the aim of harmonising international financial reporting. From 1 January 2005 at the latest, all EU listed companies are required to prepare their consolidated accounts in accordance with International Accounting Standards. An overview of the principal international standards is given in Chapter 9, together with an example of accounts prepared using these standards.

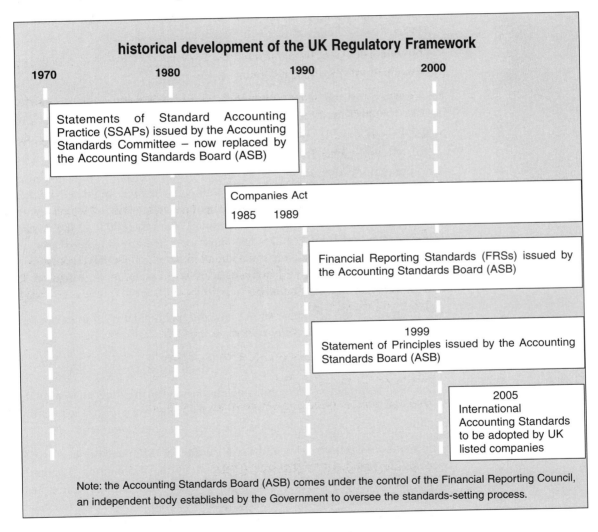

historical development of the UK Regulatory Framework

1970   **1980**   **1990**   **2000**

Statements of Standard Accounting Practice (SSAPs) issued by the Accounting Standards Committee – now replaced by the Accounting Standards Board (ASB)

Companies Act

1985   1989

Financial Reporting Standards (FRSs) issued by the Accounting Standards Board (ASB)

1999
Statement of Principles issued by the Accounting Standards Board (ASB)

2005
International Accounting Standards to be adopted by UK listed companies

Note: the Accounting Standards Board (ASB) comes under the control of the Financial Reporting Council, an independent body established by the Government to oversee the standards-setting process.

Company Law

The Companies Act 1985 (as amended by the Companies Act 1989) states the detailed accounting requirements that must be shown when preparing the financial statements of limited companies (see Chapter 3).

In particular, the 1989 Act introduced a requirement that company accounts must state that they have been prepared in accordance with applicable accounting standards and, if there have been any material departures, must give details and the reasons for such departures.

Statement of Principles for Financial Reporting

Although not an accounting standard, Statement of Principles has been developed by the Accounting Standards Board to set out the principles that should underlie the preparation and presentation of financial statements. It is designed to:

- provide a coherent frame of reference to be used in the development and review of accounting standards

- reduce the need to debate fundamental issues when accounting standards are developed or revised

- help preparers and auditors of accounts to analyse issues not covered by accounting standards

Financial Reporting Standard for Smaller Entities (FRSSE)

FRSSE has been developed for small companies and, generally, it provides a simplified version of the requirements from other accounting standards. It also allows for some disclosure requirements required by accounting standards to be excluded.

A small company satisfies two or more of the following criteria:

- turnover (sales) does not exceed £5.6m per year

- assets do not exceed £2.8m

- average number of employees does not exceed 50

THE STANDARD-SETTING PROCESS

In later chapters we will focus on the use of accounting standards – both Statements of Standard Accounting Practice (SSAPs) and Financial Reporting Standards (FRSs). Here we will look in more detail at the regulatory structure for the setting of accounting standards in the UK. The structure is shown in the diagram on the next page.

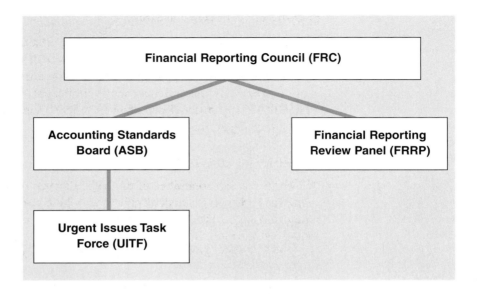

Financial Reporting Council

The role of the FRC is to promote good accounting and to give advice to government on improvements to accounting legislation. The Council has two subsidiaries – the Accounting Standards Board and the Financial Reporting Review Panel (FRRP) – to which it provides support and broad policy guidance. The FRC is funded in equal thirds by the Government, accounting firms, and companies.

Accounting Standards Board

The ASB was set up in 1990 to develop, issue and withdraw accounting standards. The aims of the Board are to establish and improve standards of financial accounting and reporting, for the benefit of users, preparers, and conductors of financial information.

accounting standards – the development process

The SSAPs which were current in 1990 at the time of the formation of the ASB were adopted by the Board. (The SSAPs had been developed between 1971 and 1990 by the ASB's predecessor, the Accounting Standards Committee.) Since 1990 a number of SSAPs have been replaced by FRSs.

The procedure for developing new standards is that appropriate topics are identified by the Board from either its own research or submissions made by interested parties. A discussion paper and consultation process then follows which may lead to the publication of a Financial Reporting Exposure Draft (FRED). A wider consultation process now takes place, with views being taken into account, before the FRED is issued as an FRS by the board.

authority of accounting standards

Although not laws in themselves, accounting standards are defined in the Companies Act 1989. The Act requires directors of companies – other than small or medium-sized companies – to disclose whether the accounts have been prepared in accordance with applicable accounting standards, particulars of any material departure from those standards, and the reasons for any such departure.

Urgent Issues Task Force

The UITF is a sub-committee of the ASB. Its main role is to assist the ASB where an accounting standard exists but where conflicting interpretations have developed. UITF seeks a consensus as to the accounting treatment that should be adopted. Once a consensus is reached, an 'Abstract' is issued, which then applies in the preparation of financial statements.

Financial Reporting Review Panel

The FRRP enquires into annual accounts of companies where there are apparent departures from the accounting requirements of the Companies Act and accounting standards. When necessary, the FRRP can seek an agreement to revise the accounts and, failing agreement, can seek an order from the court to compel revision.

Tutorial note The UK Government is currently changing the way in which the accountancy profession is regulated. Developments include the creation of a single authoritative regulator with responsibility for setting accounting standards and overseeing the regulatory functions of the accountancy bodies. Keep up-to-date by checking out the websites listed in the Web Directory (pages 6 to 7).

STATEMENT OF PRINCIPLES FOR FINANCIAL REPORTING

As we have seen earlier, Statement of Principles sets out the principles that should underlie the preparation and presentation of financial statements. It comprises eight chapters, each dealing with key issues:

1 The objective of financial statements

2 The reporting entity

3 The qualitative characteristics of financial information

4 The elements of financial statements

5 Recognition in financial statements

6 Measurement in financial statements

7 Presentation of financial information

8 Accounting for interests in other entities

For Technician Level Unit 11 the most relevant chapters are 1 to 5, and 7.

Chapter 1 **The objective of financial statements**

As we saw earlier (page 12), the objective of financial statements is *'to provide information about the reporting entity's financial performance and financial position that is useful to a wide range of users for assessing the stewardship of the entity's management and for making economic decisions'.*

Users of financial statements are:

- present and potential investors
- lenders
- suppliers and other trade creditors
- employees
- customers
- governments and their agencies
- the public

Of these users, Statement of Principles sees investors as being the primary group for whom the financial statements are prepared.

Information for users is to be provided in four areas:

1 **financial performance** – the return (from profit and loss account) an entity obtains from the resources it controls

2 **financial position** – as shown by the balance sheet, including

- the economic resources (ie assets and liabilities) controlled by an entity
- the financial structure (ie capital gearing)
- liquidity and solvency
- capacity to adapt to changes

3 **generation and use of cash** – information from the cash flow statement to show the cash from operations, investment activities and financial activities

4 **financial adaptability** – the ability of an entity to take effective action to alter the amount and timing of its cash flows, including the ability to

- raise new capital
- repay capital or debt
- sell assets (without disrupting continuing operations)
- rapidly improve cash inflows from operations

Chapter 2   The reporting entity

- an entity should prepare and publish financial statements
  - when there is a legitimate demand for the information
  - when it is a cohesive economic unit
- what activities to include
  - those activities that are under the direct or indirect control of the entity

Chapter 3   Qualitative characteristics of financial information

Four characteristics are identified by Statement of Principles:

1 relevance
2 reliability   these relate to the content of information

3 comparability
4 understandability   these relate to the presentation of information

The diagram below shows these characteristics:

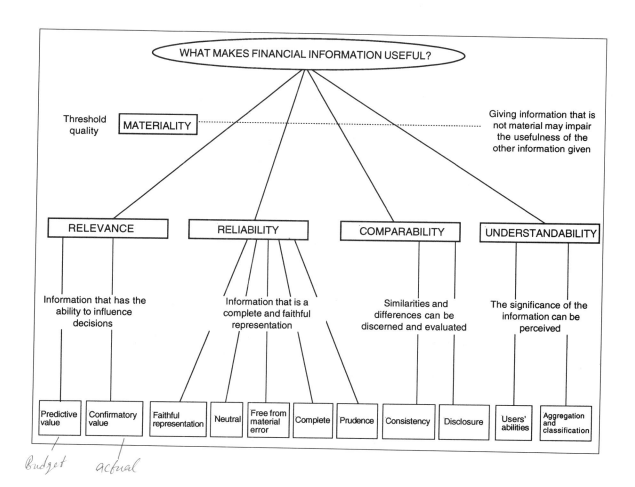

relevant information

The diagram shows that, for information to be *relevant* it must have:

- the ability to influence the economic decisions of users
- predictive value, which helps users to evaluate or assess past, present or future events
- confirmatory value, which helps users to confirm their past evaluations

reliable information

For information to be *reliable* it must be:

- a faithful representation, ie it corresponds to the effect of transactions or events
- neutral, ie it is free from deliberate or systematic bias
- free from material error, ie it is accurately recorded and reported
- complete, within the bounds of materiality
- prudent, ie a degree of caution has been applied when making judgements and estimates

comparability

Comparability enables other financial statements for the entity from other time periods to be compared so as to identify trends. It incorporates:

- consistency, ie the same accounting techniques have been used throughout the entity both within the same accounting period and also from one period to the next
- disclosure of accounting policies used in the preparation of the financial statements

understandability

Understandability means that the users of financial statements should be able to perceive the significance of the information.

materiality

This chapter of Statement of Principles also incorporates the test of *materiality*. Although materiality is rarely defined in law or accounting standards, the preparer of financial statements must make judgements as to whether or not an item is material. As Statement of Principles says: 'An item of information is material to the financial statements if its misstatement or omission might reasonably be expected to influence the economic decisions of users of those financial statements, including their assessments of management's stewardship'. It goes on to say: 'Whether information is material will depend on the size and nature of the item in question judged in the particular circumstances of the case'. Thus materiality depends very much on the size of the business: a large company may consider that items of less than £1,000 are not material; a small company will use a much lower figure. What is material, and what is not, becomes a matter of judgement, based on the overall usefulness of the financial information.

Chapter 4   The elements of financial statements

Elements of financial statements are the classes of items that financial statements comprise. The elements are listed as being:

- assets
- liabilities
- ownership interest
- gains
- losses
- contributions from owners
- distributions to owners

Statement of Principles gives a definition of each element and these have already been given earlier in this Chapter (page 12).

Chapter 5   Recognition in financial statements

The term 'recognition' means the recording in financial statements of transactions or events, eg bought vehicles for £20,000, paying by cheque; bought a stock of goods for resale £2,000 on credit; sold goods for cash £250.

There are three stages in the recognition process:

- **initial recognition**, which is where an item is recorded in the financial statements for the first time, eg bought vehicles for £20,000
- **subsequent remeasurement**, which involves changing the amount at which an already recognised asset or liability is stated in the financial statements, eg depreciation on vehicles for the year £5,000
- **derecognition**, which is where an item that has previously been recognised ceases to be recognised, eg sold vehicles for £15,000

Statement of Principles acknowledges that there are often areas of uncertainty in the recognition process – for example, in a manufacturing company, there may be uncertainty as to the point at which raw materials stock becomes work-in-progress, and again as to the point at which work-in-progress becomes finished goods. The Statement indicates that the effect of a transaction to create a new asset or liability, or add to an existing asset or liability, will be recognised if:

- sufficient evidence exists that the new asset or liability has been created or that there has been an addition to an existing asset or liability; and

- the new asset or liability or the addition to the existing asset or liability can be measured at a monetary amount with sufficient reliability

Statement of Principles acknowledges that entities operate in an uncertain business environment which can lead to uncertainty in the recognition process:

- **element uncertainty**
  - does the item exist?
  - does it meet the definitions of the elements of financial statements?
- **measurement uncertainty**
  - at what money amount should the item be recognised?

Uncertainty in the recognition process also requires the exercise of **prudence**. In particular, there needs to be stronger evidence of existence, and a greater reliability of measurement, for assets and gains when compared with liabilities and losses. However, the exercise of prudence must not lead to the omission or understatement of assets and gains, nor the deliberate overstatement of liabilities and losses.

Chapter 7   Presentation of financial information

This chapter of Statement of Principles is concerned with the good presentation of financial information so that the essential messages of the financial statements are communicated clearly and effectively and in as simple and straightforward a manner as possible.

The term 'financial statements' comprises the primary financial statements – financial performance (profit and loss account or income statement), balance sheet, and cash flow statement – together with supporting notes that amplify and explain the statements.

Statement of financial performance

Good presentation of profit and loss account (or income statement) involves:

- recognising only gains or losses
- classifying the components of the statement by function (eg production, selling, administrative) and by nature (eg employment costs, interest payable)
- identifying separately amounts that are affected by changes in economic conditions or business activity (eg from continuing and discontinued activities of the business; from geographical areas)
- identifying separately
  - items of an unusual amount
  - special items such as interest payable and taxation
  - items that relate mainly to future profits, eg research and development expenditure

Balance sheet

Good presentation of balance sheet involves:

- recognising only assets, liabilities and ownership interest
- classifying assets to help users to assess the nature, amounts and liquidity of available resources
- classifying liabilities to help users to assess the nature, amounts and timing of obligations
- classifying assets by function, eg fixed assets; current assets

Cash flow statement

Good presentation involves showing the extent to which the company's activities generate and use cash. In particular, a distinction needs to be made between cash flows from operations (eg from selling products), and from other activities (eg purchase or sale of fixed assets).

Accompanying information

This is information which accompanies and complements the financial statements, but which does not form part of the financial statements. Examples of accompanying information include directors' reports, chairman's statement, operating and financial reviews.

Good presentation involves a discussion of:

- the main factors underlying the financial performance, including the principal risks, uncertainties and trends of the main business areas and how the company is responding to them
- the strategies being adopted on capital structure
- the activities and expenditure that are being invested for the future

ACCOUNTING CONCEPTS

There are a number of accounting concepts which form the 'bedrock' of the preparation of financial statements. Some are included in Statement of Principles (see previous section), while others are discussed further in FRS 18, entitled *Accounting policies.*

Accounting concepts are illustrated in the diagram on the next page and include:

business entity

This refers to the fact that financial statements record and report on the activities of one particular entity. They do not include the personal assets and liabilities of those who play a part in owning or running the entity.

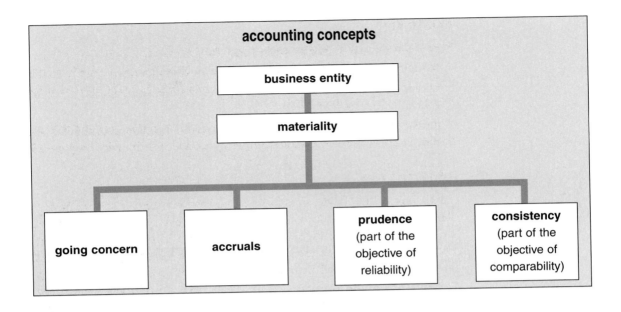

materiality

Some items are of such low value that it is not worth recording them separately in the accounting records, ie they are not 'material'. Examples include

- small expense items grouped together as sundry expenses
- small end-of-year stocks of office stationery not valued for the purpose of financial statements
- low-cost fixed assets being charged as an expense in profit and loss account

going concern

This presumes that the entity to which the financial statements relate will continue in the foreseeable future, ie there is no intention to reduce significantly the size of the entity or to liquidate it. Values based on break-up amounts – a 'gone concern' – tend not to be relevant to users seeking to assess the entity's ability to generate cash or to adapt to changing circumstances.

accruals

This means that expenses and revenues are matched so that they concern the same goods or services and the same time period. Profit and loss account shows the amount of the expense that should have been incurred and the amount of income that should have been received.

prudence

This requires that financial statements should always, when there is any doubt, report a conservative figure for profit or the valuation of assets. To this end, profits are not to be anticipated and should only be recognised when they can be reliably measured.

Note that prudence is one aspect of the overall objective of reliability for financial statements – see diagram from Statement of Principles on page 23.

consistency

This requires that, when an entity adopts particular accounting methods, it should normally continue to use such methods consistently. For example, the use of straight-line depreciation for a particular class of fixed asset would normally continue to be used in the future; however, changes can be made provided there are good reasons for so doing, and a note of explanation is included in the financial statements. By application of consistency, direct comparison between the financial statements of different years can be made.

Note that consistency is one aspect of the overall objective of comparability for financial statements – see diagram from Statement of Principles on page 23.

other concepts

There are other concepts – such as money measurement, historical cost, duality – which are followed when preparing financial statements. These will have been covered in earlier studies at NVQ Level 3 in Accounting.

Chapter Summary

- Limited companies are a common form of business unit.
- There are two main types of limited companies:
  - public limited companies (plc)
  - private limited companies (ltd)
- Virtually all limited companies are in the private sector, where they are owned by shareholders.
- The profit motive is commonly the most important objective of companies.
- The two main financial statements used by limited companies are an income statement (eg profit and loss account) and a balance sheet.
- There is a wide variety of users of financial statements – investors, lenders, employees, the public, etc.
- The elements of financial statements are: assets, liabilities, ownership interest, income, expenditure, contributions from owners, distributions to owners, gains, losses.

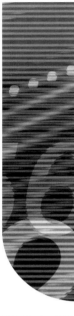

- The regulatory framework of accounting, often referred to as UK GAAP, comprises
  - Companies Act
  - Statements of Standard Accounting Practice
  - Financial Reporting Standards
  - Statement of Principles
- International Accounting Standards have been developed with the aim of harmonising international financial reporting. From 1 January 2005 at the latest, all EU listed companies are required to prepare their consolidated accounts in accordance with international standards (IASs and IFRSs).
- Statement of Principles for Financial Reporting sets out the principles that should underlie the preparation and presentation of financial statements. It comprises eight chapters, each dealing with key issues.
- Accounting concepts form the 'bedrock' of the preparation of financial statements; they include: business entity, materiality, going concern, accruals, prudence and consistency.

Key Terms

limited company	business entity in the private sector, generally owned by shareholders who are looking for profits
stewardship	the accountability of the entity's management for the safe-keeping of the organisation's resources and for their proper, efficient and profitable use
economic decisions	making use of information from financial statements to help in making decisions about investment or potential investment in the company
elements of financial statements	the building blocks from which financial statements are constructed
income statement	income *minus* expenditure *equals* gains or losses
balance sheet	assets *minus* liabilities *equals* ownership interest
SSAP	Statement of Standard Accounting Practice
FRS	Financial Reporting Standard
FRSSE	Financial Reporting Standard for Smaller Entities
IFRS	International Financial Reporting Standard
primary financial statements	financial performance (eg profit and loss account), balance sheet, and cash flow statement

Student Activities

1.1   Which one of the following statements is correct?

    (a)   assets – liabilities = ownership interest

    (b)   assets + liabilities = ownership interest

    (c)   current assets – current liabilities = ownership interest

    (d)   current assets + current liabilities = ownership interest

1.2   Which one of the following statements is correct?

    (a)   assets – expenditure = gains or losses

    (b)   income + assets = gains or losses

    (c)   income – expenditure = gains or losses

    (d)   expenditure + liabilities = gains or losses

1.3   Name three user groups of limited company financial statements indicating the type of financial information each group might be interested in.

1.4   Distinguish between 'stewardship' and 'economic decisions' in relation to financial statements.

1.5   Explain the following terms used in financial accounting.

    (a)   going concern

    (b)   prudence

    (c)   business entity

    (d)   matching/accruals

1.6   In preparing the accounts of HH Limited for the year to 31 March 20-2, the managing director, Harold Hughes, has raised a number of issues. These were as follows:

    (a)   The company bank account paid Harold's daughters' school fees for the year. *— Business entity*

    (b)   At 31 March 20-2 there was a box of pencils left in the stationery cupboard, and Harold is not sure if this should be included as closing stock. *— Materiality*

    (c)   The short-term viability of HH Limited seems extremely uncertain. *— Going concern*

(d)   During the year HH Limited paid £6,000 rent but Harold is puzzled because only £5,000 appears in the profit and loss account and £1,000 appears in the balance sheet as a prepayment. — accrual & matching

(e)   It is rumoured that one of HH Limited's customers has gone into liquidation, owing the company £500. — prudence

(f)   In previous years HH Limited has valued closing stock on a FIFO (first in first out) basis, but this year Harold believes that the company will pay less tax if the stock is valued on a LIFO (last in first out) basis. — Consistency

REQUIRED

State which accounting concept(s) relates to each of the above problems (a) - (f) and show how each concept should be applied in the case of HH Limited.

1.7   You have been asked to advise Jonathan Brown, managing director of JB Limited, on the accounting treatment of certain transactions which he considers might affect the company's financial statements for the year ended 31 December 20-5. The matters on which he would like your advice are set out below.

(a)   The company paid for an advertising campaign during the year at a cost of £2,800. It is estimated by Jonathan Brown that this will lead to an overall increase in sales of 15%. Half of this increase was achieved in 20-5 and the other half is expected to be achieved in 20-6.

(b)   Jonathan Brown took stock costing £500 from the company at the end of the year for his own use. He removed the stock on 31 December 20-5 after the year-end stock count had taken place. No adjustment was made to the stock balance to take account of this action.

(c)   Jonathan Brown has put his own house up as security for a loan made by the bank to the company. The loan was made specifically for the company and not for the personal use of Jonathan Brown.

REQUIRED

Advise Jonathan Brown on the accounting treatment of these transactions in the financial statements of JB Limited for the year ended 31 December 20-5. Explain your treatment, where relevant, by reference to accounting concepts.

1.8   Task 1

(a)   What is the objective of financial statements?

(b)   Illustrate how this objective is fulfilled by considering the financial statements of a limited company.

Task 2

(a)   Identify the elements of financial statements.

(b)   Explain how the elements are related in the balance sheet and in the profit and loss account of a limited company and the relationship between the two financial statements.

1.9   The accounting equation is often expressed as:

ASSETS – LIABILITIES = OWNERSHIP INTEREST

(a)   Explain what each of the terms 'assets', 'liabilities' and 'ownership interest' means.

(b)   Identify, in general terms only, the balances that would appear in the 'ownership interest' section of the balance sheet of a limited company.

1.10   The directors of Machier Ltd have asked you a number of questions about financial statements. Prepare notes for the directors answering the following questions:

(a)   What are the elements in a balance sheet of a company? State which of the balances in the balance sheet of Machier Ltd (shown below) fall under each element.

(b)   How are the elements related in the accounting equation? Show numerically that the accounting equation is maintained in the balance sheet of Machier Ltd.

Machier Ltd	
Balance Sheet as at 31 March 20-9	
	£000
Fixed assets	4,282
Current assets	
Stocks	448
Debtors	527
Cash	–
	975
Current liabilities	
Trade creditors	381
Dividends payable	20
Taxation	165
Bank overdraft	183
	749
Net current assets	226
Long-term loan	2,800
	1,708
Captial and reserves	
Called up share capital	200
Share premium	100
Profit and loss account	1,408
	1,708

this chapter covers . . .

In this chapter we focus on the financial statements of limited companies and look at:

- *the advantages of forming a limited company*
- *the differences between a private limited company, a public limited company, and a company limited by guarantee*
- *the information contained in a company's Memorandum of Association and Articles of Association*
- *the differences between ordinary shares and preference shares*
- *the concept of reserves, and the difference between capital reserves and revenue reserves*
- *the appropriation section of a company's profit and loss account*
- *the layout of a company's balance sheet*

NVQ PERFORMANCE CRITERIA COVERED

unit 11: DRAFTING FINANCIAL STATEMENTS

element 11.1

draft limited company financial statements

A   draft limited company financial statements from the appropriate information

B   correctly identify and implement subsequent adjustments and ensure that discrepancies, unusual features or queries are identified and either resolved or referred to the appropriate person

E   ensure that confidentiality procedures are followed at all times

ADVANTAGES OF FORMING A LIMITED COMPANY

A limited company is a separate legal entity, owned by shareholders and managed by directors.

The limited company is often chosen as the legal status of a business for a number of reasons:

limited liability

The shareholders (members) of a company can only lose the amount of their investment, being the money paid already, together with any money unpaid on their shares (unpaid instalments on new share issues, for example). Thus, if the company became insolvent (went 'bust'), shareholders would have to pay any unpaid instalments to help pay the creditors. As this happens very rarely, shareholders are usually in a safe position: their personal assets, unless pledged as security to a lender (as in the case of a director/shareholder), are not available to the company's creditors.

separate legal entity

A limited company is a separate legal entity from its owners. Anyone taking legal action proceeds against the company and not the individual shareholders.

ability to raise finance

A limited company can raise substantial funds from outside sources by the issue of shares:

- for the larger public company – from the public and investing institutions on the Stock Exchange or similar markets
- for the smaller company – privately from venture capital companies, relatives and friends

Companies can also raise finance by means of debentures (see page 40).

membership

A member of a limited company is a person who owns at least one share in that company. A member of a company is the same as a shareholder.

other factors

A limited company is usually a much larger business unit than a sole trader or partnership. This gives the company a higher standing and status in the business community, allowing it to benefit from economies of scale, and making it of sufficient size to employ specialists for functions such as production, marketing, finance and human resources.

THE COMPANIES ACT

Limited companies are regulated by the Companies Act 1985, as amended by the Companies Act 1989.

Under the terms of the 1985 Act there are two main types of limited company: the larger public limited company (abbreviated to 'Plc'), which is defined in the Act, and the smaller company, traditionally known as a private limited company (abbreviated to 'Ltd'), which is any other limited company. A further type of company is limited by guarantee.

public limited company (Plc)

A company may become a public limited company if it has:

• issued share capital of over £50,000

• at least two members (shareholders) and at least two directors

A public limited company may raise capital from the public on the Stock Exchange or similar markets – the new issues and privatisations of recent years are examples of this. A public limited company does not have to issue shares on the stock markets, and not all do so.

private limited company (Ltd)

The private limited company is the most common form of limited company. The term *private* is not set out in the Companies Act 1985, but it is a traditional description, and well describes the smaller company, often in family ownership. A private limited company has:

• no minimum requirement for issued share capital

• at least one member (shareholder) and at least one director who may be the sole shareholder

The shares are not traded publicly, but are transferable between individuals, although valuation will be more difficult for shares not quoted on the stock markets.

company limited by guarantee

A company limited by guarantee is not formed with share capital, but relies on the guarantee of its members to pay a stated amount in the event of the company's insolvency. Examples of such companies include charities, and artistic and educational organisations.

GOVERNING DOCUMENTS OF COMPANIES

There are a number of documents required by the Companies Act in the setting-up of a company. Two essential governing documents are the **Memorandum of Association** and the **Articles of Association**.

The **Memorandum of Association,** the constitution of the company, regulates the affairs of the company to the outside world and contains five main clauses:

1 the name of the company (together with the words 'public limited company' or 'limited', as appropriate)

2 capital of the company (the amount that can be issued in shares: the authorised share capital)

3 'objects' of the company, ie what activities the company can engage in; under the Companies Act the objects can be stated as being those of 'a general commercial company', ie the company can engage in any commercial activity

4 registered office of the company (not the address, but whether it is registered in England and Wales, or in Scotland)

5 a statement that the liability of the members is limited

The **Articles of Association** regulate the internal administration of the company, including the powers of directors and the holding of company meetings.

ACCOUNTING REQUIREMENTS OF THE COMPANIES ACT

The Companies Act 1985 (as amended by the Companies Act 1989) requires that companies produce sets of accounts. The Act seeks to protect the interests of shareholders, creditors, and lenders by requiring accounts to be presented in a standardised layout. This enables comparisons to be made with other companies so that users of accounts can understand and assess the progress being made. The Act also states the detailed information that must be disclosed.

For larger companies the accounts are audited by external auditors – this is a costly and time-consuming exercise (smaller and medium-sized companies are often exempt from audit). Nevertheless, the audit process enhances the reliability of the accounts for users.

The accounts must be sent to Companies House, where they are available for public inspection. The accounts are available to all shareholders, together with a report on the company's activities during the year.

In this chapter we will study the 'internal use' accounts, rather than being concerned with the detailed accounting requirements of the Companies Act. Chapter 3 will look at such 'published accounts', as they are often known.

Before we examine the financial statements in detail we will look first at the principal ways in which a company raises finance: shares. There are different types of shares which appear in a company's balance sheet as the company's share capital.

TYPES OF SHARES ISSUED BY LIMITED COMPANIES

The **authorised share capital** – also known as the nominal or registered capital – is stated in the Memorandum of Association and is the maximum share capital that the company is allowed to issue. The authorised share capital may not be the same as the **issued share capital** – also known as the called up capital. Under company law the issued capital cannot exceed the amount authorised. If a company which has issued the full extent of its authorised share capital wishes to make an increase, it must first pass the appropriate resolution at a general meeting of the shareholders.

The authorised share capital is shown on the balance sheet (or as a note to the accounts) 'for information', but is not added into the balance sheet total, as it may not be the same amount as the issued share capital. By contrast, the issued share capital – showing the classes and number of shares that have been issued – forms a part of the 'financed by' section of the balance sheet of a limited company.

The authorised and issued share capital may be divided into a number of classes or types of share; the main types are **ordinary shares** and, less commonly, **preference shares**.

ordinary (equity) shares

These are the most commonly issued class of share which carry the main 'risks and rewards' of the business: the risks are of losing part or all of the value of the shares if the business loses money or becomes insolvent; the rewards are that they take a share of the profits – in the form of **dividends** – after allowance has been made for all expenses of the business, including loan and debenture interest, taxation, and after preference dividends (if any). When a company makes large profits, it will have the ability to pay higher dividends to the ordinary shareholders; when losses are made, the ordinary shareholders may receive no dividend.

Companies rarely pay out all of their profits in the form of dividends; most retain some profits as reserves. These can always be used to enable a dividend to be paid in a year when the company makes little or no profit, always assuming that the company has sufficient cash in the bank to make the payment. Ordinary shareholders, in the event of the company becoming insolvent, will be the last to receive any repayment of their investment: other creditors will be paid off first.

Ordinary shares usually carry voting rights – thus shareholders have a say at the annual general meeting and at any other shareholders' meetings.

preference shares

Whereas ordinary share dividends will vary from year-to-year, preference shares usually carry a fixed percentage rate of dividend – for example, ten per cent of nominal value. Their dividends are paid in preference to those of ordinary shareholders; but they are only paid if the company makes profits. In the event of the company ceasing to trade, the preference shareholders will also receive repayment of capital before the ordinary shareholders.

Preference shares do not normally carry voting rights.

nominal and market values of shares

Each share has a **nominal value** – or face value – which is entered in the accounts. Shares may be issued with nominal values of 5p, 10p, 25p, 50p or £1, or indeed for any amount. Thus a company with an authorised share capital of £100,000 might state in its Memorandum of Association that this is divided up into:

100,000 ordinary shares of 50p each	£50,000
50,000 ten per cent preference shares of £1 each	£50,000
	£100,000

The nominal value usually bears little relationship to the **market value**. The market value is the price at which issued – or 'secondhand' – shares are traded. Share prices of a quoted public limited company may be listed in the *Financial Times*.

issue price

This is the price at which shares are issued to shareholders by the company – either when the company is being set up, or at a later date when it needs to raise more funds. The issue price is either **at par** (ie the nominal value), or above nominal value. In the latter case, the amount of the difference between issue price and nominal value is known as a **share premium** (see page 42): for example – nominal value £1.00; issue price £1.50; therefore share premium is 50p per share.

LOANS AND DEBENTURES

In addition to money provided by shareholders, who are the owners of the company, further funds can be obtained by borrowing in the form of loans or debentures:

- **Loans** are monies borrowed by companies from lenders – such as banks – on a medium or long-term basis. Generally repayments are made throughout the period of the loan, but can often be tailored to suit the needs of the borrower. Invariably lenders require security for loans so that, if the loan is not repaid, the lender has an asset – such as property – that can be sold.

  Smaller companies are sometimes also financed by directors' loans.

- **Debentures** are formal certificates issued by companies raising long-term finance from lenders and investors. Debenture certificates issued by large public limited companies are often traded on the Stock Exchange. Debentures are commonly secured against assets such as property that, in the event of the company ceasing to trade, could be sold and used to repay the debenture holders.

Loans and debentures usually carry fixed rates of interest that must be paid, just like other business overheads, whether a company makes profits or not. As loan and debenture interest is a business expense, this is shown in the profit and loss account along with all other overheads. In the event of the company ceasing to trade, loan and debenture-holders would be repaid before any shareholders.

TRADING AND PROFIT AND LOSS ACCOUNT

A limited company uses the same form of financial statements as a sole trader or partnership. However there are two overhead items commonly found in the profit and loss account of a limited company that are not found in those of other business types:

- **directors' remuneration** – ie amounts paid to directors; as directors are employed by the company, their pay appears amongst the overheads of the company

- **debenture interest** – as already noted, when debentures are issued by companies, the interest is shown as an overhead in the profit and loss account

A limited company follows the profit and loss account with an *appropriation section.* This shows how net profit has been distributed and includes:

- corporation tax – the tax payable on company profits
- dividends paid and proposed – on both ordinary and preference shares, including *interim dividends* (usually paid just over half-way through the financial year) and *final dividends* (proposed at the end of the year, and paid early in the next financial year)
- transfers to and from reserves – see below

The diagram on pages 44 and 45 shows an example of a limited company's trading and profit and loss account for internal use.

BALANCE SHEET

Balance sheets of limited companies follow the same layout as those we have seen earlier, but the capital section is more complex because of the different classes of shares that may be issued, and the various reserves. The diagram on pages 46 and 47 shows the internal use balance sheet of Orion Limited as an example (published accounts are covered in the next chapter).

RESERVES

A limited company rarely distributes all its profits to its shareholders. Instead, it will often keep part of the profits earned each year in the form of reserves. As the balance sheet of Orion Limited shows (page 47), there are two types of reserves:

- capital reserves, which are created as a result of a non-trading profit
- revenue reserves, which are retained profits from profit and loss account

capital reserves

Examples of capital reserves (which cannot be used to fund dividend payments) include:

- **Revaluation reserve.** This occurs when a fixed asset, most probably property, is revalued (in an upwards direction) in the balance sheet. The amount of the revaluation is placed in a revaluation reserve where it increases the value of the shareholders' investment in the company. Note, however, that this is purely a 'book' adjustment – no cash has changed hands.

  In the example on the next page a company revalues its property upwards by £250,000 from £500,000 to £750,000.

BALANCE SHEET (EXTRACTS)

	£
Before revaluation	
Fixed asset: property at cost	500,000
Share capital: ordinary shares of £1 each	500,000
After revaluation	
Fixed asset: property at revaluation	750,000
Share capital: ordinary shares of £1 each	500,000
Capital reserve: revaluation reserve	250,000
	750,000

- **Share premium account.** An established company may issue additional shares to the public at a higher amount than the nominal value. For example, Orion Ltd (page 47) seeks finance for further expansion by issuing additional ordinary shares. Although the shares have a nominal value of £1 each, because Orion is a well-established company, the shares are issued at £1.50 each. Of this amount, £1 is recorded in the issued share capital section, and the extra 50p is the share premium.

revenue reserves

Revenue reserves are profits generated from trading activities; they have been retained in the company to help build the company for the future. Revenue reserves include the balance of the appropriation section of the profit and loss account: this balance is commonly described as 'profit and loss account balance' or 'balance of retained profits'. Alternatively, a transfer may be made from the appropriation section to a named revenue reserve account, such as *general reserve*, or a revenue reserve for a specific purpose, such as *reserve for the replacement of machinery*. Transfers to or from these named revenue reserve accounts are made in the appropriation section of the profit and loss account.

reserves: profits not cash

It should be noted that reserves – both capital and revenue – are not cash funds to be used whenever the company needs money, but are in fact represented by assets shown on the balance sheet. The reserves record the fact that the assets belong to the shareholders via their ownership of the company.

EXAMPLE ACCOUNTS

On the next four pages are set out the trading and profit and loss account and balance sheet for Orion Limited, a private limited company. Note that these are the 'internal use' accounts – the detailed accounting requirements of the Companies Act are covered in Chapter 3.

Explanations of the financial statements are set out on the left-hand page.

ACCESSIBILITY AND CONFIDENTIALITY OF ACCOUNTS

accessibility

Limited company accounts are far more readily accessible to interested parties than the accounts of sole traders and partnerships:

– all limited companies must submit accounts to Companies House where they are available for public inspection

– a copy of the accounts is available to all shareholders, together with a report on the company's activities during the year

– the profit statements and balance sheets of larger public limited companies are commented on and discussed in the media

– the accounts of larger public limited companies are freely available to potential investors, lenders and other interested parties

confidentiality

Although company accounts are readily accessible, great care must be taken when they are being prepared. Confidentiality procedures must be observed at all times:

– during the preparation of year-end financial statements

– during the period after the accounts have been prepared but before they are sent to the shareholders and disclosed to the public

– for information that has been used in the preparation of the accounts but which is not required to be disclosed under the Companies Act (see also Chapter 3, which follows)

The **appropriation section** (or account) is the part of the profit and loss account which shows how net profit is distributed. It includes corporation tax, dividends paid and proposed, and transfers to and from reserves.

The **overheads** of a limited company include directors' remuneration and interest paid on debentures (if debentures have been issued).

The company has recorded a **net profit** of £43,000 in its profit and loss account – this is brought into the appropriation section.

Corporation tax, the tax that a company has to pay, based on its profits, is shown in the appropriation section. We shall not be studying the calculations for corporation tax in this book. It is, however, important to see how the tax is recorded in the financial statements.

The company has already paid **interim dividends** on the two classes of shares it has in issue (ordinary shares and preference shares); these would, most probably, have been paid just over half-way through the company's financial year. The company also proposes to pay a **final dividend** to its shareholders: these will be paid in the early part of the next financial year. Note that a dividend is often expressed as an amount per share, based on the nominal value, eg 5p per £1 nominal value share (which is the same as a five per cent dividend).

Added to **net profit** is a **balance** of £41,000. This represents profits of the company from previous years that have not been distributed as dividends. Note that the appropriation section shows a balance of retained profits at the year-end of £50,000. Such retained profits form a revenue reserve (see page 42) of the company.

ORION LIMITED

TRADING AND PROFIT AND LOSS ACCOUNT

for the year ended 31 December 2004

	£	£
Sales		725,000
Opening stock	45,000	
Purchases	381,000	
	426,000	
Less closing stock	50,000	
Cost of sales		376,000
Gross profit		349,000
Less overheads:		
Directors' remuneration	75,000	
Debenture interest	6,000	
Other overheads	225,000	
		306,000
Net profit for year before taxation		43,000
Less corporation tax		15,000
Profit for year after taxation		28,000
Less interim dividends paid		
ordinary shares	5,000	
preference shares	2,000	
final dividends proposed		
ordinary shares	10,000	
preference shares	2,000	
		19,000
Retained profit for year		9,000
Add balance of retained profits at beginning of year		41,000
Balance of retained profits at end of year		50,000

Limited company balance sheets usually distinguish between:

intangible fixed assets, which do not have material substance but belong to the company and have value, eg goodwill (the amount paid for the reputation and connections of a business that has been taken over), patents and trademarks; intangible fixed assets are depreciated (or amortised) in the same way as tangible fixed assets.

tangible fixed assets, which have material substance, such as premises, equipment, vehicles.

As well as the usual **current liabilities**, for limited companies, this section also contains the amount of proposed dividends (but not dividends that have been paid in the year) and the amount of corporation tax to be paid within the next twelve months. The amounts for both of these items are also included in the appropriation section of the profit and loss account.

Long-term liabilities are those that are due to be repaid more than twelve months from the date of the balance sheet, eg loans and debentures.

Authorised share capital is included on the balance sheet 'for information', but is not added into the balance sheet total, as it may not be the same amount as the issued share capital.

Issued share capital shows the classes and number of shares that have been issued. In this balance sheet, the shares are described as being fully paid, meaning that the company has received the full amount of the value of each share from the shareholders. Sometimes shares will be partly paid, eg ordinary shares of £1, but 75p paid. This means that the company can make a call on the shareholders to pay the extra 25p to make the shares fully paid.

Capital reserves are created as a result of non-trading profit.

Revenue reserves are retained profits from profit and loss account.

The total for **shareholders' funds** represents the stake of the shareholders in the company. It comprises share capital (ordinary and preference shares), plus reserves (capital and revenue reserves).

ORION LIMITED
Balance sheet as at 31 December 2004

Fixed Assets	Cost £	Dep'n to date £	Net £
Intangible			
Goodwill	50,000	20,000	30,000
Tangible			
Freehold land and buildings	180,000	20,000	160,000
Machinery	230,000	90,000	140,000
Fixtures and fittings	100,000	25,000	75,000
	560,000	155,000	405,000

Current Assets		
Stock		50,000
Debtors		38,000
Bank		22,000
Cash		2,000
		112,000

Less Current Liabilities		
Creditors	30,000	
Proposed dividends	12,000	
Corporation tax	15,000	
	57,000	
Working Capital*		55,000
		460,000

Less Long-term Liabilities	
10% debentures	60,000
NET ASSETS	400,000

FINANCED BY
Authorised Share Capital

100,000 10% preference shares of £1 each	100,000
600,000 ordinary shares of £1 each	600,000
	700,000

Issued Share Capital

40,000 10% preference shares of £1 each, fully paid	40,000
300,000 ordinary shares of £1 each, fully paid	300,000
	340,000

Capital Reserve

Share premium account	10,000

Revenue Reserve

Profit and loss account	50,000
SHAREHOLDERS' FUNDS	400,000

* working capital is often referred to as 'net current assets'

Chapter Summary

- A limited company has a separate legal entity from its owners.

- A company is regulated by the Companies Act 1985 (as amended by the Companies Act 1989), and is owned by shareholders and managed by directors.

- A limited company may be either a public limited company or a private limited company.

- The liability of shareholders is limited to any money unpaid on their shares.

- The main types of shares that may be issued by companies are ordinary shares and preference shares.

- Borrowings in the form of loans and debentures are a further source of finance.

- The final accounts of a company include an appropriation section, which follows the profit and loss account.

- The balance sheet of a limited company is similar to that of sole traders and partnerships but the capital and reserves section reflects the ownership of the company by its shareholders:
  - a statement of the authorised and issued share capital
  - details of capital reserves and revenue reserves

Key Terms

limited company	a separate legal entity owned by shareholders and managed by directors
limited liability	shareholders of a company are liable for company debts only to the extent of any money unpaid on their shares
shareholder	person who owns at least one share in a limited company; a shareholder is also a member of a company
public limited company	a company, registered as a plc, with an issued share capital of over £50,000 and at least two members and at least two directors; it may raise funds on the stock markets
private limited company	any limited company with share capital other than a public limited company
Memorandum of Association	the document setting out the constitution of the company, which regulates the affairs of the company to the outside world
Articles of Association	the document regulating the internal administration of the company

ordinary shares	commonly issued type of shares which take a share in the profits of the company but which also carry the main risks
preference shares	shares which carry a fixed rate of dividend paid, subject to sufficient profits, in preference to ordinary shareholders; in event of repayment of capital, rank before the ordinary shareholders
debentures	issued by companies raising long-term finance; debenture interest is an overhead in profit and loss account
nominal value	the face value of the shares entered in the accounts
issue price	the price at which shares are issued to shareholders by the company
market value	the price at which shares are traded
directors' remuneration	amounts paid to directors as employees of the company; an overhead in profit and loss account
appropriation section	the part of profit and loss account which shows how net profit is distributed, and includes corporation tax, dividends paid and proposed, and transfers to and from reserves
dividends	amounts paid to shareholders from the profit of the company; an interim dividend is paid just over half-way through a financial year; a final dividend is paid early in the following year
authorised share capital	amount of share capital authorised by the company's Memorandum of Association
issued share capital	the classes and number of shares that have been issued by the company; cannot exceed the authorised share capital
reserves	profits retained by the company; two main types: – capital reserves, created as a result of a non-trading profit – revenue reserves, retained profits from profit and loss account
revaluation reserve	capital reserve created by the upwards revaluation of a fixed asset, most usually property; cannot be used to fund dividend payments
share premium account	capital reserve created by the issue of shares at a price higher than nominal value, the excess being credited to share premium; cannot be used to fund dividend payments

Student Activities

2.1 In limited company financial statements, directors salaries are:

(a) ╱ debited to the profit and loss appropriation account.

(b) debited to the profit and loss account.

(c) credited to the profit and loss appropriation account.

(d) credited to the profit and loss account.

2.2 The authorised share capital of a limited company is:

(a) the amount of shares issued to shareholders.

(b) the amount paid for shares by the shareholders.

(c) ╱ the maximum amount of shares that can be issued.

(d) the minimum amount of shares that can be issued.

2.3 Which one of these items would not appear in the appropriation account of a limited company?

(a) ╱ debenture interest payable.

(b) ordinary dividend proposed.

(c) interim preference dividend paid.

(d) the retained profit for the year.

2.4 What are the main differences between preference shares and ordinary shares?

2.5 List four differences between a profit and loss account of a limited company and that of a sole trader business.

2.6 The following trial balance has been extracted from the books of account of Gretton plc as at 31 March 20-2

	Dr	Cr
	£000	*£000*
Administrative expenses	210	
Issued share capital (ordinary shares of £1 fully paid)		600
Debtors	670	
Cash at bank and in hand	15	
Share premium		240
Distribution costs	420	
Rent, rates and insurance	487	
Plant and machinery		
At cost	950	
Accumulated depreciation (at 1 April 20-1)		220
Profit and loss (at 1 April 20-1)		182
Purchases	960	
Stock (at 1 April 20-1)	140	
Trade creditors		260
Sales turnover		2,350
	3,852	3,852

Additional information

- Stock at 31 March 20-2 was valued at £180,000.

- The corporation tax charged based on the profits for the year is estimated to be £32,000.

- A final ordinary dividend of 10p per share is proposed.

- It is company policy to depreciate the plant and machinery based on an annual rate of 10% on cost.

REQUIRED

Prepare the financial statements of Gretton plc for the year ended 31 March 20-2.

2.7   Hickson plc prepares its accounts to 30 September each year. At 30th September 20-2 its trial balance was as follows:

	Dr £	Cr £
Equipment at cost	140,000	
Depreciation to 01.10.20-1		20,000
Fixtures and fittings at Cost	40,000	
Depreciation to 01.10.20-1		10,000
Motor vehicles at cost	80,000	
Depreciation to 01.10.20-1		30,000
Stock at 01.10.20-1	25,000	
Purchases	125,000	
Sales		280,000
Wages and salaries	40,000	
Directors fees	29,000	
Printing, telephone and stationery	7,000	
General expenses	6,000	
Rent, rates and insurance	11,000	
Trade debtors	26,000	
Trade creditors		14,000
Cash at bank	5,000	
Cash in hand	1,000	
Ordinary shares 25p each		80,000
10% Preference shares £1 each		30,000
Share premium account		6,000
Profit and loss account		15,000
8% Debenture loan		50,000
	535,000	535,000

Additional information

- Closing stock is valued at £49,000

- The interest on the debenture loan needs to be accrued for, for the whole year.

- Depreciation of the fixed assets is to be provided for as follows:
    Equipment   10% on cost
    Fixtures & fittings   15% on cost
    Motor vehicles   25% Reducing balance method

- The directors now propose to pay the following dividends:
    All of the preference dividend for the year
    An ordinary dividend of 2p per share

- Provision of £8,000 corporation tax is to be made.

REQUIRED

Prepare the financial statements of Hickson plc for the year ended 30 September 20-2.

2.8 The following list of balances has been extracted from the books of Grayson plc as at 31 December 20-2:

	Dr £	Cr £
Sales		2,640,300
Administration expenses	120,180	
Selling and distribution costs	116,320	
Wages and Salaries	112,800	
Directors Salaries and Fees	87,200	
Interest paid on loan stock	10,000	
Postage and Telephone	7,900	
Bank Loan Account		50,000
Purchases	2,089,600	
Stock at 01.01.20-2	318,500	
Cash at bank	20,640	
Trade debtors	415,800	
Provision for doubtful debts at 01.01.20-2		10,074
Bad debts	8,900	
Creditors		428,250
10% loan stock		200,000
Motor Expenses	12,280	
Bank charges and loan interest	7,720	
Office Equipment at net book value	110,060	
Vehicles at net book value	235,000	
50p Ordinary shares		200,000
Profit and loss account at 01.01.20-2		144,276
	3,672,900	3,672,900

Additional information

- Provide for £10,000 loan stock interest which is payable on 01.01.20-3. *— Accrual*

- Provide for administration expenses paid in advance at 31.12.20-2 £12,200 and distribution costs of £21,300 owing at 31.12.20-2. *— prepayment & Accrual*

- Provision for doubtful debts is to be maintained at 3% of debtors.

- Stock at 31.12.20-2 is £340,600.

- Provide for corporation tax of £45,000 payable on 01.10.20-3.

- The directors recommend a dividend of 15 pence per share.

- Depreciation on the fixed assets has already been calculated for the year and charged to administration costs and distribution costs accordingly.

REQUIRED

Prepare the financial statements of Grayson plc for the year ended 31 December 20-2.

3 Published accounts of limited companies

this chapter covers . . .

- the financial statements required by the Companies Act

- the reasons for, and the layout of, published accounts

- interpretation of the auditors' report

- the accounting policies followed by a particular company

- bonus issues and rights issues of shares

Towards the end of the Chapter (page 79) we see how a trial balance for a company is converted into the layout of published accounts.

NVQ PERFORMANCE CRITERIA COVERED

unit 11: DRAFTING FINANCIAL STATEMENTS

element 11.1

draft limited company financial statements

A   draft limited company financial statements from the appropriate information

B   correctly identify and implement subsequent adjustments and ensure that discrepancies, unusual features or queries are identified and either resolved or referred to the appropriate person

C   ensure that limited company financial statements comply with relevant accounting standards and domestic legislation and with the organisation's policies, regulations and procedures

E   ensure that confidentiality procedures are followed at all times

INTRODUCTION

All limited companies have shareholders. Each shareholder owns a part of the company and, although they do not take part in the day-to-day running of the company (unless they are also directors), they are entitled to know the financial results of the company.

Every limited company, whether public or private, is required by law to produce financial statements, which are also available for anyone to inspect if they so wish. We need to distinguish between the *statutory accounts* and the *report and accounts*. The **statutory accounts** are those which are required to be produced under company law, and a copy of these is filed with the Registrar of Companies. Smaller companies – see page 76 – can file abbreviated accounts.

The **report and accounts** – often referred to as the **corporate report** – is available to every shareholder and contains:

- directors' report

- auditors' report (where required)

- profit and loss account

- balance sheet

- cash flow statement (where required)

- notes to the accounts, including a statement of the company's accounting policies

The report and accounts of large well-known companies are often presented in the form of a glossy booklet, well illustrated with photographs and diagrammatic presentations. Some companies, by agreement with individual shareholders, issue a simpler form of annual review, including a **summary financial statement**, the full report and accounts being available on request.

Company law not only requires the production of financial statements, but also states the detailed information that must be disclosed. The legal requirements are detailed in the relevant sections of the Companies Act 1985 (as amended by the Companies Act 1989).

Large companies that are listed on the Stock Exchange or similar markets usually also include an **Operating and Financial Review** (OFR) as a part of their corporate report. Such a review provides a discussion of the main factors underlying the company's financial performance and position. It is of assistance to users of accounts who wish to assess for themselves the future potential of the business. Sub-headings used within the OFR include:

OPERATING REVIEW

- operating results for the period
- investment for the future
- profit for the financial year, dividends and earnings per share
- accounting policies

FINANCIAL REVIEW

- capital structure
- taxation
- funds from operating activities and other sources of cash
- current liquidity
- going concern confirmation
- balance sheet value

The Accounting Standards Board has issued a Statement to guide companies as to the framework of the OFR. The Statement is neither an accounting standard nor is it mandatory. However, the UK Government is currently reviewing company law and a proposal is that, in due course, the publication of an OFR should be mandatory for large companies.

RESPONSIBILITIES OF DIRECTORS

The directors of a limited company are responsible for ensuring that the provisions of the Companies Act 1985 which relate to accounting records and statements are followed. The main provisions of the Act are that:

- a company's accounting records must:
  - show and explain the company's transactions
  - disclose with reasonable accuracy at any time the financial position of the company
  - enable the directors to ensure that the company's profit and loss account and balance sheet comply with the Act and give a true and fair view of the company's financial position
- a company's accounting records must contain:
  - day-to-day entries of money received and paid, together with details of the transactions
  - a record of the company's assets and liabilities
  - details of stock held at the end of the year

Every company director has a responsibility to ensure that the statutory accounts are produced and filed with the Registrar of Companies, where they are available for public inspection. The annual accounts must be approved by the company's board of directors and the copy of the balance sheet filed with the Registrar of Companies must be signed by one of the directors on behalf of the board. The directors must prepare a directors' report (see page 63) – this must be approved by the board and the copy to be filed with the Registrar of Companies signed on behalf of the board by a director (or the company secretary). The statutory accounts must be laid before the company at the annual general meeting, and they must be circulated beforehand to shareholders, debenture holders and any other persons entitled to attend the meeting.

The statutory accounts are normally included in the corporate report (see page 55), together with a range of other financial and general information about the company.

STATEMENTS REQUIRED BY THE COMPANIES ACT

The financial statements required by the Companies Act are:
*   profit and loss account
*   balance sheet
*   directors' report
*   auditors' report
*   consolidated accounts, where appropriate (see Chapter 8)

When producing financial statements, companies have to take note of the requirements of the Companies Act, accounting standards (SSAPs and FRSs or, from 2005, International Accounting Standards), and Urgent Issues Task Force (UITF) Abstracts. The overall objective is to produce financial statements which give a true and fair view. If compliance with the Companies Act, accounting standards, or UITF Abstracts is inconsistent with the requirement to give a true and fair view, then they should be departed from only to the extent necessary to give a true and fair view.

The reporting procedures of smaller companies allow for simpler and less detailed disclosure requirements (see pages 76-77).

PROFIT AND LOSS ACCOUNT

The published profit and loss account does not, by law, have to detail every single overhead incurred by the company – to do so would be to disclose important management information to competitors. Instead, the main items are summarised; however, the Companies Act requires that certain items must be detailed either in the profit and loss account itself, or in separate notes to the accounts (see page 68).

The profit and loss account must follow one of two standard formats set out in the Act, and the example on the next page shows the one that is most commonly used by trading companies, and is adapted to take note of the requirements of FRS 3 – see below and page 144. (The other format is appropriate for manufacturing companies.) Specimen figures have been shown – the presentation is in vertical style.

As mentioned above, much of the detail shown in profit and loss account is summarised. For example:

- turnover incorporates the figures for sales and sales returns
- cost of sales includes opening stock, purchases, purchases returns, carriage inwards and closing stock
- distribution costs include warehouse costs, post and packing, delivery drivers' wages, running costs of vehicles, depreciation of vehicles, etc
- administrative expenses include office costs, rent and rates, heating and lighting, depreciation of office equipment, etc.

A recent profit and loss account for Tesco PLC is shown on page 60. This gives the consolidated (or group) profit and loss account, together with the figures for the previous year. Group accounts are covered in Chapter 8.

continuing and discontinued operations

Limited company profit and loss accounts are also required (by FRS 3 *Reporting financial performance*) to show the financial results of any changes to the structure of the company, eg the purchase of another company, or the disposal of a section of the business. To this end the profit and loss account must distinguish between:

- results of continuing operations, ie from those parts of the business that have been kept throughout the year
- results of acquisitions, ie from businesses bought during the year
- results of discontinued operations, ie from parts of the business that have been sold or terminated during the year
- exceptional items (see page 60) of which the following are to be disclosed:
  - profits or losses on the sale or termination of an operation
  - costs of fundamental reorganisation
  - profits or losses on the disposal of fixed assets
- extraordinary items (see page 61)

The objective of these requirements is to give more information to users of accounts.

XYZ PLC
Profit and Loss Account for the year ended 31 December 2004

	£000s	£000s
Turnover		
Continuing operations	22,000	
Acquisitions	3,000	
	25,000	
Discontinued operations	2,000	27,000
Cost of sales		16,500
Gross profit		10,500
Distribution costs		4,250
Administrative expenses		4,000
Operating profit		
Continuing operations	2,000	
Acquisitions	200	
	2,200	
Discontinued operations	50	2,250
Profit on disposal of discontinued operations		250
		2,500
Other operating income		250
Income from shares in group undertakings		–
Income from participating interests		–
Income from other fixed asset investments		100
Other interest receivable and similar income		–
Amounts written off investments		–
Profit on ordinary activities before interest		2,850
Interest payable and similar charges		200
Profit on ordinary activities before taxation		2,650
Tax on profit on ordinary activities		725
Profit on ordinary activities after taxation		1,925
Extraordinary items		–
Profit for the financial year		1,925
Dividends		1,125
Retained profit for the financial year		800

group profit and loss account

52 weeks ended 23 February 2002

	note	2002 £m	Restated[†] 2001 £m
Sales at net selling prices	2	25,654	22,773
Turnover including share of joint ventures		23,804	21,096
Less: share of joint ventures' turnover		(151)	(108)
Group turnover excluding value added tax	2/3	23,653	20,988
Operating expenses			
– Normal operating expenses		(22,273)	(19,770)
– Employee profit-sharing	4	(48)	(44)
– Goodwill amortisation	12	(10)	(8)
Operating profit	2/3	1,322	1,166
Share of operating profit of joint ventures and associates		42	21
Net loss on disposal of fixed assets		(10)	(8)
Profit on ordinary activities before interest and taxation		1,354	1,179
Net interest payable	8	(153)	(125)
Profit on ordinary activities before taxation	5	1,201	1,054
Profit before net loss on disposal of fixed assets and goodwill amortisation		1,221	1,070
Net loss on disposal of fixed assets		(10)	(8)
Goodwill amortisation		(10)	(8)
Tax on profit on ordinary activities	9	(371)	(333)
Profit on ordinary activities after taxation		830	721
Minority interests		–	1
Profit for the financial year		830	722
Dividends	10	(390)	(340)
Retained profit for the financial year	25	440	382
		Pence	Pence
Earnings per share	11	12.05	10.63
Adjusted for net loss on disposal of fixed assets after taxation		0.14	0.12
Adjusted for goodwill amortisation		0.14	0.12
Adjusted earnings per share[†]	11	12.33	10.87
Diluted earnings per share	11	11.86	10.42
Adjusted for net loss on disposal of fixed assets after taxation		0.14	0.12
Adjusted for goodwill amortisation		0.14	0.12
Adjusted diluted earnings per share[†]	11	12.14	10.66
Dividend per share	10	5.60	4.98
Dividend cover (times)		2.17	2.14

Accounting policies and notes forming part of these financial statements are on pages 20 to 39.

[†] Excluding net loss on disposal of fixed assets and goodwill amortisation.

[‡] Prior year comparatives have been restated due to the adoption of Financial Reporting Standard (FRS) 19, 'Deferred Tax'. See note 1 page 22.

Profit and loss account of Tesco PLC

(note that, for comparison, figures for both the current year and last year are shown)

non-recurring profits and losses

FRS 3 distinguishes between three categories of non-recurring profits and losses:

Exceptional items are defined as 'material items which derive from events or transactions that fall within the ordinary activities of the reporting entity and which individually or, if of a similar type, in aggregate, need to be disclosed by virtue of their size or incidence if the financial statements are to give a true and fair view'.

Extraordinary items are defined as 'material items possessing a high degree of abnormality which arise from events or transactions that fall outside the ordinary activities of the reporting entity and which are not expected to recur'. As extraordinary items are recorded in profit and loss account 'below the line' – ie after profit on ordinary activities – FRS 3 requires virtually all one-off transactions to be classified as exceptional items and shown 'above the line'.

Prior period adjustments are defined as 'material adjustments applicable to prior periods arising from changes in accounting policies or from the correction of fundamental errors'.

Any such adjustments are accounted for by restating the figures for the prior period and by adjusting the opening balance of retained profits for the current year.

statement of total recognised gains and losses

FRS 3 requires that a statement of total recognised gains and losses is included in the year-end financial statements and is given the same prominence as profit and loss account and balance sheet. As its name implies, it shows total recognised gains and losses – from profit and loss account, together with *unrealised* profits (for example, the revaluation of fixed assets) – to record the total movement in shareholders' funds for the accounting period.

The statement starts with the figure of profit for the financial year (from profit and loss account before deduction of dividends) and then adjusts for unrealised gains and losses, differences arising from changes in foreign currency exchange rates, and prior period adjustments. An example is given below:

XYZ PLC
Statement of Total Recognised Gains and Losses
for the year ended 31 December 2004

	£000s
Profit for the financial year	1,925
Unrealised surplus on revaluation of properties	1,000
Total recognised gains	2,925
Prior year adjustment	(100)
Total gains and losses for year	2,825

other notes required by FRS 3

As well as the accounting requirements of FRS 3 described above, the standard requires two notes to the accounts to be shown:

- the reconciliation of movements in shareholders' funds
- the note of historical cost profit and losses

These two notes are described fully in Chapter 5, pages 144-146.

BALANCE SHEET

The Companies Act 1985 sets out the standard formats for balance sheets. The example shown on the next page is presented in the layout most commonly used. As with the profit and loss account, extra detail is often shown in the notes to the balance sheet (see page 68).

The layout of the balance sheet follows that which we have used for limited companies in the previous chapter. However, some of the terms used need further explanation:

- **intangible fixed assets** – those assets which do not have material substance but belong to the company, eg goodwill (the amount paid for the reputation and connections of a business that has been taken over), patents and trademarks

- **tangible fixed assets** – those assets which have material substance, such as premises, equipment, vehicles

- **investments** – shares held in other companies, or government securities: classed as fixed asset investments if there is the intention to hold them for a long time, and as current asset investments where they are likely to be sold within twelve months of the balance sheet date

- **creditors: amounts falling due within one year** – the term used in company balance sheets to mean current liabilities, ie amounts that are due to be paid within twelve months of the balance sheet date

- **creditors: amounts falling due after more than one year** – the term used to mean long-term liabilities, ie amounts that are due to be paid more than twelve months from the balance sheet date, eg loans and debentures

- **provisions for liabilities and charges** – an estimate of possible liabilities to be paid in the future: see FRS 12 for provisions (page 138), and FRS 19 for deferred tax (page 131)

XYZ PLC
Balance Sheet as at 31 December 2004

	£000s	£000s
Fixed assets		
Intangible assets		50
Tangible assets		6,750
Investments		1,000
		7,800
Current assets		
Stock	1,190	
Debtors	1,600	
Investments	–	
Cash at bank and in hand	10	
	2,800	
Creditors: amounts falling due within one year	1,800	
Net current assets		1,000
Total assets *less* current liabilities		8,800
Creditors: amounts falling due after more than one year		1,500
Provisions for liabilities and charges		100
		7,200
Capital and reserves		
Called up share capital		2,800
Share premium		400
Revaluation reserve		1,500
Profit and loss account		2,500
		7,200

A recent balance sheet for Tesco PLC is shown on the next page. This gives the consolidated (or group) balance sheet, together with the figures for the previous year; group accounts are covered in Chapter 8.

DIRECTORS' REPORT

The report contains details of the following:

* a statement of the principal activities of the company
* review of the activities of the company over the past year and of likely developments in the future, including research and development activity
* directors' names and their shareholdings

continued on page 66

balance sheets

23 February 2002

	note	£m	2002 £m	£m	Group Restated[‡] 2001 £m	Company 2002 £m	2001 £m
Fixed assets							
Intangible assets	12		154		154	–	–
Tangible assets	13		11,032		9,580	–	–
Investments	14		69		101	6,704	5,774
Investments in joint ventures	14						
Share of gross assets		1,480		1,283			
Less: share of gross liabilities		(1,266)		(1,094)			
Goodwill		18		14			
			232		203	156	146
Investments in associates	14		16		–	–	–
			11,503		10,038	6,860	5,920
Current assets							
Stocks	15		929		838	–	–
Debtors	16		454		322	3,060	874
Investments	17		225		255	5	2
Cash at bank and in hand			445		279	–	–
			2,053		1,694	3,065	876
Creditors:							
falling due within one year	18		(4,809)		(4,389)	(4,707)	(2,518)
Net current liabilities			(2,756)		(2,695)	(1,642)	(1,642)
Total assets less current liabilities			8,747		7,343	5,218	4,278
Creditors:							
falling due after more than one year	19		(2,741)		(1,927)	(2,609)	(1,819)
Provisions for liabilities and charges	22		(440)		(402)	–	–
Net assets			5,566		5,014	2,609	2,459
Capital and reserves							
Called up share capital	24		350		347	350	347
Share premium account	25		2,004		1,870	2,004	1,870
Other reserves	25		40		40	–	–
Profit and loss account	25		3,136		2,721	255	242
Equity shareholders' funds			5,530		4,978	2,609	2,459
Minority interests			36		36	–	–
Total capital employed			5,566		5,014	2,609	2,459

Accounting policies and notes forming part of these financial statements are on pages 20 to 39.

[‡] Prior year comparatives have been restated due to the adoption of FRS 19, 'Deferred Tax'. See note 1 on page 22.

Terry Leahy
Andrew Higginson
Directors

Financial statements approved by the Board on 9 April 2002.

Balance sheet of Tesco PLC

(note that both the 'group' and 'company' balance sheets are shown – see also consolidated accounts, covered in Chapter 8)

group cash flow statement

52 weeks ended 23 February 2002

	note	2002 £m	2001 £m
Net cash inflow from operating activities	32	2,038	1,937
Dividends from joint ventures and associates			
Income received from joint ventures and associates		15	–
Returns on investments and servicing of finance			
Interest received		44	49
Interest paid		(232)	(206)
Interest element of finance lease rental payments		(4)	(4)
Net cash outflow from returns on investments and servicing of finance		(192)	(161)
Taxation			
Corporation tax paid		(378)	(272)
Capital expenditure and financial investment			
Payments to acquire tangible fixed assets		(1,877)	(1,953)
Receipts from sale of tangible fixed assets		42	43
Purchase of own shares		(85)	(58)
Net cash outflow from capital expenditure and financial investment		(1,920)	(1,968)
Acquisitions and disposals			
Purchase of subsidiary undertakings		(31)	(41)
Invested in joint ventures		(46)	(35)
Invested in associates and other investments		(19)	–
Net cash outflow from acquisitions and disposals		(96)	(76)
Equity dividends paid		(297)	(254)
Cash outflow before management of liquid resources and financing		(830)	(794)
Management of liquid resources			
Decrease in short-term deposits		27	–
Financing			
Ordinary shares issued for cash		82	88
Increase in other loans		916	928
New finance leases		–	13
Capital element of finance leases repaid		(24)	(46)
Net cash inflow from financing		974	983
Increase in cash		171	189
Reconciliation of net cash flow to movement in net debt			
Increase in cash		171	189
Cash inflow from increase in debt and lease financing		(892)	(895)
Cash inflow from decrease in liquid resources		(27)	–
Amortisation of 4% unsecured deep discount loan stock, RPI and LPI bonds		(14)	(7)
Other non-cash movements		(12)	(8)
Foreign exchange differences		18	(23)
Increase in net debt		(756)	(744)
Opening net debt	33	(2,804)	(2,060)
Closing net debt	33	(3,560)	(2,804)

Accounting policies and notes forming part of these financial statements are on pages 20 to 39.

Cash flow statement of Tesco PLC

- proposed dividends
- significant differences between the book value and market value of land and buildings
- political and charitable contributions
- policy on employment of disabled people
- health and safety at work of employees
- action taken on employee involvement and consultation
- policy on payment of creditors

CASH FLOW STATEMENTS

FRS 1 requires that all but the smaller limited companies must include, as part of their published accounts, a cash flow statement, which we will look at in detail in Chapter 6. Such a statement shows where the funds (money) have come from during the course of a financial year, and how such funds have been used. The statement also provides a direct link between the previous year's balance sheet and the current one. A recent cash flow statement for Tesco PLC is shown on the previous page.

AUDITORS' REPORT

Larger companies must have their accounts audited by external auditors, who are appointed by the shareholders to check the accounts. The auditors' report, which is printed in the published accounts, is the culmination of their work. The three main sections of the auditors' report are:

- **respective responsibilities of directors and auditors** – the directors are responsible for preparing the accounts, while the auditors are responsible for forming an opinion on the accounts
- **basis of opinion** – the framework of Auditing Standards (issued by the Auditing Practices Board) within which the audit was conducted, other assessments, and the way in which the audit was planned and performed
- **opinion** – the auditors' view of the company's accounts

An *'unqualified'* auditors' opinion will read as follows:

'In our opinion the financial statements give a true and fair view of the state of affairs of the Company at .... 20.., and of the profit, and cash flows of the Company for the year then ended, and have been properly prepared in accordance with the Companies Act 1985.'

A '*qualified*' auditors' report will raise points that the auditors consider have not been dealt with correctly in the accounts. Where such points are not too serious, the auditors will use phrases such as 'except for …' or 'subject to … the financial statements give a true and fair view'. Much more serious is where the auditors' statement says that the accounts 'do not show a true and fair view' or 'we are unable to form an opinion …'. These indicate a major disagreement between the company and the auditors, and a person involved with the company – such as an investor or creditor – should take serious note.

Note that smaller private companies are exempt from audit requirements if their turnover (sales) for the year is below a certain figure.

ACCOUNTING POLICIES

The Companies Act requires companies to include a statement of their accounting policies in the published accounts. FRS 18 *Accounting policies* (see also page 97) defines accounting policies as '*those principles, bases, conventions, rules and practices applied by an entity that specify how the effects of transactions and other events are to be reflected in its financial statements through*

*   *recognising*
*   *selecting measurement bases for, and*
*   *presenting*

assets, liabilities, gains, losses and changes to shareholders' funds'.

The objective of FRS 18 is to ensure that:

*   an entity adopts the accounting policies most appropriate to its particular circumstances for the purpose of giving a true and fair view
*   accounting policies adopted are reviewed regularly to ensure that they remain appropriate, and changes are made as necessary
*   sufficient information is disclosed in the financial statements to enable users to understand the accounting policies adopted and their implementation

When selecting accounting policies, the four criteria from Statement of Principles of relevance, reliability, comparability and understandability (see diagram in Chapter 1 on page 23) need to be considered.

Estimation techniques – such as straight-line and reducing balance depreciation methods, discounting of expected cash flows, and provisions for bad debts – are not accounting policies but, instead, are ways in which money amounts are arrived at under accounting policies. An accounting policy may say 'we depreciate computers over five years', but an estimation technique – eg straight-line depreciation – is used to calculate the money amounts shown in the financial statements.

An extract from the accounting policies of Tesco PLC is shown on the next page.

NOTES TO THE ACCOUNTS

The Companies Act 1985, as well as requiring the presentation of financial statements in a particular layout, also requires additional information to be provided. These *notes to the accounts* include:

- disclosure of accounting policies (see previous section)
- details of authorised and allotted share capital
- movements on fixed assets
- details of listed investments
- movements on reserves
- provision for deferred tax
- analysis of indebtedness
- details of charges and contingent liabilities
- details of interest or similar charges on loans and overdrafts
- basis of computation of UK Corporation Tax and details of tax charge
- directors' emoluments including Chairman's emoluments where necessary
- auditor's remuneration

We will look at each of these in turn.

details of authorised and allotted share capital

These details include:

- where appropriate, the different classes of shares (eg ordinary, preference), the number of shares and the total nominal value
- the amount of share capital allotted and called up
- details of any changes made during the year

An example (at 31 December 2004) is shown on page 70.

accounting policies

BASIS OF PREPARATION OF FINANCIAL STATEMENTS

These financial statements have been prepared under the historical cost convention, in accordance with applicable accounting standards and the Companies Act 1985.

In November and December 2000, the Accounting Standards Board issued FRS 17, 'Retirement Benefits' and FRS 19, 'Deferred Tax' respectively.

FRS 17 will be adopted by the Group over the next two years. The FRS has an extended transitional period during which certain disclosures will be required in the notes to the financial statements. The Group is required to make these phased disclosures in the current year, which are are shown in note 27(b).

FRS 19 has been adopted with effect from 25 February 2001. This standard addresses the recognition, on a full provision basis, of deferred tax assets and liabilities arising from timing differences between the recognition of gains and losses in the financial statements and their recognition in a tax computation. Prior to 25 February 2001, the Group's accounting policy was to provide for the deferred tax which was likely to be payable or recoverable.

BASIS OF CONSOLIDATION

The Group financial statements consist of the financial statements of the parent company, its subsidiary undertakings and the Group's share of interests in joint ventures and associates. The accounts of the parent company's subsidiary undertakings are prepared to dates around 23 February 2002 apart from Global T.H., Tesco Polska Sp. z o.o., Tesco Stores ČR a.s., Tesco Stores SR a.s., Samsung Tesco Co. Limited, Tesco Taiwan Co. Limited and Ek-Chai Distribution System Co. Ltd which prepared accounts to 31 December 2001. In the opinion of the Directors it is necessary for the above named subsidiaries to prepare accounts to a date earlier than the rest of the Group to enable the timely publication of the Group financial statements.

The Group's interests in joint ventures are accounted for using the gross equity method. The Group's interests in associates are accounted for using the equity method.

TURNOVER

Turnover consists of sales through retail outlets and sales of development properties excluding value added tax.

STOCKS

Stocks comprise goods held for resale and properties held for, or in the course of, development and are valued at the lower of cost and net realisable value. Stocks in stores are calculated at retail prices and reduced by appropriate margins to the lower of cost and net realisable value.

MONEY MARKET DEPOSITS

Money market deposits are stated at cost. All income from these investments is included in the profit and loss account as interest receivable and similar income.

FIXED ASSETS AND DEPRECIATION

Fixed assets are carried at cost and include amounts in respect of interest paid on funds specifically related to the financing of assets in the course of construction.

Depreciation is provided on a straight-line basis over the anticipated useful economic lives of the assets.

The following rates applied for the year ended 23 February 2002:

- Land premia paid in excess of the alternative use value – at 2.5% of cost.
- Freehold and leasehold buildings with greater than 40 years unexpired – at 2.5% of cost.
- Leasehold properties with less than 40 years unexpired are amortised by equal annual instalments over the unexpired period of the lease.
- Plant, equipment, fixtures and fittings and motor vehicles – at rates varying from 10% to 33%.

GOODWILL

Goodwill arising from transactions entered into after 1 March 1998 is capitalised and amortised on a straight-line basis over its useful economic life, up to a maximum of 20 years.

All goodwill arising from transactions entered into prior to 1 March 1998 has been written off to reserves.

IMPAIRMENT OF FIXED ASSETS AND GOODWILL

Fixed assets and goodwill are subject to review for impairment in accordance with FRS 11, 'Impairment of Fixed Assets and Goodwill'. Any impairment is recognised in the profit and loss account in the year in which it occurs.

LEASING

Plant, equipment and fixtures and fittings which are the subject of finance leases are dealt with in the financial statements as tangible fixed assets and equivalent liabilities at what would otherwise have been the cost of outright purchase.

Rentals are apportioned between reductions of the respective liabilities and finance charges, the latter being calculated by reference to the rates of interest implicit in the leases. The finance charges are dealt with under interest payable in the profit and loss account.

Leased assets are depreciated in accordance with the depreciation accounting policy over the anticipated working lives of the assets which generally correspond to the primary rental periods. The cost of operating leases in respect of land and buildings and other assets is expensed as incurred.

Extract from the accounting policies of Tesco PLC

	£000s
Authorised share capital	
3,000,000 ordinary shares of £1 each	3,000
500,000 6% preference shares of £1 each	500
	3,500
Issued share capital	
2,500,000 ordinary shares of £1 each, fully paid	2,500
300,000 6% preference shares of £1 each, fully paid	300
	2,800

movements on fixed assets (tangible & intangible)

This section of the notes requires the company to:

- disclose amounts of cost or valuation
  - at the beginning of the year
  - at the end of the year
- disclose the amount of depreciation (or amortisation of intangibles, such as goodwill)
  - at the beginning of the year
  - at the end of the year
- give details of changes during the year
  - acquisitions
  - disposals
  - revaluations (giving the date and basis of valuation)
  - depreciation (or amortisation)

An example (at 31 December 2004) is shown on the opposite page.

details of listed investments

Listed investments are those that are quoted on a stock exchange. Investments to be held for the foreseeable future are treated as fixed assets; short-term investments are treated as current assets. The notes will show:

- the cost price, together with any additions or disposals during the year
- the market value where it differs from the carrying value (ie book value)

An example (at 31 December 2004) is shown on page 72.

INTANGIBLE FIXED ASSETS

	Goodwill
	£000s
Cost at 1 Jan and 31 Dec 2004	100
Amortisation	
at 1 Jan 2004	40
Charge for year	10
at 31 Dec 2004	50
Net book value:	
at 1 Jan 2004	60
at 31 Dec 2004	50

TANGIBLE FIXED ASSETS

	Freehold land and buildings	*Plant and machinery*	*Total*
	£000s	£000s	£000s
Cost or valuation:			
at 1 Jan 2004	5,200	1,000	6,200
Additions	–	200	200
Revaluations	1,000	–	1,000
Disposals	–	(100)	(100)
at 31 Dec 2004	6,200	1,100	7,300
Depreciation:			
at 1 Jan 2004	200	500	700
Charge for year	90	110	200
Revaluation	(290)	–	(290)
Disposals	–	(60)	(60)
at 31 Dec 2004	–	550	550
Net book value:			
at 1 Jan 2004	5,000	500	5,500
at 31 Dec 2004	6,200	550	6,750

- Included in freehold land and buildings is land valued at £700,000 which is not depreciated.
- The freehold land and buildings were valued on the basis of open market values on 31 December 2004 by Petham & Co, Chartered Surveyors.

Listed investments	£000s
Cost:	
at 1 Jan 2004	950
Additions	100
Disposals	(50)
at 31 Dec 2004	1,000
Valuation:	
market value	1,232

movements on reserves

Notes in the accounts for reserves (eg profit and loss account, revaluation reserve, share premium account) show

- opening balance, movements and closing balance
- changes in provisions for liabilities and charges, disclosed in the same way (see provision for deferred tax, below)

An example (at 31 December 2004) is shown below.

Reserves	£000s
Profit and loss account:	
at 1 Jan 2004	1,700
Retained profit for year	800
at 31 Dec 2004	2,500
Revaluation reserve:	
at 1 Jan 2004	500
Revaluation surplus	1,000
at 31 Dec 2004	1,500

provision for deferred tax

Deferred tax (see page 131) is a potential liability that may have to be paid to the Inland Revenue. A deferred tax account is included in the balance sheet under the heading 'provisions for liabilities and charges'. The notes will show the opening balance, movements and the closing balance.

An example (at 31 December 2004) is shown on the next page.

Provisions for liabilities and charges	£000s
Deferred taxation:	
at 1 Jan 2004	75
Transfer from profit and loss account	25
Transfer to profit and loss account	(–)
at 31 Dec 2004	100

analysis of indebtedness

Indebtedness in all forms – eg trade creditors, bank loans, overdrafts, debentures, taxation, social security costs, etc – is split between amounts due within one year and amounts due in more than one year (the balance sheet layout – see page 63 – shows this).

Notes to the accounts disclose amounts due for each form of indebtedness:

- for creditors falling due after five years, the notes must state in respect of each item shown the total amounts of debts which

  - are repayable, other than by instalments, more than five years after the end of the financial year

  - are repayable by instalments, any of which fall due after the five-year period, with the total amount of the instalments falling due after the end of that time also stated

- the terms of repayment and the rates of interest are normally to be stated for debts falling due after five years

- where creditors are secured, there must be stated the total amount of debts for which security has been given and an indication of the nature of those securities

- for debentures issued during the financial year, details should be given which include the amount of money raised by the issue

- FRS 4, *Capital instruments*, requires additional information to be given in the notes – see page 137

An example (at 31 December 2004) is shown on the next page.

Creditors: amounts falling due within one year   £000s

Bank overdraft	20
Trade creditors	630
Corporation tax	700
Social security costs	50
Proposed final dividend	400
	1,800

The bank overdraft is secured by a floating charge on the assets of the company

Creditors: amounts falling due after more than one year

10% debentures repayable in 2012	1,500

The debentures are secured by a fixed charge on the freehold property

details of charges and contingent liabilities

- for liabilities and charges show
  - opening balance
  - movements
  - closing balance
- provision for deferred tax (see page 72, and page 131) is to be disclosed separately
- contingent liabilities should be disclosed as a note to the accounts with an estimate of the financial effect, its legal nature and details of any security
- FRS 12, *Provisions, contingent liabilities and contingent assets,* sets out the principles of accounting for these items – see page 138
- an example (at 31 December 2004) is shown below:

Contingent liabilities

A customer has commenced an action against the company in respect of faulty goods supplied. Legal proceedings are due to commence in March 2005; if the action is successful it has been estimated that the liability is £15,000. The company has been advised by its lawyers that it is possible, but not probable, that the action will be successful. Accordingly no provision for any liability has been made in this year's accounts.

interest or similar charges on loans and overdrafts

Separate disclosure is required of interest and other charges on

- bank loans and overdrafts
- other loans

An example (for year to 31 December 2004) is shown below.

Interest payable and similar charges	£000s
Bank loans and overdrafts	50
Other loans	150
	200

basis of computation of UK Corporation Tax and details of tax charge

The notes will disclose the total charge for tax on profit on ordinary activities distinguishing between major components such as:

- UK corporation tax
- deferred tax
- foreign tax

FRS 16, *Current tax,* discusses corporation tax in more detail – see page 131. An example (at 31 December 2004) is shown below.

Taxation on profit on ordinary activities	£000s
UK corporation tax at 30%	700
Deferred tax	25
	725

directors' emoluments

The notes should show the total of directors' emoluments (note that the term 'emoluments' includes salaries, fees and bonuses, allowances which are taxed, and the value of benefits in kind).

The notes should also disclose the highest paid director's emoluments (only required to be shown for listed companies, and where total directors' emoluments exceed £200,000 per year).

Look at the example (for year to 31 December 2004) shown on the next page.

Directors' emoluments	£000s
Emoluments	250
The amount is respect of the highest paid director is:	
Emoluments	95

auditors' remuneration

These notes disclose the amount of auditors' remuneration, including expenses. An example (for year to 31 December 2004) is shown below.

	£000s
Auditors' remuneration	15

SMALL AND MEDIUM-SIZED COMPANIES

The Companies Act allows small and medium-sized *private* companies to file modified accounts with the Registrar of Companies. However, accounts must still be prepared in full form for presentation to their members. A company qualifies to be treated as small or medium-sized if it satisfies any two or more of the following conditions:

	small	*medium*
• turnover (sales) does not exceed	£5.6m	£22.8m
• assets do not exceed	£2.8m	£11.4m
• average number of employees does not exceed	50	250

small companies

A small company need not file a profit and loss account. The directors' report can be abbreviated and details of directors' emoluments need not be disclosed. The balance sheet can list only the main asset and liability headings, with notes to the accounts reduced to include only details of accounting policies, share capital, indebtedness, and figures for the previous year.

For taxation purposes, the Inland Revenue accepts a simple profit and loss account which is used to calculate the amount of corporation tax due.

medium-sized companies

Concessions for medium-sized companies are more limited: details of sales turnover and the make-up of cost of sales need not be given; instead, the profit and loss account starts with the figure for gross profit. In all other respects, a full set of accounts must be filed.

Note: the above concessions apply only to private limited companies; public limited companies of all sizes must file full accounts.

BONUS ISSUES AND RIGHTS ISSUES

Limited companies – and particularly plcs – quite often increase their capital by means of either **bonus issues** or **rights issues** of shares. Whilst both of these have the effect of increasing the number of shares in issue, they have quite different effects on the structure of the company balance sheet.

bonus issues

A bonus issue is made when a company issues free shares to existing shareholders; it does this by using reserves that have built up and capitalising them (ie they are turned into permanent share capital). The bonus issue is distributed on the basis of existing shareholdings – for example, one bonus share for every two shares already held.

With a bonus issue no cash flows in or out of the company. The shareholders are no better off: with more shares in issue the stock market price per share will fall in proportion to the bonus issue, ie the company's net assets are now spread among a greater number of shares.

Bonus issues are made in order to acknowledge the fact that reserves belong to shareholders. Often a build-up of reserves occurs because a company hasn't the cash to pay dividends, so a bonus issue is a way of passing the reserves to shareholders.

Note that capital or revenue reserves can be used for bonus issues. If there is a choice, then capital reserves are used first – this is because it is one of the few uses of a capital reserve, which cannot be used to fund the payment of dividends.

rights issues

A rights issue is used by a company seeking to raise further finance through the issue of shares. Instead of going to the considerable expense of offering additional shares to the public, it is cheaper to offer shares to existing shareholders at a favourable price (usually a little below the current market price). As with a bonus issue the extra shares are offered in proportion to the shareholders' existing holding. The shareholder may take up the rights by subscribing for the shares offered; alternatively the rights can often be sold on the stock market.

SEVERN PLC AND WYE PLC:
BONUS ISSUES AND RIGHTS ISSUES

situation

The following are the summary balance sheets of Severn plc and Wye plc:

	Severn	Wye
	£	£
Fixed assets	300,000	300,000
Current assets (including bank)	100,000	100,000
	400,000	400,000
Ordinary shares of £1 each	200,000	200,000
Reserves (capital and revenue)	200,000	200,000
	400,000	400,000

Severn is planning a one-for-two bonus issue.

Wye is seeking finance for a capital expenditure programme through a one-for-two rights issue at a price of £1.80 per share (the current market price is £2.10).

solution

After the issues, the balance sheets appear as:

	Severn	Wye
	£	£
Fixed assets	300,000	300,000
Current assets (including bank)	100,000	280,000
	400,000	580,000
Ordinary shares of £1 each	300,000	300,000
Share premium account (capital reserve)	–	80,000
Reserves	100,000	200,000
	400,000	580,000

The changes are:

Severn   Reserves are reduced by £100,000, whilst share capital is increased by the same amount; the ordinary share capital is now more in balance with fixed assets; no cash has been received.

Wye   The bank balance has increased by £180,000, being 100,000 shares (assuming that all shareholders took up their rights) at £1.80; share capital has increased by £100,000, whilst 80p per share is the share premium, ie £80,000 in total. The company now has the money to finance its capital expenditure programme. There are also significant reserves which could be used for a bonus issue in the future.

tutorial note – preparing for examination

In the AAT Examination for the Unit covered by this book you will often be presented with a limited company's trial balance (or sometimes an extended trial balance). Points of further information will also be given to you.

You will then be required to produce a profit and loss account and/or a balance sheet using the figures from the trial balance and incorporating the further information. A specimen layout of the financial statement(s) is normally provided in the answer booklet.

In the Case Study which follows we will see how the profit and loss account and balance sheet are prepared in published accounts format from the figures given in a trial balance.

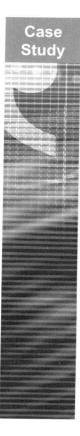

Case Study

AMARILLO LIMITED: PREPARING THE ACCOUNTS FROM A TRIAL BALANCE

situation

You have been asked to help prepare the financial statements of Amarillo Limited for the year ended 30 June 2004. The trial balance of the company as at 30 June 2004 is set out below.

Amarillo Limited
Trial balance as at 30 June 2004

	Debit £000	Credit £000
Interest	200	
Distribution costs	5,468	
Administrative expenses	2,933	
Trade debtors	4,610	
Trade creditors		1,872
Interim dividend	250	
Ordinary share capital		5,000
Sales		25,840
Long-term loan		4,000
Land – cost	6,000	

continued on next page

Buildings – cost	2,298	
Fixtures and fittings – cost	1,865	
Vehicles – cost	2,145	
Office equipment – cost	1,783	
Purchases	12,965	
Bank	609	
Profit and loss account as at 1 July 2003		3,875
Stock as at 1 July 2003	4,285	
Share premium		1,500
Buildings – accumulated depreciation		424
Fixtures and fittings – accumulated depreciation		597
Vehicles – accumulated depreciation		1,410
Office equipment – accumulated depreciation		893
	45,411	45,411

Further information available to you:

- The authorised share capital of the company, all of which has been issued, consists of ordinary shares with a nominal value of £1.

- The company paid an interim dividend of 5p per share during the year but has not provided for the proposed final dividend of 10p per share.

- The stock at the close of business on 30 June 2004 was valued at cost at £5,162,000.

- The corporation tax charge for the year has been calculated as £1,475,000.

- An advertising campaign was undertaken during the year at a cost of £22,000. No invoices have yet been received for this campaign.

- Interest on the long-term loan has been paid for six months of the year. No adjustment has been made for the interest due for the final six months of the year. Interest is charged on the loan at a rate of 10% per annum.

- The land has been revalued by professional valuers at £7,000,000. The revaluation is to be included in the financial statements for the year ended 30 June 2004.

- All of the operations are continuing operations.

From the further information given above you are to make the journal entries required (dates and narratives are not required).

Notes:

- show any workings relevant to these adjustments

- ignore any effect of these adjustments on the tax charge for the year given above

Draft a profit and loss account for the year ended 30 June 2004, and a balance sheet for Amarillo Limited as at that date, making any adjustments required as a result of the further information given above (notes to the accounts are not required).

solution

JOURNAL ENTRIES

				£000	£000
1.	DR	Dividend		500	
	CR	Dividend proposed			500
2.	DR	Stock (balance sheet)		5,162	
	CR	Stock (trading account)			5,162
3.	DR	Taxation		1,475	
	CR	Taxation payable			1,475
4.	DR	Distribution expenses		22	
	CR	Accruals			22
5.	DR	Interest		200	
	CR	Interest payable			200
6.	DR	Land		1,000	
	CR	Revaluation reserve			1,000

tutorial notes:
(all figures £000)

Dividend: £5,000 x 10p = £500

Interest: £4,000 x 10% x 6 months = £200

Revaluation: £7,000 – £6,000 = £1,000

AMARILLO LIMITED
Profit and Loss Account for the year ended 30 June 2004

	£000
Turnover	
Continuing operations	25,840
Cost of sales (note 1)	12,088
Gross profit	13,752
Distribution costs (note 2)	5,490
Administrative expenses	2,933
Operating profit	
Continuing operations	5,329
Interest payable and similar charges (note 3)	400
Profit on ordinary activities before taxation	4,929
Tax on profit on ordinary activities	1,475
Profit on ordinary activities after taxation	3,454
Dividends (note 4)	750
Retained profit for the financial year	2,704

Balance Sheet as at 30 June 2004

	£000	£000
Fixed assets (note 5)		
Tangible assets		11,767
Current assets		
Stock	5,162	
Debtors	4,610	
Bank	609	
	10,381	
Creditors: amounts falling due within one year (note 6)	(4,069)	
Net current assets		6,312
Total assets *less* current liabilities		18,079
Creditors: amounts falling due after more than one year		(4,000)
		14,079
Capital and reserves		
Called up share capital		5,000
Share premium		1,500
Revaluation reserve		1,000
Profit and loss account (note 7)		6,579
		14,079

tutorial notes

(All figures £000)

The profit and loss account and balance sheet are presented in a suitable form for publication: however, the full notes to the accounts are not required.

1 Calculation of cost of sales:

Opening stock	4,285
Purchases	12,965
	17,250
less Closing stock	5,162
Cost of sales	12,088

2 Distribution costs:

5,468 + 22 (advertising accrual) = 5,490

3   Interest payable:

200 + 200 (half-year's interest on 10% long-term loan accrued) = 400

4   Dividends:

Interim dividend paid	250
Final dividend proposed	500
	750

5   Fixed Assets:

	Cost	Accumulated depreciation	Net book value
Land	7,000	–	*7,000
Buildings	2,298	424	1,874
Fixtures and fittings	1,865	597	1,268
Vehicles	2,145	1,410	735
Office equipment	1,783	893	890
	15,091	3,324	11,767

* Land: 6,000 + 1,000 = 7,000

6   Creditors: amounts falling due within one year:

Trade creditors	1,872
Corporation tax payable	1,475
Dividends proposed (see above)	500
Accruals (advertising 22 + interest 200)	222
	4,069

7   Profit and loss account:

at 1 July 2003	3,875
Retained profit for the year	2,704
at 30 June 2004	6,579

This Case Study asked you to prepare the profit and loss account and balance sheet from a trial balance. However, if an examination question asks you to prepare a balance sheet only, you need to think about how you are going to get the figure for profit and loss account which goes in the balance sheet. In such circumstances you will need to do a working note which summarises the profit and loss account transactions, ie sales, less cost of sales, costs and expenses, taxation and dividends.

CONFIDENTIALITY PROCEDURES

The published accounts of limited companies are readily available to shareholders and interested parties either from the company itself or from Companies House (www.companieshouse.gov.uk). Nevertheless, as noted in this chapter, only certain information has to be disclosed in the published accounts.

For those involved in the preparation of the accounts, confidentiality procedures must be observed at all times:

– during the preparation of published accounts

– during the period after the accounts have been prepared but before they are sent to the shareholders, filed at Companies House, and disclosed to the public

– for detailed information that is needed in the preparation of the accounts but is not required to be disclosed under the Companies Acts

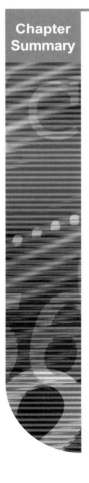

Chapter Summary

- The Companies Act 1985 (as amended by the Companies Act 1989) requires a considerable amount of detail to be disclosed in the published accounts of limited companies.

- The Act requires all limited companies to produce:
  – a profit and loss account
  – a balance sheet
  – a directors' report
  – an auditors' report
  – consolidated accounts (where appropriate)

- The Act lays down formats for profit and loss account and balance sheet.

- Besides the requirements of the Companies Act, companies must also abide by the Statements of Standard Accounting Practice (SSAPs) and Financial Reporting Standards (FRSs), as laid down by the Accounting Standards Board, together with Urgent Issues Task Force (UITF) Abstracts.

- Most companies also include in their published accounts a cash flow statement which shows where the funds (money) has come from during the course of the financial year, and how it has been used.

- For larger companies, external auditors report to the shareholders on the state of affairs of the company.

- The directors establish the accounting policies which the company will follow.

- Bonus issues and rights issues increase the number of shares in issue – only the latter brings in cash to the company.

Key Terms		
	statutory accounts	financial statements required by law, a copy of which is filed at Companies House, where it can be inspected
	report and accounts	the corporate report of the company which is available to every shareholder
	summary financial statement	a shorter version of the report and accounts which, by agreement with individual shareholders, can be sent in place of the report and accounts
	exceptional items	'material items which derive from events or transactions that fall within the ordinary activities of the reporting entity and which individually or, if of a similar type, in aggregate, need to be disclosed by virtue of their size or incidence if the financial statements are to give a true and fair view' (FRS 3)
	extraordinary items	'material items possessing a high degree of abnormality which arise from events or transactions that fall outside the ordinary activities of the reporting entity and which are not expected to recur' (FRS 3)
	prior period adjustments	'material adjustments applicable to prior periods arising from changes in accounting policies or from the correction of fundamental errors' (FRS 3)
	auditors' report	gives the auditors' opinion on the company's financial statements as to whether they give a true and fair view of the state of affairs of the company
	accounting policies	the specific accounting principles, bases, conventions, rules and practices that the directors of a company choose to follow
	bonus issue	the capitalisation of reserves – either capital or revenue – in the form of free shares issued to existing shareholders in proportion to their holdings; no cash flows into the company
	rights issue	the raising of cash by offering shares to existing shareholders, in proportion to their holdings, at a favourable price

Student Activities

Osborne Books is grateful to the AAT for their kind permission to use past assessment material for the following activity: 3.10.

3.1 Which one of the following statements is not part of the corporate report?

(a) profit and loss account

(b) auditors' report

(c) directors' report

(d) chairman's statement

3.2 Which one of the following is not a non-recurring profit and loss, as defined by FRS3 'Reporting Financial Performance'?

(a) exceptional items

(b) extraordinary items

(c) Post balance sheet events

(d) prior period adjustments

3.3 According to the Companies Act 1985 which one of the following features is applicable to a medium sized company?

(a) turnover of £15m

(b) turnover of £10m

(c) assets of £8m

(d) average number of employees 300

3.4 Which one of the following transactions does not involve the movement of cash?

(a) bonus issue of shares

(b) rights issue of shares

(c) redemption of shares

(d) issue of non-cumulative preference shares

3.5 Briefly outline the benefits to a company's shareholders when a business produces a statement of total recognised gains and losses as part of its corporate report.

3.6 List four items that need to be included in a directors' report.

3.7   The following trial balance has been extracted from the books of account of Proudlock PLC as at 31 March 20-2.

	£000	£000
Administration expenses	240	
Issued share capital (£1 ordinary shares)		700
Debtors	600	
Cash in bank	75	.
Accruals		15
Share premium account		200
Distribution costs	500	
Other creditors		80
Fixed asset investments	600	
Plant machinery at cost	1,000	
Accumulated depreciation as at 31.03.20-2		500
Profit and loss account b/f		210
Purchases	1,200	
Stock at 01.04.20-1	160	
Trade creditors		300
Sales		2,295
Dividends received		75
	4,375	4,375

Additional information

- Stock at 31 March 20-2 was valued at £180,000.

- Corporation tax charge based on the profits for the year is estimated to be £65,000.

- A final ordinary dividend of 40 pence per share is proposed.

Students should note that depreciation has already been provided for in the list of balances above and allocated to administration expenses and distribution costs accordingly.

REQUIRED

Task 1

Prepare journal entries for the adjustments listed above under 'additional information'.

Task 2

In so far as the information permits, prepare the company's published profit and loss account for the year to 31 March 20-2 and a balance sheet as at that date in accordance with the Companies Act 1985 and FRS3 (revised).

Note – A statement of accounting policies is NOT required and no formal notes should be submitted, but where relevant, working notes should be attached to your answer.

3.8   The following information has been extracted from the books of Broadfoot plc for the year to 31 March 20-2.

	Dr £000	Cr £000
Administrative expenses	185	
Issued share capital (£1 ordinary shares)		200
Cash at bank and in hand	15	
Accruals		90
Distribution costs	240	
Land and buildings: at cost	210	
accumulated depreciation (at 1 April 20-1)		48
Plant and machinery: at cost	125	
accumulated depreciation (at 1 April 20-1)		75
Profit and loss account (at 1 April 20-1)		350
Purchases	470	
Sales		1,300
Stock (at 1 April 20-1)	150	
Trade creditors		60
Trade debtors	728	
	2,123	2,123

Additional information

- Stock at 31 March 20-2 was valued at £250,000.

- Buildings and plant and machinery are depreciated on a straight-line basis (assuming no residual value) at the following rates:

On cost:	%
Buildings	5
Plant and machinery	20

  Land at cost was £110,000. Land is not depreciated.

  There were no purchases or sales of fixed assets during the year to 31 March 20-2.

  The depreciation charges for the year to 31 March 20-2 are to be apportioned as follows:

	%
Cost of sales	60
Distribution costs	20
Administrative expenses	20

- Corporation tax for the year to 31 March 20-2 (based on profits for that year at a rate of 35%) is estimated to be £135,000.

- The directors propose to pay a dividend of 150p per share.

REQUIRED

Task 1

Prepare journal entries for the adjustments listed above under 'additional information'.

Task 2

As far as the information permits, prepared Broadfoot plc's profit and loss account for the year to 31 March 20-2 and a balance sheet as at that date in accordance with the minimum disclosure requirements of the Companies Act 1985, FRS3 (revised) and related statements of standard accounting practice. (Note: A statement of accounting policies is *not* required and no formal notes should be submitted, but where relevant, working notes should be attached to your answer).

3.9   The following list of balances was extracted from the books of Grandware plc on 31 December 20-2

	£
Sales	2,640,300
Administration expenses	220,180
Selling and distribution costs	216,320
Interest paid on loan stock	10,000
Dividends received	2,100
Share Premium Account	40,000
Purchases	2,089,600
Stocks at 01.01.20-2	318,500
Cash at bank	20,640
Trade debtors	415,800
Provision for doubtful debts at 01.01.20-2	10,074
Bad debts	8,900
Creditors	428,250
10% loan stock	200,000
Long-term investments in listed companies	20,000
Office equipment	110,060
Vehicles	235,000
£1 ordinary shares	200,000
Profit and loss account at 01.01.20-2	144,276

Notes:

•   Accrue for the 6 months £10,000 loan stock interest due, which is payable 01.01.20-3.

•   Provide for administration expenses of £12,200 paid in advance at 31.12.20-2 and distribution costs of £21,300 owing at 31.12.20-2.

•   Provision for doubtful debts is to be maintained at 3% of debtors.

- Stocks at 31.12.20-2 were valued at £340,600.

- Provide for corporation tax £45,000 which is payable 31.12.20-3.

- The directors recommend a dividend of 28 pence per share.

- Depreciation on tangible fixed assets has already been allocated for the year and apportioned to the respective expense accounts in the list of balances provided.

REQUIRED

Task 1

Prepare journal entries for the adjustments listed above under 'notes'.

Task 2

Prepare for presentation to the shareholders a profit and loss account for the year ended 31 December 20-2 and a balance sheet as at that date, which comply, in so far as the information given allows, with the requirements of the Companies Act 1985 and FRS3 (revised).

Formal notes are not required but working notes should be attached to your answer.

3.10   You have been asked to help prepare the financial statements of Hightink Limited for the year ended 31 March 2002. The trial balance of the company as at 31 March 2002 is set out below.

	Dr	Cr
	£000	£000
Interest	240	
Distribution costs	6,852	
Administrative expenses	3,378	
Trade debtors	5,455	
Trade creditors		2,363
Interim dividend	400	
Ordinary share capital		4,000
Sales		31,710
Long-term loan		6,000
Land – cost	5,000	
Buildings – cost	3,832	
Fixtures and fittings – cost	2,057	
Motor vehicles – cost	3,524	
Office equipment – cost	2,228	
Purchases	15,525	
Cash at bank	304	
Profit and loss account		6,217
Stock as at 1 April 2001	6,531	

continued on next page

Share premium		2,000
Buildings – accumulated depreciation		564
Fixtures and fittings – accumulated depreciation		726
Motor vehicles – accumulated depreciation		1,283
Office equipment – accumulated depreciation		463
	55,326	55,326

Further information:

- The authorised share capital of the company, all of which has been issued, consists of ordinary shares with a nominal value of £1.

- The company paid an interim dividend of 10p per share during the year but has not provided for the proposed final dividend of 15p per share.

- The stock at the close of business on 31 March 2002 was valued at cost at £7,878,000.

- The corporation tax charge for the year has been calculated as £1,920,000.

- Credit sales relating to April 2002 amounting to £204,000 had been entered incorrectly into the accounts in March 2002.

- Interest on the long-term loan has been paid for six months of the year. No adjustment has been made for the interest due for the final six months of the year. Interest is charged on the loan at a rate of 8% per annum.

- The land has been revalued by professional valuers at £5,500,000. The revaluation is to be included in the financial statements for the year ended 31 March 2002.

- All of the operations are continuing operations.

REQUIRED

Task 1

Make the journal entries required as a result of the further information given above. Dates and narratives are not required.

- You must show any workings relevant to these adjustments.

- Ignore any effect of these adjustments on the tax charge for the year given above.

Task 2

Making any adjustments required as a result of the further information given above, draft a profit and loss account for the year ended 31 March 2002, and a balance sheet for Hightink as at that date.

Note: You are *not* required to produce notes to the accounts.

3.11 You have been asked to assist in the preparation of the financial statements of Wyvern Office Products Limited for the year ended 31 December 2004. The company sells office equipment and supplies to businesses and individuals through its shops and warehouses.

You have been provided with the extended trial balance of Wyvern Office Products Limited as at 31 December 2004 as shown on the next page.

The following information is available to you:

- the authorised share capital of the businesses, all of which has been issued, consists of ordinary shares with a nominal value of £1

- depreciation has been calculated on the fixed assets of the business and has already been transferred into the balances for distribution costs and administration expenses shown on the extended trial balance

- the corporation tax charge for the year has been calculated as £215,000

- the company paid an interim dividend of 6p per share during the year but has not provided for a proposed final dividend of 10p per share

- interest on the 10% debentures has been paid for the first six months of the year only

REQUIRED

From the extended trial balance, and the information provided above, you are to draft a profit and loss account for the year ended 31 December 2004 and a balance sheet as at that date.

Notes:

- journal entries are not required for any necessary adjustments to the figures in the extended trial balance

- ignore the effect of any of the adjustments to the tax charge for the year

- show workings relevant to the figures appearing in the financial statements

EXTENDED TRIAL BALANCE   **WYVERN OFFICE PRODUCTS LIMITED**   **31 DECEMBER 2004**

Description	Trial balance Dr £000	Trial balance Cr £000	Adjustments Dr £000	Adjustments Cr £000	Profit and loss Dr £000	Profit and loss Cr £000	Balance sheet Dr £000	Balance sheet Cr £000
Sales		10,641				10,641		
Purchases	7,028				7,028			
Returns inwards	65				65			
Returns outwards		48				48		
Stock	2,220		2,533	2,533	2,220	2,533	2,533	
Distribution costs	1,524		176		1,700			
Administration expenses	1,103		308		1,411			
Accruals				67				67
Prepayments			24				24	
Interest	80				80			
Land – cost	510						510	
Buildings – cost	1,490						1,490	
Fixtures and fittings – cost	275						275	
Vehicles – cost	316						316	
Office equipment – cost	294						294	
Investments	1,850						1,850	
Buildings – accumulated depn		407		298				705
Fixtures and fittings – accumulated depn		142		55				197
Vehicles – accumulated depn		124		48				172
Office equipment – accumulated depn		107		30				137
Trade debtors	1,592						1,592	
Provision for bad debts		70		10				80
Bank	44						44	
Trade creditors		2,051						2,051
10% Debentures		1,600						1,600
Interim dividend	120				120			
Share capital		2,000						2,000
Share premium		750						750
Profit and loss account		571						571
Profit					598			598
	18,511	18,511	3,041	3,041	13,222	13,222	8,928	8,928

In this chapter we focus on the accounting standards (SSAPs and FRSs) that impact on the way in which assets are accounted for in both profit and loss account and balance sheet. We look first of all at the selection of accounting policies (FRS 18), and then consider the importance of reporting the commercial substance of transactions in financial statements (FRS 5). We then focus on the fixed assets, to cover:

- *goodwill, intangible assets, and impairment of fixed assets (FRSs 10 and 11)*
- *fixed assets (FRS 15)*
- *investment properties (SSAP 19)*
- *hire purchase and leasing (SSAP 21)*
- *research and development expenditure (SSAP 13)*
- *government grants (SSAP 4)*

For current assets we look at accounting for stocks (SSAP 9).

NVQ PERFORMANCE CRITERIA COVERED

unit 11: DRAFTING FINANCIAL STATEMENTS

element 11.1

draft limited company financial statements

A   *draft limited company financial statements from the appropriate information*

B   *correctly identify and implement subsequent adjustments and ensure that discrepancies, unusual features or queries are identified and either resolved or referred to the appropriate person*

C   *ensure that limited company financial statements comply with relevant accounting standards and domestic legislation and with the organisation's policies, regulations and procedures*

E   *ensure that confidentiality procedures are followed at all times*

HOW TO STUDY THE ACCOUNTING STANDARDS

As we have seen in earlier chapters, accounting standards – in the form of Statements of Standard Accounting Practice (SSAPs) and Financial Reporting Standards (FRSs) – play a major role in the presentation and detail of financial statements. International Accounting Standards – see Chapter 9 – will play an increasingly important role in the preparation of financial statements over the next few years. (Note that, in most cases, compliance with an FRS automatically ensures compliance with the relevant international standard – each FRS includes a section explaining how it relates to the IAS or IFRS dealing with the same topic.)

The NVQ Unit *Drafting Financial Statements* requires knowledge of a large number of standards – in this book we have attempted, as far as possible, to group standards together where they relate to particular topics. Accordingly, this chapter focuses on those standards that relate to assets. The next chapter looks at the standards covering liabilities and profit and loss account; Chapter 8 deals with consolidated accounts, so the standards which cover group accounts (and also associated companies) are covered there. The cash flow statement is detailed in an accounting standard (FRS 1) and this is detailed in Chapter 6. A few standards do not fit readily to such groupings and so these have been included at what seems to be the most logical place. We believe that this 'grouping' approach is preferable to explaining the standards in their numerical order, which results in a long 'list' where often unrelated topics follow one another.

the accounting standards

The table that follows shows the current UK accounting standards, together with their titles and the page in this book where each is covered. Note that the index also shows page numbers for the various standards.

---

coverage of UK accounting standards

SSAP 4	Accounting for government grants	page 114
SSAP 5	Accounting for value added tax	page 134
SSAP 9	Stocks and long-term contracts	page 116
SSAP 13	Accounting for research and development	page 112
SSAP 17	Accounting for post balance sheet events	page 142
SSAP 19	Accounting for investment properties	page 105
SSAP 20	Foreign currency translation	page 150
SSAP 21	Accounting for leases and hire purchase contracts	page 108

continued . . .

organising your study of accounting standards

In this textbook we cover the aspects of each accounting standard that are assessable under *Drafting Financial Statements*. Note, however, that some standards cover more detailed issues that are not assessable. The texts of all current standards are available from the Accounting Standards Board.

For learning the key points of accounting standards, it is strongly recommended that you use a system of index cards: put the number and name of each standard on the top of an index card and then outline the key points of the standards on the cards, using bullet point format. The set of index cards (don't use very small cards!) then forms a useful learning and revision aid which can be carried around and easily referred to at almost any time.

It is also important to keep up-to-date with any changes to accounting standards – use accountancy magazines and web sites. The Accounting Standards Board's web site www.asb.org.uk is especially useful for this purpose.

FRS 18 – ACCOUNTING POLICIES

FRS 18 defines accounting policies as *'those principles, bases, conventions, rules and practices applied by an entity that specify how the effects of transactions and other events are to be reflected in its financial statements through*

- *recognising*

- *selecting measurement bases for, and*

- *presenting*

assets, liabilities, gains, losses and changes to shareholders' funds'.

An entity should adopt accounting policies that enable its financial statements to give a true and fair view. The accounting policies should be consistent with the requirements of accounting standards, Urgent Issues Task Force (UITF) Abstracts, and companies legislation. Where compliance with accounting standards or UITF Abstracts is inconsistent with the requirement to give a true and fair view, then they should be departed from to the extent necessary to give a true and fair view. Two accounting concepts – going concern and accruals (see page 28) – play a pervasive (ie spread throughout) role in financial statements and, hence, in the selection of accounting policies.

In the choice of accounting policies an entity must consider the objectives of

- **relevance** – the financial information is useful to users of accounts

- **reliability** – the financial information can be depended upon by users

- **comparability** – financial information can be compared with that from previous accounting periods

- **understandability** – users can understand the financial information provided

Once selected, accounting policies are to be reviewed regularly to ensure that they remain appropriate, and are changed when necessary.

In the financial statements, an entity must disclose sufficient information to enable users to understand the accounting policies adopted and how they have been implemented.

FRS 5 – REPORTING THE SUBSTANCE OF TRANSACTIONS

FRS 5 requires that transactions should be treated in the financial statements in accordance with their underlying **commercial substance** (reality), rather than their technical **legal form** – a case of 'substance over form'.

In most cases, commercial substance and legal form are the same: if a company buys a property it is shown as a fixed asset in the balance sheet because the company owns it. However a number of techniques – often connected with financing – have been devised that enable a business to receive economic benefits from an asset without showing it on the balance sheet. An example of this is a finance lease (see page 108), where the user of an asset, such as a machine or vehicle, is not the legal owner but, nevertheless, benefits from the asset. FRS 5 identifies three common features of transactions where commercial substance and legal form may differ:

- where the beneficiary of an asset is not the legal owner of the asset

- where a transaction is one of a series of similar transactions – the whole series will need to be considered in order to determine the commercial substance

- where there is an option – for example for the original owner to repurchase – which is likely to be exercised

Case Study

WYVERN TOYS LIMITED: SUBSTANCE OVER FORM

situation

Wyvern Toys Limited is coming towards the end of its financial year at 31 December 2004. Unfortunately trade has been poor in the run-up to Christmas and the company has £50,000 too much stock in its warehouse. The Managing Director, Alexandra Foster, has come up with an idea to improve the look of the company's year-end balance sheet. What she proposes is that the company should 'do a deal' with a nearby business, Mercia Retail Limited, to:

- sell £50,000 of stock to Mercia Retail for cash in December

- enter into a repurchase agreement to buy the stock back for £55,000 by the end of January 2005 unless Mercia has already sold them at a higher price

As Alexandra explains: 'This is a 'win-win' situation; we reduce our stock figure for the balance sheet and improve our bank balance – that should keep the bank happy! For Mercia Retail, they earn £5,000 'interest' on their money in a month! It won't affect their balance sheet as I know that their year-end is 30 June. We've done business with Mercia Retail before and I've spoken to their MD who is pleased to help us. What do you think?'

How should this transaction be recorded in the financial statements of Wyvern Toys Limited?

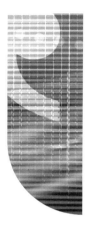

solution

Under the circumstances of this sale and repurchase agreement, Wyvern Toys has the option to buy back the goods, provided they have not already been sold by Mercia Retail. As it seems that the option is likely to be exercised, the transaction should be treated as a loan instead of being classed as a sale of goods. Accordingly, Wyvern Toys must keep the stock on its balance sheet and record the money from Mercia Retail as a loan (in the current liabilities section of its balance sheet, as the loan is repayable in January 2005).

The commercial substance of the transaction is that it is a loan instead of the legal form of a sale of goods: under FRS 5 'substance over form' prevails and it will be recorded as a loan. Users of the financial statements will have a clearer view of the state of the business.

FRS 10 – GOODWILL AND INTANGIBLE ASSETS

goodwill

The value of a well-established and profitable business is often greater than the value of the separate assets and liabilities which comprise the business. This is because, if the business were to be sold, a buyer would be prepared to pay above the value of the tangible assets and liabilities to acquire the existing products, customers, reputation, etc: this extra amount paid is for the **goodwill** of the business.

Goodwill may be defined as the difference between the value of a business as a whole and the aggregate (total) of the fair value of its separate net assets. For example, an existing business is bought for £500,000, with the net assets being worth £400,000; goodwill is, therefore, £100,000. Note that:

- goodwill can be either positive, where the value is greater than the net assets (as above), or negative, where the value is less than the net assets
- fair value is, effectively, the price at which assets and liabilities would be sold for on the open market (see FRS 7 *Fair values in acquisition accounting*, on page 239, for a formal definition).
- goodwill is an asset but it cannot be sold separately from the business as a whole

FRS 10 distinguishes between:

- **purchased goodwill**, which is the amount of goodwill arising on the purchase of a business
- **non-purchased goodwill,** which is goodwill other than that which has been purchased; for example, the owner of a business says that she has built up goodwill since setting up the business – this is non-purchased (or internally generated) goodwill

Only purchased goodwill can be recognised in accounting statements. The accounting treatment is to capitalise (ie record) it on the balance sheet as an intangible fixed asset (note that negative goodwill is shown in the assets section – below positive goodwill – and is deducted) and then:

- either, amortised (depreciated) through profit and loss account over its estimated useful economic life (generally up to a maximum of 20 years)

- or, if its estimated useful economic life is considered to be indefinite, the goodwill need not be amortised

Note that FRS 10 presumes that goodwill does not have a useful economic life of more than 20 years; however, the Standard accepts that there may be arguments for a life which is greater than 20 years. A business, or other entity, would need to disclose, as a note to the accounts, why it believed the useful economic life exceeded 20 years.

intangible assets

Intangible assets are fixed assets that do not have physical substance but which are identifiable and are controlled by an entity through custody or legal rights. Examples include licences, quotas, patents, copyrights, franchises and trade marks.

The accounting treatment for intangible assets is the same as that for goodwill:

- they should be recognised in the financial statements by capitalising them on the balance sheet as fixed assets at cost price

- when intangible assets are acquired as part of a takeover of another business, they should be capitalised separately from goodwill if their fair value can be measured reliably; where such value cannot be measured reliably, the intangible assets can be subsumed (included) into goodwill

- they should be amortised through profit and loss account over the assets' useful economic life; where this is considered to be indefinite, the assets need not be amortised

- as with goodwill, FRS 10 presumes that intangible assets do not have a useful economic life of more than 20 years; however the Standard accepts that there may be arguments for a life which is greater than 20 years, or even indefinite (in which case the business, or other entity, needs to disclose why it believes this to be the case)

FRS 11 – IMPAIRMENT OF FIXED ASSETS AND GOODWILL

objectives

The objectives of FRS 11 are to ensure that:

- fixed assets and goodwill are recorded in the financial statements at no more than their recoverable amount

- any resulting impairment loss is measured and recognised on a consistent basis

- sufficient information is disclosed for users of accounts to understand the impact of impairment on the financial performance of the organisation

The standard defines impairment as 'a reduction in the recoverable amount of a fixed asset or goodwill below its carrying amount'. (The 'carrying amount' is the cost of the asset less depreciation to date.)

The principle of the standard is that fixed assets (excluding investment properties) and goodwill need be reviewed for impairment only when there is evidence that impairment has taken place. Therefore a review may not be required every year (except for goodwill and other intangibles with an indefinite or over 20-year life – see FRS 10), but is only needed when something happens to the asset or economic circumstances change.

indicators of impairment

FRS 11 gives a number of indicators of impairment

- persistent operating losses or negative cash flows from operations

- a significant fall in the asset's market value

- physical damage to, or obsolescence of, the asset

- an adverse change in the company's competitive or regulatory environment

- a significant reorganisation

- a loss of key employees

- a significant increase in market interest rates or other market rates of return

the impairment review

The three steps to carry out an impairment review are as follows (see also the Case Study, on the next page):

STEP 1   What is the asset's carrying amount (net book value, ie cost less depreciation to date)?

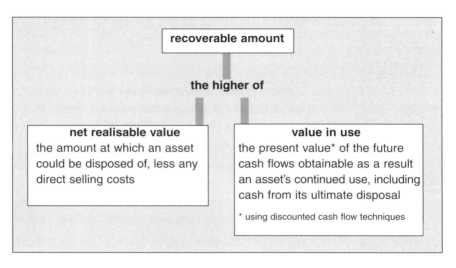

STEP 2   What is the asset's recoverable amount? See the diagram above.

STEP 3   If carrying value is greater than recoverable amount, then the asset
               is impaired and should be written down to its recoverable amount.
               The amount of the impairment is written down as an expense in
               profit and loss account (unless it arises on a previously revalued
               fixed asset when it is normally taken to the statement of total
               recognised gains and losses).

**Case
Study**

INITIAL TRAINING PLC: THE IMPAIRMENT REVIEW

situation

Initial Training plc is a large training organisation providing government-sponsored
'return-to-work' courses.

You are helping to prepare the company's year-end accounts and have been asked by
your boss, the company accountant, to carry out an impairment review on fixed assets
held at the training centre at Rowcester. Today you have obtained details of the two
photocopiers in the print room at Rowcester:

• **Machine 1** is six years old and is a relatively slow photocopier based on old
  technology. The cost of this machine was £8,000 and depreciation to date (the year-
  end) is £4,800, giving it a net book value of £3,200. Since the arrival of the other
  photocopier, this machine has been relegated to 'standby' use.

• **Machine 2** is only a few months old. It is a digital copier incorporating the latest
  technology. It is very fast and versatile, and has the capacity to meet the needs of
  the entire training centre. It cost £15,000 and depreciation to the end of the financial
  year will be £1,500, giving it a net book value of £13,500. This machine is much
  preferred by the staff who use it as a first choice.

solution

The impairment review you carry out is as follows:

Machine 1

- Carrying value (ie net book value): £3,200
- The company accountant has given you the following information to enable you to calculate the recoverable amount:

  the higher of
  - net realisable value: £1,000 resale value of machine on the secondhand market
  - value in use: £2,000 being the present value of the future benefits from continued use as a standby machine

  Therefore the recoverable amount is £2,000.
- As carrying value (£3,200) is greater than the machine's recoverable amount (£2,000), the asset is impaired. Accordingly, the amount of the impairment (£1,200) is to be shown as an overhead in profit and loss account, and the value of the machine will be shown on the company's balance sheet at the recoverable amount of £2,000.

Machine 2

- Carrying value (ie net book value): £13,500
- You are given the following information to enable you to calculate the recoverable amount:

  the higher of
  - net realisable value: £10,000 resale value of machine on the secondhand market
  - value in use: £55,000 being the present value of the future benefits from continued use as the main machine

  Therefore recoverable amount is £55,000.
- As carrying value (£13,500) is less than the machine's recoverable amount (£55,000), the asset is not impaired and does not need to be written down. Accordingly, the machine will be shown in the year-end accounts at cost price less depreciation to date.

FRS 15 – TANGIBLE FIXED ASSETS

This standard sets out the principles of accounting for tangible fixed assets:

- initial measurement
- valuation
- depreciation

Note that investment properties are covered by SSAP 19 (see page 105).

initial measurement

Tangible fixed assets are initially measured at cost (ie purchase price, less any trade discounts). Note that:

*   included in cost (ie capitalised) can be other costs which are *directly attributable* to bringing the asset into working condition, eg installation costs, legal fees, finance costs
*   where finance costs are capitalised the policy of capitalisation should be applied consistently to all tangible fixed assets when finance costs are incurred

valuation

Revaluation of tangible fixed assets is not compulsory, but where a policy of revaluation is implemented . . .

*   – all assets of the same class are to be revalued
*   – the carrying value (or book value) of the assets should be their current value as at the balance sheet date
*   – valuations are to be kept up-to-date by undertaking full valuations every five years, with at least one interim valuation during year 3 (where there is thought to be a material change in value, interim valuations in years 1, 2 and 4 should be undertaken)
*   – valuations are normally undertaken by qualified external valuers (eg Chartered Surveyors), interim valuations can be conducted by qualified external or internal valuers
*   – all gains are to be recorded in the statement of total recognised gains and losses (unless they reverse losses previously charged to profit and loss account – in which case the gain is credited to profit and loss account)
*   – losses are normally charged to profit and loss account

Also note that:

*   properties of a non-specialist nature are valued on the basis of existing use value
*   tangible fixed assets other than properties are valued at either market value, or depreciated replacement cost (ie replacement cost less deduction for proportion of useful economic life used)

depreciation

The objective of depreciation is to reflect in operating profit the cost of the use of the tangible fixed assets in the period.

All tangible fixed assets having a known useful economic life are to be depreciated (the most common exception is land).

Note that:

- non-depreciation of fixed assets is usually ruled out on the grounds that

  - residual values are normally assumed to be negligible

  - maintenance alone will not normally extend an asset's life indefinitely

- under exceptional circumstances a long useful economic life, or high residual value, can give rise to immaterial depreciation

- when depreciation is not charged on grounds of immateriality, and where the estimated useful economic life exceeds 50 years, annual impairment reviews are required

- any acceptable depreciation method can be used to spread the cost of the asset over its estimated useful economic life: two of the more common methods are straight-line and reducing balance

- where fixed assets are revalued, depreciation is based on the revalued amount

SSAP 19 – ACCOUNTING FOR INVESTMENT PROPERTIES

An investment property is defined by the standard as:

'an interest in land and/or buildings:

(a)   in respect of which construction work and development have been completed;

and

(b)   which is held for its investment potential, any rental income being negotiated at arm's length.'

Thus a property owned and occupied by an entity for its own purpose is not an investment property, nor is a property let to and occupied by another group company.

SSAP 19 states that it is the current value of investment properties, and changes in that current value, that are of prime importance – rather than a calculation of systematic annual depreciation. As a consequence, a different accounting treatment is used:

- Investment properties are not depreciated on the basis of FRS 15, except for leasehold properties – which are depreciated at least over the period during which the unexpired term of the lease is 20 years or less.

- Investment properties are shown in the fixed assets section of the balance sheet at their open market value, with the name or qualification of the valuer being disclosed together with the valuation bases used.

- The valuation need not be made by a professional valuer who can, in fact, be an employee of the entity. The exception to this is where investment properties represent a substantial proportion of the total assets of a major enterprise (such as a company listed on a stock market): here a professional external valuer should be used at least every five years.

- Changes in the value of investment properties should not be taken to profit and loss account but should be disclosed as a movement on an *investment revaluation reserve*, shown in the balance sheet, and reported through the statement of total recognised gains and losses.

- If investment revaluation reserve has a debit balance representing unrealised losses (ie the value of investment properties has fallen) and the losses are considered to be permanent, then the full amount can be charged to profit and loss account. A debit balance which is considered to be temporary is allowed to remain.

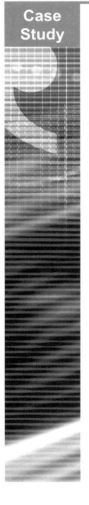

Case Study

WYVERN CARS LIMITED:
ACCOUNTING FOR INVESTMENT PROPERTIES

situation

Wyvern Cars Limited is a 'niche' manufacturer of hand-built sports cars. On 1 January 2003 it buys an office block near to the works for £2m. The office block will not be used by Wyvern Cars, but is to be held as an investment property.

During the next few years the valuation of the office block at 31 December (the financial year-end of Wyvern Cars) is as follows:

31 December 2003	£2.4m
31 December 2004	£2.2m
31 December 2005	£1.9m*

* the professional valuers used by Wyvern Cars consider this fall to be temporary

Show how the investment property will be shown in the balance sheets of Wyvern Cars.

solution

Year-ended 31 December 2003

	£m
Fixed assets	
Investment property at cost	2.0
Revaluation	0.4
	2.4
Capital and reserves	
Investment revaluation reserve:	
Revaluation in year	0.4
	0.4

- The increase in valuation is credited to revaluation reserve (ie is not credited to profit and loss account).

- The £0.4m revaluation is reported through the statement of total recognised gains and losses.

Year-ended 31 December 2004

Fixed assets	£m
Investment property at revaluation	2.4
Revaluation	(0.2)
	2.2

Capital and reserves	
Investment revaluation reserve:	
Balance at start of year	0.4
Revaluation in year	(0.2)
Balance at end of year	0.2

- The decrease in valuation is debited to revaluation reserve (ie is not debited to profit and loss account).

- The £0.2m decrease in valuation is reported through the statement of total recognised gains and losses.

Year-ended 31 December 2005

Fixed assets	£m
Investment property at revaluation	2.2
Revaluation	(0.3)
	1.9

Capital and reserves	
Investment revaluation reserve:	
Balance at start of year	0.2
Revaluation in year	(0.3)
Balance at end of year	(0.1)

- The decrease in valuation is debited to revaluation reserve.

- As the decrease in valuation is considered to be temporary, then the £0.1m negative balance on the investment revaluation reserve can remain.

- The £0.3m decrease in valuation is reported through the statement of total recognised gains and losses.

- If the decrease in valuation was considered to be permanent then:

  - revaluation reserve would be debited with £0.2m, being the amount remaining in the account

  - profit and loss account would be debited with £0.1m

  - the £0.2m decrease in investment revaluation reserve would be reported through the statement of total recognised gains and losses

SSAP 21 – LEASES AND HIRE PURCHASE CONTRACTS

Leasing and hire purchase contracts are means by which companies obtain the right to use or purchase fixed assets, such as machinery or vehicles. The lessee (under a leasing contract), or the hirer (under a hire purchase contract), makes agreed payments for a period of time to a lessor or vendor (often a finance company). There is normally no provision in a lease contract for legal title to the leased asset to pass to the lessee. By contrast, under a hire purchase contract, which has similar features to a lease, the hirer may acquire legal title by exercising an option to purchase the asset.

SSAP 21 sets out the accounting treatment where fixed assets are obtained for use by a business under:

– an **operating lease** (a short-term lease, where there is no transfer of the risks and rewards of ownership to the lessee)

– a **finance lease** (a long-term lease, under which substantially all of the risks and rewards of ownership are transferred to the lessee)

– a **hire purchase agreement** (under which the hirer has the use of the asset while paying for it by instalments over an agreed period of time)

A simple example illustrates the difference between these: hiring a van for the weekend to move some furniture is an operating lease; a business that leases a van under a four or five year contract does so under a finance lease; under a four or five year hire purchase contract the business will own the van (subject to the terms of the contract).

In more technical terms, a finance lease is when, at the inception of the lease, the present value of the minimum lease payments amounts to substantially all (normally 90 per cent or more) of the asset's fair value. As such, the lessee enjoys substantially all of the risks and rewards of ownership – apart from legal title. An operating lease, by contrast, involves the lessee paying a rental for the use of the asset for a time period which is normally substantially less than its total useful economic life; also, the lessor retains the risks and rewards of ownership of the asset and is responsible for the costs of repairs and maintenance.

With an operating lease, the rental payments are shown as an overhead in the profit and loss account of the lessee.

With a finance lease and hire purchase agreement:

• the cost of the fixed asset (excluding interest) is capitalised on the balance sheet of the lessee or hirer, as if they were the purchaser of the asset outright (this is the application of 'substance over form' – see FRS 5, page 98)

• the asset is depreciated over its estimated useful economic life, with depreciation charged to profit and loss account

- interest payable to the finance company is shown as an overhead in profit and loss account

- the amount due to the finance company for the capital amount (ie excluding interest) is shown as a liability on the balance sheet, and is split between long-term liabilities and current liabilities, as appropriate

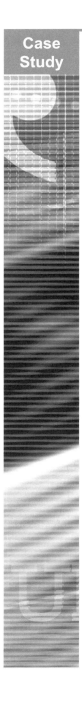

WYVERN ENGINEERING LIMITED: ACCOUNTING FOR LEASING

situation

Wyvern Engineering Limited is leasing two machines for use in its business:

1 A **portable compressor** is leased from The Hire Shop as and when it is needed at a cost of £100 per week; usage was as follows:

2003	5 weeks
2004	3 weeks
2005	6 weeks
2006	10 weeks

When the machine is not being used, Wyvern Engineering returns it to The Hire Shop where it is available for hire by other customers. The estimated useful economic life of the machine is six years.

2 A **pressing machine** is leased from Mercia Finance plc from 1 January 2003. The details are:

cost price of machine	£10,000
leasing period	4 years
estimated useful economic life	4 years
leasing payments	£3,500 per year (payable monthly on 1st of each month in advance)

Explain how these two leases will be recorded in the accounts of the lessee. Show relevant extracts from the profit and loss account and balance sheet for the years ending 31 December 2003, 2004, 2005 and 2006.

solution

1 The **portable compressor** is being leased under an operating lease because

– the lessee is renting the machine for a period which is substantially less than its total useful economic life

– the lessor retains the risks and rewards of ownership of the asset and is responsible for the costs of repairs and maintenance

The only accounting entries will be a charge to profit and loss account of the lease rentals payable in each financial year.

2   The **pressing machine** is being leased under a finance lease because

- the present value of the leasing payments amounts to substantially all of the asset's fair value, ie *£14,000 (£3,500 x 4 years), compared with £10,000

- substantially all of the risks and rewards of ownership are transferred to the lessee

The accounting entries are shown below.

* For simplicity, the £14,000 has not been discounted; at a 10% discount rate the present value would be approximately £12,000 – well above the 90% or more of the asset's fair value set by SSAP 21.

accounting entries: operating lease for the portable compressor

Debit profit and loss account with lease rentals, ie

	£
2003	500
2004	300
2005	600
2006	1,000

accounting entries: finance lease for the pressing machine

The first step is to apportion the leasing payments between finance charges and capital payments. With total leasing payments of £14,000 and the cost price of the machine at £10,000, the finance charges and capital payments are as follows:

	leasing payment	finance charge	capital payment
	£	£	£
2003	3,500	1,000	2,500
2004	3,500	1,000	2,500
2005	3,500	1,000	2,500
2006	3,500	1,000	2,500
	14,000	4,000	10,000

Note that the finance charge has been calculated here using the straight-line method. This is acceptable under SSAP 21, as are other methods which weight the finance charge more to the early years of the contract.

Depreciation on the machine (using the straight-line method) will be:

$$\frac{£10,000}{4 \text{ years}} = £2,500 \text{ per year}$$

profit and loss account extracts

	£
2003	
Operating lease rental	500
Finance charge under finance lease	1,000
Depreciation of machinery	2,500
	4,000

2004

Operating lease rental	300
Finance charge under finance lease	1,000
Depreciation of machinery	2,500
	3,800

2005

Operating lease rental	600
Finance charge under finance lease	1,000
Depreciation of machinery	2,500
	4,100

2006

Operating lease rental	1,000
Finance charge under finance lease	1,000
Depreciation of machinery	2,500
	4,500

balance sheet extracts

Note: only the finance lease appears on the balance sheet.

2003 £

Fixed assets

Machinery under finance lease at cost	10,000
Less depreciation to date	2,500
	7,500

Liabilities

Current – obligations under finance lease	*2,500
Long-term – obligations under finance lease	5,000
	7,500

* next year's payments are a current liability

2004 £

Fixed assets

Machinery under finance lease at cost	10,000
Less depreciation to date	5,000
	5,000

Liabilities

Current – obligations under finance lease	2,500
Long-term – obligations under finance lease	2,500
	5,000

2005	£
Fixed assets	
Machinery under finance lease at cost	10,000
Less depreciation to date	7,500
	2,500
Liabilities	
Current – obligations under finance lease	2,500

2006 – this balance sheet will show neither asset nor liability, as the leasing contract will terminate on 31 December 2006.

SSAP 13 – ACCOUNTING FOR RESEARCH AND DEVELOPMENT

The accounting treatment of research and development expenditure can lead to the creation of an intangible fixed asset when it is not fully written off to the profit and loss account in the year in which it is incurred. SSAP 13 sets out three categories of research and development expenditure:

- **pure (or basic) research** – experimental or theoretical work undertaken primarily to acquire new scientific or technical knowledge for its own sake rather than directed towards any specific aim or application
- **applied research** – original or critical investigation undertaken in order to gain new scientific or technical knowledge and directed towards a specific practical aim or objective
- **development** – use of scientific or technical knowledge in order to produce new or substantially improved products, services, or systems prior to the commencement of commercial production or commercial applications, or to improving substantially those already produced or installed

SSAP 13 requires that expenditure on pure and applied research is to be written off as revenue expenditure to profit and loss account in the year in which it is incurred. However, capital expenditure on fixed assets – such as a new research laboratory – is to be recorded as fixed assets and depreciated over the useful lives of the assets.

Development expenditure should, generally, be written off to profit and loss account as it is incurred. It may, however, be *capitalised* and treated as an intangible fixed asset if it relates to an ultimately profitable project. The criteria for this are:

- there is a clearly defined project
- the related expenditure is separately identifiable

- the outcome of such a project has been assessed with reasonable certainty as to
  - its technical feasibility, and
  - its ultimate commercial viability, taking into account factors such as likely market conditions (including competing products), public opinion, consumer and environmental legislation
- estimated future profits are reasonably expected to exceed past and future development costs
- adequate resources are available to complete the project

Provided that all these criteria can be satisfied, the development expenditure can be capitalised as an intangible fixed asset and recorded on the balance sheet. The intangible asset will then be amortised (depreciated down to zero) in proportion to sales of the product as they materialise.

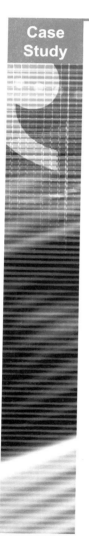

Case Study

POMONA AGROCHEMICAL COMPANY: RESEARCH AND DEVELOPMENT COSTS

situation

Pomona Agrochemical Company has the following account in its book-keeping system:

Dr	Research and Development Expenditure Account		Cr
2004	£	2004	£
24 Mar Bank (research)	24,000		
18 Nov Bank (development)	40,000		

The development costs have been incurred in respect of a new agricultural chemical, WACL X123. This product has been on sale since 1 January 2005 and sales in the first few weeks look very promising.

It is now February 2005 and you are preparing the company's accounts for the financial year ended 31 December 2004. How will you deal with the research and development expenditure?

solution

research expenditure

The research expenditure of £24,000 will be charged as an overhead in the profit and loss account for the year ended 31 December 2004.

development expenditure

The development expenditure of £40,000 should be charged to profit and loss account unless it meets the criteria set out in SSAP 13. Here, the development of the new chemical does appear to be a clearly defined project, for which the related expenditure is separately identifiable, and for which the outcome is technically feasible and has

commercial viability. Thus, the development expenditure can be capitalised and shown on Pomona's balance sheet as an intangible fixed asset with a value of £40,000 at 31 December 2004.

As the new chemical is now in production, the asset must now be amortised over its expected life, so the question for the following year's accounts (2005) will be to decide how long sales of the product will last – this will determine the amount of amortisation to be shown in the profit and loss account for the year ended 31 December 2005, and the reduced value of the intangible fixed asset for the year-end balance sheet.

SSAP 4 – ACCOUNTING FOR GOVERNMENT GRANTS

Various types of grants are available to businesses and other entities from government departments and similar bodies, whether local, national or international (including grants from the European Union).

revenue grants

These are grants which contribute to profit and loss account expenditure. Examples include grants towards the training costs of employees, grants towards the costs of employing particular categories of employees (such as those who have just left school, or those who have previously been unemployed), grants towards the rent and rates of premises in order to encourage businesses to establish in certain areas.

The accounting treatment of revenue grants is that they should be credited to profit and loss account in the same period as the expenditure to which they contribute was incurred. This fits in with the concept of matching (accruals).

capital grants

These grants contribute to the cost of capital expenditure (eg premises, machinery, equipment). The accounting treatment is that such grants should be credited to profit and loss account over the expected useful economic lives of the assets to which they relate. The usual way of dealing with this is to treat the amount of the grant as a deferred credit, a portion of which will be credited to profit and loss account each year. The part of the grant that has not yet been transferred to profit and loss account shows on the balance sheet as deferred income – under either the heading of creditors, or a separate liability heading for 'accruals and deferred income' (see Case Study, below).

disclosure in financial statements

For government grants the following information should be disclosed:

• the accounting policy adopted for government grants

- the effects of government grants on the results for the period and/or the financial position of the enterprise

- any potential liability to repay grants (see also FRS 12, *Provisions, contingent liabilities and contingent assets* – page 138)

- if appropriate, the material effects of government assistance, other than grants, on the financial statements

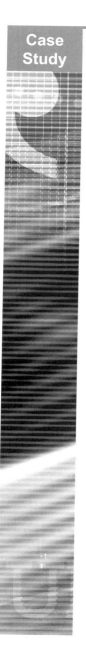

Case Study

MEREFORD MANUFACTURING LIMITED: ACCOUNTING FOR GRANTS

situation

In January 2003 Mereford Manufacturing Limited re-equips its factory with computer-controlled machinery at a cost of £250,000. The Wyvern Development Agency, a government-sponsored body charged with the task of developing business in its area, gives a 20 per cent grant towards the cost of Mereford's new machinery. The grant is paid in February 2003. The useful economic life of the machinery is expected to be five years, after which it will have a scrap value of £10,000.

The expected profit of Mereford, before accounting for depreciation on the new machinery, is expected to be £100,000 each year for the next five years.

Show how the grant will be treated in the financial statements of Mereford for each of the five years ending 31 December 2003 - 2007.

solution

Depreciation on new machinery (using the straight-line method) is

$$\frac{£250,000 - £10,000}{5 \text{ years}} = £48,000 \text{ per year}$$

Profit and loss account (extracts)

	2003 £000	2004 £000	2005 £000	2006 £000	2007 £000
Profit before depreciation	100	100	100	100	100
Grant*	10	10	10	10	10
Depreciation	(48)	(48)	(48)	(48)	(48)
Profit	62	62	62	62	62

* £250,000 x 20% = £50,000 ÷ 5 years = £10,000 per year

Balance sheet (extracts)

Fixed assets	2003 £000	2004 £000	2005 £000	2006 £000	2007 £000
Machinery at cost	250	250	250	250	250
Less depreciation to date	48	96	144	192	240
Net book value	202	154	106	58	10

Balance sheet extracts continued

Deferred income**

Government grant – deferred credit	40	30	20	10	–

** shown either under the heading of creditors, or under a separate liability heading for 'accruals and deferred income'.

SSAP 9 – STOCKS AND LONG-TERM CONTRACTS

Note that for the NVQ Unit *Drafting Financial Statements*, the valuation of long-term contracts is not examined.

Businesses often have stocks of goods in various forms:

- stocks of raw materials, for use in a manufacturing process

- stocks of work-in-progress (partly manufactured goods)

- stocks of finished goods, made by the business and ready for resale to customers

- stocks of finished goods, which have been bought in by the business for resale

The principle of stock valuation, as set out in SSAP 9, is that stocks should be valued at 'the lower of cost and net realisable value'. This valuation applies the prudence concept and is illustrated by the following diagram:

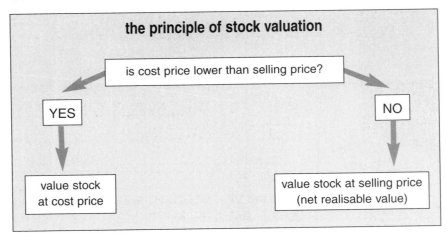

Thus two different stock values are compared:

- cost, including additional costs to bring the product or service to its present location and condition

- net realisable value (the expected selling price less any further costs such as selling and distribution)

The lower of these two values is taken, and *different items or groups of stock are compared separately*. These principles are illustrated in the two Case Studies which follow.

Case Study

THE CLOTHING STORE: STOCK VALUATION

situation

The Clothing Store bought in a range of 'designer' beachwear in the Spring, with each item costing £15 and retailing for £30. Most of the stock is sold but, by Autumn, ten items remain unsold. These are put on the 'bargain rail' at £18 each. On 31 December, at the end of the store's financial year, five items remain unsold. At what price will they be included in the year-end stock valuation?

Twelve months later, three items still remain unsold and have been reduced further to £10 each. At what price will they now be valued in the year-end stock valuation?

solution

- At 31 December, the five items will be valued at a cost of £15 each,

  ie 5 x £15 = £75.

- Twelve months later, the three items remaining unsold will be valued at a net realisable value of £10 each, ie 3 x £10 = £30.

Important note: Stock is never valued at selling price when selling price is above cost price. The reason for this is that selling price includes profit, and to value stock in this way would recognise the profit in the accounts before it has been realised.

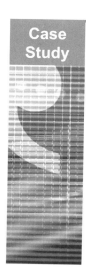

Case Study

PAINT AND WALLPAPER SUPPLIES: STOCK VALUATION

situation

The year-end stocks for the two main groups of stock held by the business Paint and Wallpaper Supplies are found to be:

	Cost	Net Realisable Value
	£	£
Paints	2,500	2,300
Wallpapers	5,000	7,500
	7,500	9,800

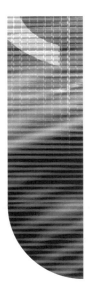

Which of the following stock valuations do you think is correct?

(a)   £7,500

(b)   £9,800

(c)   £7,300

(d)   £10,000

solution

Stock valuation (c) is correct, because it has taken the 'lower of cost and net realisable value' for each *group* of stock, ie

Paints (at net realisable value)	£2,300
Wallpapers (at cost)	£5,000
	£7,300

You will also note that this valuation is the lowest of the four possible choices, indicating that stock valuation follows the *prudence concept*.

commonly used stock valuation methods

Businesses use different methods to calculate the cost price of stock. Three commonly used methods are:

- **FIFO** (first in, first out) – this method assumes that the first stocks acquired are the first to be used, so that the valuation of stock on hand at any time consists of the most recently acquired stock.

- **LIFO*** (last in, first out) – here it is assumed that the last stocks acquired are the first to be used, so that the stock on hand is made up of earlier purchases.

- **AVCO** (average cost) – here the average cost of items held at the beginning of the period is calculated; as new stocks are acquired a new average cost is calculated (usually based on a weighted average, using the number of units bought as the weighting).

  * Note that SSAP 9 discourages the use of LIFO because it usually does not provide an up-to-date valuation (being based on older stock); however, the Companies Act 1985 does permit the use of LIFO.

The use of a particular method does not necessarily correspond with the method of physical distribution adopted in a firm's stores. For example, in a car factory, one car battery of type X is the same as another, and no-one will be concerned if the storekeeper issues one from the latest batch received, even if the FIFO system has been adopted. However, perishable goods are always physically handled on the basis of first in, first out, even if the accounting stock records use another method.

Having chosen a suitable stock valuation method, a business would continue to use that method unless there were good reasons for making the change. This is in line with the consistency concept of accounting.

closing stock valuation for a manufacturer

The principles of SSAP 9 are applied to a manufacturer, who may hold three types of stock at the year-end:

- raw materials
- work-in-progress
- finished goods

For **raw materials,** the comparison is made between cost (which can be found using techniques such as FIFO, LIFO, or AVCO) and net realisable value.

For stocks of both **work-in-progress** and **finished goods**, SSAP 9 requires that the cost valuation includes expenditure not only on direct materials but also on direct labour, direct expenses and production overheads. Thus for work-in-progress and finished goods, 'cost' comprises:

- direct materials
- direct labour
- direct expenses
- production overheads (to bring the product to its present location or condition)
- other overheads, if any, attributable to bringing the product or service to its present location and condition

Such 'cost' is then compared with net realisable value, and the lower figure is taken as the stock valuation (remember that different items or groups of stock are compared separately).

Case Study

XYZ MANUFACTURING: STOCK VALUATION

situation

XYZ Manufacturing started in business on 1 July 2003 producing security devices for doors and windows. During the first year 2,000 units were sold and at the end of the year, on 30 June 2004, there were 200 finished units in stock and 20 units which were exactly half-finished as regards direct materials, direct labour and production overheads.

Costs for the first year were:

	£
Direct materials used	18,785
Direct labour	13,260
Production overheads	8,840
Non-production overheads	4,420
TOTAL COST FOR YEAR	45,305

At 30 June 2004 it was estimated that the net realisable value of each completed security device was £35. At the same date, the company holds stocks of raw materials as follows:

	cost	net realisable value
	£	£
Material X	1,400	1,480
Material Y	400	360
Material Z	260	280

Calculate the stock valuation at 30 June 2004 for:

- raw materials
- work-in-progress
- finished goods

solution

RAW MATERIALS

Using the SSAP 9 rule of 'the lower of cost and net realisable value' the total value is:

	£	
Material X	1,400	(cost)
Material Y	360	(net realisable value)
Material Z	260	(cost)
	2,020	

WORK-IN-PROGRESS

To calculate the value of work-in-progress and finished goods we need to know the production cost, ie direct materials, direct labour and production overheads. This is:

	£
Direct materials used	18,785
Direct labour	13,260
Production overheads	8,840
PRODUCTION COST FOR YEAR	40,885

All these costs must be included because they have been incurred in bringing the product to its present location or condition. Non-production overheads are not included because they are not directly related to production. Thus, a production cost of £40,885 has produced:

Units sold	2,000
Closing stock of completed units	200

calculation continued . . .

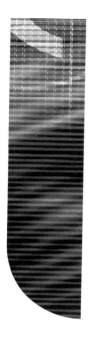

Closing stock of work-in-progress –

20 units exactly half-finished equals

10 completed units	10
PRODUCTION FOR YEAR	2,210

The **cost per unit** is: $\dfrac{£40,885}{2,210}$ = **£18.50 per unit**

The 20 half-finished units have a cost of (20 ÷ 2) x £18.50 = **£185**. They have a net realisable value of (20 ÷ 2) x £35 = £350. The value of work-in-progress will, therefore, be shown in the accounts as £185, which is the lower of cost and net realisable value.

FINISHED GOODS

The completed units in stock at the end of the year have a production cost of 200 x £18.50 = £3,700, compared with a net realisable value of 200 x £35 = £7,000. Applying the rule of lower of cost and net realisable value, finished goods stock will be valued at **£3,700**.

CONFIDENTIALITY PROCEDURES

It is a requirement of the Companies Act for directors of companies – other than most small or medium-sized companies – to disclose whether the accounts have been prepared in accordance with applicable accounting standards, particulars of any material departure from the standards and the reasons for the departure. Whilst this information is readily available to users of accounts, for those involved in the preparation of the accounts, confidentiality procedures must be observed at all times:

– regarding any discussion about accounting standards with the directors

– regarding how the standards have been applied to a particular set of financial statements

– concerning any figures used but not disclosed in the accounts; for example, the calculation of stock valuations at cost price and net realisable value, or the calculation of amortisation of goodwill

– concerning any investigations to determine whether to treat an item in one way rather than another; for example, confidential information about the development of a new product, the outcome of which will determine whether costs are to be capitalised on the balance sheet or, alternatively, written off to profit and loss account

- Accounting standards comprise SSAPs and FRSs.

- **FRS 18** 'Accounting policies' sets out the principles of selecting accounting policies. The accounting concepts of going concern and accruals play an important part in the selection and application of policies.

- **FRS 5** 'Reporting the substance of transactions' requires that business transactions should be treated in the financial statements in accordance with their underlying commercial substance, rather than their technical legal form, ie 'substance over form'.

- **FRS 10** 'Goodwill and intangible assets' covers the recognition of purchased goodwill and intangible assets in financial statements. The usual accounting treatment is for amortisation through profit and loss account over the asset's estimated useful economic life.

- **FRS 11** 'Impairment of fixed assets and goodwill' requires an impairment review to be carried out when there is evidence that impairment has taken place. The standard gives a number of indicators of impairment.

- **FRS 15** 'Tangible fixed assets' sets out the principles of accounting for tangible fixed assets:
  - initial measurement
  - valuation
  - depreciation

- **SSAP 19** 'Accounting for investment properties' requires investment properties to be shown on the balance sheet at their open market value. Changes in value are reported through an investment revaluation reserve.

- **SSAP 21** 'Leases and hire purchase contracts' sets out the accounting treatment for
  - operating leases
  - finance leases
  - hire purchase agreement

- **SSAP 13** 'Accounting for research and development' requires that
  - research expenditure is written off as revenue expenditure to profit and loss account in the year in which it is incurred
  - development expenditure should generally be written off to profit and loss account as it is incurred, but may be capitalised and treated as an intangible fixed asset if certain criteria are met

- **SSAP 4** 'Accounting for government grants' distinguishes between revenue grants and capital grants:
  - revenue grants are to be credited to profit and loss account in the same

period as the expenditure to which they contribute was incurred

– capital grants are to be credited to profit and loss account over the expected useful economic lives of the assets to which they relate; this is usually accounted for by treating the grant as a deferred credit, a portion of which will be credited to profit and loss account each year

• **SSAP 9** 'Stocks and long-term contracts' requires that stock is normally valued at the lower of cost and net realisable value. Stock valuation methods include:

– FIFO (first in, first out)

– LIFO (last in, first out)

– AVCO (average cost, based on a weighted average)

Key Terms		
SSAP		Statement of Standard Accounting Practice; part of the rules of accounting
FRS		Financial Reporting Standard; part of the rules of accounting
accounting policies		those principles, bases, conventions, rules and practices applied by an entity that specify how the effects of transactions and other events are to be reflected in its financial statements
goodwill		the difference between the value of a business as a whole and the aggregate (total) of the fair value of its separate net assets
intangible assets		fixed assets that do not have physical substance but which are identifiable and are controlled by an entity through custody or legal rights
amortisation		technique of writing down intangible assets through profit and loss account
impairment		a reduction in the recoverable amount of fixed assets or goodwill below its carrying amount
depreciation		the objective of depreciation is to reflect in operating profit the cost of the use of the tangible fixed assets in the period
investment property		an interest in land and/or buildings:
		(a) in respect of which construction work and development have been completed; and

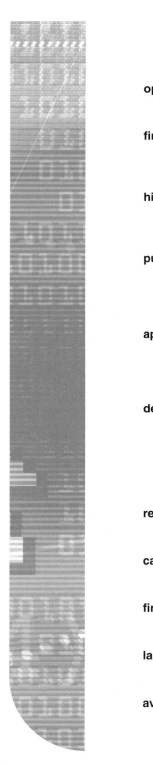

(b) where it is held for its investment potential, any rental income being negotiated at arm's length

operating lease

a short-term lease, where there is no transfer of the risks and rewards of ownership to the lessee

finance lease

a long-term lease, under which substantially all of the risks and rewards of ownership are transferred to the lessee

hire purchase

agreement under which the hirer has the use of the asset while paying for it by instalments over an agreed period of time

pure research

experimental or theoretical work undertaken primarily to acquire new scientific or technical knowledge for its own sake rather than directed towards any specific aim or application

applied research

original or critical investigation undertaken in order to gain new scientific or technical knowledge and directed towards a specific practical aim or objective

development expenditure

use of scientific or technical knowledge in order to produce new or substantially improved products, services, or systems prior to the commencement of commercial production or commercial applications, or to improving substantially those already produced or installed

revenue grants

grants which contribute to profit and loss account expenditure

capital grants

grants which contribute to the cost of capital expenditure

first in, first out (FIFO)

stock valuation method which assumes that the first stocks acquired are the first to be used

last in, first out (LIFO)

stock valuation method which assumes that the last stocks acquired are the first to be used

average cost (AVCO)

stock valuation method which calculates an average cost (based on a weighted average) whenever new stocks are acquired

Student Activities

Osborne Books is grateful to the AAT for their kind permission to use past assessment material for the following activities: 4.14, 4.15.

4.1   Which of the following statements, according to SSAP 9 *Stock and long term contracts*, best describes the valuation of stock at the end of the financial year?

(a)   the lower of cost and net realisable value

(b)   the higher of cost and net realisable value

(c)   all stock should be valued at historic cost

(d)   all stock should be valued at net realisable value

4.2   Joe Yates runs a garage buying and selling cars. At the end of his financial year he has the following cars in stock. What is the correct valuation to be recorded according to SSAP 9?

	Cost £	Net realisable value £
Vauxhall Vectra	2,800	3,500
Landrover Discovery	10,000	15,000
Nissan Primera	3,400	2,600
Ford Focus	6,000	7,500
Volkswagon Polo	1,200	500

(a)   £23,400

(b)   £21,900

(c)   £30,600

(d)   £29,100

4.3   The Betterland Company Limited purchased a freehold warehouse on 1st January 20-0 for £250,000. The directors decided to depreciate the warehouse over its anticipated economic life of 50 years. At 1 January 20-5, the building is valued at £345,000, and the directors decide to incorporate this valuation into the books of account from this date.

1   What is the amount to be transferred to the asset revaluation account?

(a)   £120,000

(b)   £100,000

(c)   £125,000

(d)   £250,000

2   Assuming that the asset's life still has 46 years to run as from the 1st January 20-5, what would be the depreciation charge from the 31st December 20-5 onwards?

(a)   £5,000

(b)   £10,000

(c)   £7,500

(d)   £2,500

4.4 In certain circumstances research and development expenditure can be deferred to later periods and carried forward on a company balance sheet as an intangible asset. Which broad category best describes this deferral process?

(a)   basic research

(b)   development research

(c)   applied research

(d)   basic, applied and development research

4.5 During 20-3 The Hassan Trading Company Limited acquired another business for £180,000 in cash and in exchange for 50,000 £1 ordinary shares valued at £2.50 each.

The fair value of separable net assets of the company acquired at the date of purchase was:

	£
Land and Buildings	100,000
Plant and Equipment	60,000
Stock	35,000
Debtors	25,000
	220,000

All liabilities were discharged by the previous owner.

What is the correct valuation for goodwill?

(a)   £10,000

(b)   £60,000

(c)   £85,000

(d)   £165,000

4.6 Machin Limited has three assets in use

	Net book Value	Net realisable Value	Value in use
	£	£	£
Compressor	8,000	12,000	10,000
Fork lift truck	20,000	18,000	19,000
Dumper truck	10,000	7,000	13,000

Which of the above assets is impaired and needs to be written down as indicated?

(a)   compressor written down by £2,000

(b)   fork lift truck written down by £2,000

(c)   fork lift truck written down by £1,000

(d)   dumper truck written down by £3,000

4.7 Briefly explain the accounting treatment available to companies, when dealing with capital and revenue based grants. Your answer should make specific reference to SSAP 4.

4.8 Briefly outline the three broad classifications for research and development expenditure. Your answer should make specific reference to SSAP 13.

4.9 What are the main differences between an operating lease and a finance lease, as defined by SSAP 21?

4.10 Briefly explain the difference in accounting treatment, between an owner occupied freehold property, and that of a freehold investment property. You should make specific reference to FRS 15 and SSAP 19.

4.11 On 1 January 20-0, Makeshift Enterprises plc purchased a freehold property, Castle Hamlets at a cost of £400,000, which it intended to hold as an investment property.

In subsequent years, the valuation of the property was as follows:

At 31 December	20-1	20-2	20-3
	£000	£000	£000
	440	460	380

The valuation made in 20-3 is assumed to be a permanent valuation at that time.

Task 1

Show how the property and the revaluation surpluses and deficits would be recorded in the books of account and the financial statements for the years to 31 December 20-0 to 20-3.

Task 2

How would the accounts and book-keeping differ if we had been told that the valuation made on 31 December 20-3 was a temporary one?

4.12 Chemco plc has its own research and development department, the breakdown of costs for the year to 31 December 20-3 are as follows:

(a) Project Xchem was started in July 20-3, researching into the possibility that an arm patch could be used to cure the common cold. Some minor testing had been completed but the results had proved to be disappointing and no real benefits recorded. It was unlikely that the project would continue in the foreseeable future and the costs to date amounted to £295,000.

(b) Project Zchem had also started this year, investigating the possibility of producing insulin in tablet form to help sufferers of diabetes. Results to date had proved to be most encouraging, and matters were progressing at a pace. Production is due to start next year (20-4) and demand for this type of product initially, is likely to be very high and lucrative. The product has already been patented and its planned selling price is likely to yield a high level of profit, until competition can enter the market in 20-9. Costs for the year to date amounted to £435,000.

The company has sufficient finance and resources to complete both projects.

Task

How should the total research and development expenditure be dealt with in the financial statements for 20-3 and subsequent years (if appropriate)?

4.13 Sampson plc has recently acquired a new business – Delia Limited. The purchase consideration has led the business to account for purchased goodwill.

The directors are keen to know more about what it is.

Task 1
Define purchased goodwill.

Task 2
List five aspects of Delia Limited which may give rise to goodwill.

Task 3
Account for the difference in prescribed accounting practice for purchased and non-purchased goodwill. Your answer should make reference to FRS 10 – *Goodwill and intangible assets*.

4.14 Answer the following questions which the directors of Poussin Limited have asked. Justify your answers, where appropriate, by reference to accounting concepts, SSAPs and or FRSs.

(a)   Why are we carrying forward development costs of £351,572 on the balance sheet? Should these costs be written off in the profit and loss account in the year in which they are incurred? Under what circumstances can these costs be carried forward in the balance sheet and how will they be treated in the future?

(b)   The auditors have asked us to reduce the value of some of our stock – from the cost of £147,213 to £60,648, the amount at which we sold stock after the year end. Why should something that happened after the year end be at all relevant to the balances at the year end?

4.15 You have been assigned to assist in the preparation of the financial statements of Dowango Limited for the year ended 31 March 20-6. The company is a cash and carry operation that trades from a large warehouse on an industrial estate.

You have recently received a letter from the directors of Dowango Limited, the contents of which are listed below.

DOWANGO LIMITED

Dear AAT student,

In preparation for discussions about a possible loan to Dowango Limited, the bank has asked to see the latest financial statements of Dowango. We wish to ensure that the financial statements show the company in the best light. In particular, we wish to ensure that the assets of the business are shown at their proper value. We would like to discuss with you the following issues:

1   The fixed assets of our company are undervalued. We have received a professional valuation of the land and buildings which shows that they are worth more than is stated in

our financial statements. The land has a current market value of £641,000 and the buildings are valued at £558,000.

2   The investments are recorded in our trial balance at cost. We realise that the market value of the investment is less than the cost, but since we have not yet sold it, we have not made a loss on it and so we should continue to show it at cost.

3   Stocks are recorded in our balance sheet at cost. Most of our stock is worth more than this as we could sell it for more than we paid for it. Only a few items would sell for less than we paid for them. We have worked out the real value of our stock as follows:

	Cost	Sales price
	£000	£000
Undervalued items	340	460
Overvalued items	25	15
Total	365	475

We have set out a number of questions we would like answered at our meeting in an appendix to this letter. We would also like you to advise us at that meeting on the profitability and return on capital of the two companies targeted for takeover (whose financial statements we have already sent to you) and on the reporting implications if we purchase one of the companies.

Yours sincerely

The Directors

Dowango Limited

Tasks

The questions from the appendix to the directors' letter are shown below. Write a memo to the directors answering these questions, which relate to the financial statements of Dowango Limited. Explain your answers, where relevant, by reference to company law, accounting concepts and applicable accounting standards.

1   (a)   Can we show the land and buildings at valuation rather than cost?

(b)   If we did so, how would the valuation of land and buildings be reflected in the financial statements?

(c)   Would revaluing the land and buildings have any effect upon the gearing ratio of the company and would this assist us in our attempt to get a loan from the bank?

(d)   What effect would a revaluation have upon the future results of the company?

2   Can we continue to show the investments at cost?

The investments consist of shares in a retail company that were purchased with a view to resale at a profit. Dowango Limited owns 2 per cent of the share capital of the company. At the end of the year a valuation of the shares was obtained with a view to selling the shares in the forthcoming year. The shares were valued at £56,000, but originally cost Dowango £64,000.

3   What is the best value for stock that we can show in our balance sheet in the light of the information we have given you about sales price?

this chapter covers . . .

This chapter focuses on the accounting standards (SSAPs and FRSs) that impact mainly on the way in which liabilities are accounted for in both the profit and loss account and balance sheet. We then turn our attention to those standards that affect principally the profit and loss account.

For the liabilities side of the balance sheet we consider standards that cover:
- *taxation, including VAT (FRS 16, FRS 19 and SSAP 5)*
- *hire purchase and leasing (SSAP 21)*
- *capital instruments (FRS 4)*
- *provisions and contingencies (FRS 12)*
- *accounting for post balance sheet events (SSAP 17)*

Accounting standards which affect mainly the profit and loss account include:
- *tangible fixed assets (FRS 15)*
- *reporting financial performance (FRS 3)*
- *earnings per share (FRS 14)*
- *segmental reporting (SSAP 25)*
- *foreign currencies (SSAP 20)*
- *retirement benefits (FRS 17)*
- *related party disclosures (FRS 8)*

NVQ PERFORMANCE CRITERIA COVERED

unit 11: DRAFTING FINANCIAL STATEMENTS

element 11.1

draft limited company financial statements

A   draft limited company financial statements from the appropriate information

B   correctly identify and implement subsequent adjustments and ensure that discrepancies, unusual features or queries are identified and either resolved or referred to the appropriate person

C   ensure that limited company financial statements comply with relevant accounting standards and domestic legislation and with the organisation's policies, regulations and procedures

E   ensure that confidentiality procedures are followed at all times

ACCOUNTING STANDARDS COVERING TAXATION

There are three standards which show how aspects of taxation, including VAT, are to be accounted for:

- FRS 16   – Current tax
- FRS 19   – Deferred tax
- SSAP 5   – Accounting for value added tax

FRS 16 – Current tax

The profits of limited companies are subject to corporation tax at various rates set out by the Chancellor of the Exchequer in budget announcements.

The date (or dates) of payment of corporation tax due vary depending on the size of the company. For example, a small company pays all its corporation tax to the Inland Revenue (the tax collector) nine months after the company's year-end; thus a small company with a financial year-end of 31 December 2004 will pay the corporation tax due on its profits for 2004 by the end of September 2005. Larger companies pay part of their tax due every three months, with some amounts due to be paid in the following accounting period.

In the financial statements there will be shown:

- in profit and loss account, an estimate of corporation tax due on the year's profits (there may also be an entry in the statement of total recognised gains and losses – see below)
- in balance sheet, a current liability for the estimated amount of corporation tax to be paid (or remaining to be paid) on the year's profits

FRS 16 requires that current tax (ie the amount of tax estimated to be due on the profits of the accounting period) is to be recognised in profit and loss account. However, where a gain (or loss) has been recognised directly in the statement of total recognised gains and losses, the tax relating to the gain (or loss) is recognised directly in that statement.

The amount of current tax is to be measured in the financial statements using the tax rates applicable at the balance sheet date.

The Case Study on page 135 illustrates how corporation tax is dealt with in the financial statements of a company.

FRS 19 – Deferred tax

The standard defines deferred tax as 'estimated future tax consequences of transactions and events recognised in the financial statements of the current and previous periods'.

Deferred tax comes about because the taxable profit of a business is often different from the net profit shown in profit and loss account. One reason for this is because the Inland Revenue disallows depreciation and amortisation shown in profit and loss account and, instead, allows a capital allowance against tax for the purchase of fixed assets.

An example of a capital allowance is 25 per cent reducing balance, which is allowed on office equipment, machinery and most vehicles. For example, the capital allowances on a machine costing £10,000 will be:

	£
Cost price	10,000
Year 1 capital allowance at 25%	2,500
	7,500
Year 2 capital allowance at 25%	1,875
	5,625
Year 3 capital allowance at 25%	1,406
	4,219
	and so on . . .

If the company owning the machine had a net profit of £15,000 in year 1 after allowing for depreciation on the machine of, say, £1,000, the taxable profit would be calculated as follows:

	£
Net profit in year 1	15,000
Add back depreciation charge	1,000
	16,000
Less capital allowance	2,500
Taxable profit	13,500

Thus the company would pay tax on profits of £13,500 rather than £15,000. This is because the capital allowance is higher than the depreciation charge. As the tax benefit of the capital allowance has been received earlier than the depreciation charge, the company will make a transfer from profit and loss account to deferred tax account to record a possible liability to the Inland Revenue. The transfer will be for £2,500 – £1,000 = £1,500 x the company's tax rate. The possible liability to the Inland Revenue is that, if the machine was sold at the end of year 1 for £9,000 (ie cost, less depreciation to date), the Inland Revenue would claim for a balancing charge of £1,500, ie £9,000 – (£10,000 – £2,500 capital allowance) x the company's tax rate.

In the ordinary course of events, amounts transferred to deferred tax account will reverse (ie be transferred back to profit and loss account) over time – see Case Study on the next page.

In the circumstances described above, the balance of deferred tax account is shown as a liability on the balance sheet under the heading of 'provisions for liabilities and charges'.

Deferred tax account can also be an asset – for example, where a company has taxable losses in the past and is carrying them forward to reduce future taxable profits.

Case Study

RAVEN LIMITED:
ACCOUNTING FOR DEFERRED TAX

situation

Raven Limited buys a machine for £10,000. The machine is expected to last for ten years and have a nil scrap value. The company uses straight-line depreciation.
The Inland Revenue gives capital allowances of 25 per cent reducing balance on the machine.
Raven Limited pays corporation tax at the rate of 30 per cent.

solution

- Depreciation is at £1,000 per year (ie 10 per cent, using the straight-line method).
- Capital allowances are at 25 per cent reducing balance.
- The amounts are shown in the table below:

YEARS	1	2	3	4	5	6	7	8	9	10
	£	£	£	£	£	£	£	£	£	£
depreciation	1,000	1,000	1,000	1,000	1,000	1,000	1,000	1,000	1,000	1,000
capital allow'nce	2,500	1,875	1,406	1,054	791	593	445	334	250	188
difference	(1,500)	(875)	(406)	(54)	209	407	555	666	750	812

◾ The difference multiplied by the tax rate is transferred (to) or from deferred tax account, as follows:

Dr	**Deferred tax account**	Cr
	Year 1 Transfer from profit and loss	450*

* £1,500 difference x 30%

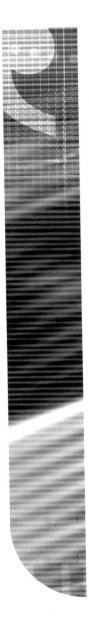

■ The year 1 profit and loss account will show a transfer to deferred tax of £450, as follows:

Profit and loss account – year 1

	£
Net profit for year	x
Less corporation tax	(x)
Transfer to deferred tax account	(450)
Transfer from deferred tax account	x
Profit after tax	x

■ The balance sheet will show a potential liability to the Inland Revenue of £450 under the heading of 'provisions for liabilities and charges', as follows:

Balance sheet – year 1

	£
Fixed Assets	x
Current Assets	x
Current Liabilities	(x)
Long-term Liabilities	(x)
Provisions for Liabilities and Charges	
Provision for deferred tax	(450)
Net assets	x

■ In years 2, 3 and 4, further transfers will be debited to profit and loss account and credited to deferred tax account. From year 5 onwards, the capital allowances will begin to reverse by debiting deferred tax account with the difference multiplied by the tax rate, and crediting profit and loss account with a 'transfer from deferred tax account'.

■ When the machine is finally sold any small discrepancies between capital allowances and the sale proceeds will be resolved by means of a balancing charge or allowance.

SSAP 5 – Accounting for value added tax

This accounting standard applies to organisations which are registered for Value Added Tax (VAT).

VAT is a tax on the supply of goods and services, which is eventually borne by the final consumer but is collected at each stage of the production and distribution chain.

The treatment of VAT in the accounts of a business should reflect the business' role as a tax collector, and VAT should not be included in income and expenditure – whether for capital or revenue items (although there are some exceptions, such as the purchase of cars, where VAT cannot be reclaimed and the tax is therefore included as part of the cost of the items).

SSAP 5 requires that:

- the turnover figure in profit and loss account is to be shown net of VAT
- irrecoverable VAT on fixed assets (eg cars) is to be included in their cost
- the net amount due to, or from, HM Customs and Excise (the VAT authority) is to be included in the figures for creditors and debtors respectively, and need not be disclosed separately

Case Study

SANTA PLC:
SHOWING THE TAX LIABILITIES

situation

The following balances are taken from the accounting system of Santa plc as at 31 December 2004:

	£	£
Value Added Tax payable		20,800
Provision for deferred tax		8,000
Stock	51,200	
Tangible fixed assets at cost or revaluation	250,000	
Bank	24,500	
Issued ordinary shares		100,000
Share premium account		25,000
Creditors		75,400
Debtors	102,800	
Revaluation reserve		50,000
Loan (repayable in 2009)		20,000
Net profit for year before taxation		68,300
Retained profit at start of year		61,000
	428,500	428,500

Notes:

- Corporation tax liability on the profits for the year is estimated to be £25,400
- £4,000 is to be transferred to deferred tax account
- The company proposes to pay a final dividend on its ordinary shares of £30,000

You are helping with the year-end accounts and are asked to prepare:

- profit and loss account, starting with net profit
- balance sheet, using the Companies Act layout for the financial year ended 31 December 2004.

solution

SANTA PLC
Profit and loss account (extract) for the year ended 31 December 2004

	£
Net profit for year before taxation	68,300
Less: corporation tax	25,400
transfer to deferred tax account	4,000
Profit for year after taxation	38,900
Less proposed final ordinary dividend	30,000
Retained profit for year	8,900
Add balance of retained profits at beginning of year	61,000
Balance of retained profits at end of year	69,900

Balance sheet as at 31 December 2004

	£	£
Fixed Assets		
Tangible assets at cost or revaluation		250,000
Current Assets		
Stock	51,200	
Debtors	102,800	
Bank	24,500	
	178,500	
Creditors: amounts falling due within one year		
Creditors	75,400	
VAT payable	20,800	
Corporation tax payable	25,400	
Proposed dividends	30,000	
	151,600	
Net current assets		26,900
Total assets less current liabilities		276,900
Creditors: amounts falling due after one year		20,000
Provisions for liabilities and charges		
Provision for deferred tax		*12,000
NET ASSETS		244,900

* £8,000 + £4,000 transfer = £12,000

Financed by:	£
Issued share capital	100,000
Share premium account	25,000
Revaluation reserve	50,000
Profit and loss account	69,900
	244,900

LIABILITIES SIDE OF BALANCE SHEET

Four further accounting standards impact mainly on the liabilities side of the balance sheet:

    SSAP 21   – Leases and hire purchase contracts

    FRS 4   – Capital instruments

    FRS 12   – Provisions, contingent liabilities and contingent assets

    SSAP 17   – Accounting for post balance sheet events

Note that these standards often also have an effect on both profit and loss account and on the assets side of the balance sheet.

SSAP 21 – Leases and hire purchase contracts

This standard has already been looked at in detail in Chapter 4 (pages 108 - 109).

With finance leases and hire purchase agreements, the liabilities side of the balance sheet shows the amount due to the finance company for the capital amount (ie excluding interest); the amount is split between long-term and current liabilities, as appropriate.

FRS 4 – Capital instruments

Capital instruments is the term used to describe the means of financing a business – shares, debentures, loans and debt instruments.

The objective of FRS 4 is to ensure that financial statements provide a clear, coherent and consistent treatment of capital instruments – in particular the classification into debt, ordinary shares, and other classes of shares.

The standard defines capital instruments as 'all instruments that are issued by reporting entities as a means of raising finance, including shares, debentures, loans and debt instruments, options and warrants that give the holder the right to subscribe for or obtain capital instruments'.

FRS 12 – Provisions, contingent liabilities and contingent assets

These three items – provisions, contingent liabilities, contingent assets – represent uncertainties that may have an effect on future financial statements. They need to be accounted for consistently so that users of accounts can have a fuller understanding of their effect on financial statements.

The objective of FRS 12 is to ensure that appropriate recognition criteria and measurement bases are applied to provisions, contingent liabilities and contingent assets and that sufficient information is disclosed in the notes to the financial statements to enable users to understand their nature, timing and amount.

provisions

A **provision** is a liability that is of uncertain timing or amount, to be settled by the transfer of economic benefits.

A provision should be recognised (ie recorded) as a liability in the financial statements when:

- an entity has a present obligation as a result of a past event
- it is probable that a transfer of economic benefits will be required to settle the obligation
- a reliable estimate can be made of the amount of the obligation

Unless all of these conditions are met, no provision should be recognised.

FRS 12 uses the word 'probable', in connection with the transfer of economic benefits, as being more likely to occur than not, ie a more than 50% likelihood of its occurrence.

The 'reliable estimate' of the amount of the obligation should be the best estimate of the expenditure required to settle the present obligation at the balance sheet date.

FRS 12 identifies and lists a number of specific classes of provision:

- future operating losses: provisions should not be recognised
- onerous contracts, where the unavoidable costs of meeting the obligations of the contract exceed the economic benefits expected to be received under it: provisions should be recognised for the present obligation under the contract
- restructuring, such as the sale or termination of part of the business, and changes in the management structure; restructuring costs can only be recognised as a provision when the business has an obligation to restructure

The amount of a provision is recorded as an overhead in profit and loss account, and a liability is shown on the balance sheet (under the heading 'provisions for liabilities and charges').

Disclosure in the notes to the financial statements requires:

- details of changes in the amount of provisions between the beginning and end of the year

- a description of the provision(s) and expected timings of any resulting transfers

- an indication of the uncertainties regarding the amount or timing of any resulting transfers

contingent liabilities

A **contingent liability** is either:

- a possible obligation arising from past events whose existence will be confirmed only by the occurrence of one or more uncertain future events not wholly within the entity's control; or

- a present obligation that arises from past events but is not recognised because:

  (a) it is not probable that a transfer of economic benefits will be required to settle the obligation; or

  (b) the obligation cannot be measured with sufficient reliability

Note that a contingent liability is a *possible* obligation, ie less than 50% likelihood of its occurrence (contrast this with the *probable* obligation of a provision, ie more than 50% likelihood of its occurrence).

A contingent liability is not recognised (ie recorded) in the financial statements; however, it should be disclosed as a note which includes:

- a brief description of the nature of the contingent liability

- an estimate of its financial effect

- an indication of the uncertainties relating to the amount or timing of any outflow

- the possibility of any re-imbursement

Note that where a contingent liability is considered to be remote (contrast with 'possible') then no disclosure is required.

contingent assets

A **contingent asset** is a possible asset arising from past events whose existence will be confirmed only by the occurrence of one or more uncertain future events not wholly within the entity's control.

A business should not recognise (ie record) a contingent asset in its financial statements (because it could result in the recognition of profit that may never be realised). However, when the realisation of the profit is virtually certain, then the asset is no longer contingent and its recognition is appropriate.

A contingent asset is disclosed where an inflow of economic benefits is probable; disclosure should include:

- – a brief description of the nature of the contingent asset
- – an estimate of its financial effect

summary

The diagram below summarises the ways in which provisions, contingent liabilities and contingent assets are to be handled in the financial statements.

PROVISIONS (more than 50% likelihood of occurrence)		CONTINGENT LIABILITIES (less than 50% likelihood of occurrence)	
Probable • provision recognised in financial statements as a liability • disclosure of provision in notes		*Possible* • no liability recognised in financial statements • disclosure of contingent liability in notes	*Remote* • no liability recognised in financial statements • no disclosure in notes
CONTINGENT ASSETS			
Virtually certain • no longer contingent • accrue asset in financial statements		*Probable* • no asset recognised in financial statements • disclosure of contingent asset in notes	*Not probable* • no asset recognised in financial statements • no disclosure of contingent asset in notes

Case Study

WYVERN WATER: WHAT SHOULD BE SHOWN IN THE FINANCIAL STATEMENTS?

situation

Wyvern Water Limited is a producer of spa water which is bottled at source high in the Wyvern Hills. The company also produces a very successful high energy drink – with a secret mix of Wyvern Water, glucose, and vitamins – marketed under the 'Dr Wyvern' label to sports enthusiasts.

You are helping to prepare the year-end financial statements and have been asked to decide how the following should be reported in the accounts to 31 December 2004.

1   Earlier in the year, a small batch of bottles of spa water was contaminated with oil from the bottling machinery. Although the problem was spotted by quality control checks, and most bottles were withdrawn from sale, some were sold to the public. In a few instances consumers of the water suffered severe stomach upsets and had to spend a night in hospital. These consumers are currently suing Wyvern Water for damages. The company's legal representatives consider that it is probable that the company will lose the case and that damages of £50,000 will be awarded against the company.

2   Wyvern Water holds worldwide patents and trademarks for the 'Dr Wyvern' energy drink. However, it has recently had letters from somebody claiming to be a Dr Wyvern who says that he devised the secret formula for the drink over fifty years ago. The mysterious Dr Wyvern is claiming royalties on sales of the drink for the past fifty years and says he will sue the company for £10m if he is not paid. Wyvern Water has checked carefully and found that the formula for the high energy drink was devised ten years ago by its own development team and that all applicable patents and trademarks are held. The company has sought legal advice and been advised that it is extremely unlikely that the claimant's case, if it gets to court, will be successful.

3   During the year Wyvern Water Limited has formed a separate company, Wyvern Foods Limited, to manufacture 'homestyle' pies and cakes. Wyvern Water has given a guarantee to Mercia Bank plc in respect of bank overdraft facilities provided to Wyvern Foods. At 31 December 2004 it is considered possible (but not probable) that Wyvern Water will have to make payment under the guarantee.

solution

1   Court case for damages

- The present obligation is the potential liability to pay damages from a past event, ie the sale of contaminated bottled water.

- It is probable that the company will lose the case and have to pay damages.

- The amount of damages is reliably estimated at £50,000.

- The company will record a provision as an expense in its profit and loss account and will record a liability in its balance sheet (under the heading 'provisions for liabilities and charges').

- Details of the provision will be given in the notes to the financial statements.

2   Claim for past royalties

- This is a possible obligation arising from past events, ie the sale of 'Dr Wyvern' energy drink.

- However, the possible obligation will be confirmed only by a future event – a court case.

- Legal advice considers the claimant's chances of success in a court case to be remote.

- This is a contingent liability, which will not be recognised in the accounts.

- Because the likelihood of losing the case is remote, there will be no disclosure of the contingent liability in the notes.

3 Bank guarantee

- The guarantee is a present obligation arising from a past event, ie the giving of the bank guarantee.
- However, at 31 December 2004, no transfer of economic benefits is probable to settle the obligation.
- This is a contingent liability, which will not be recognised in the accounts.
- Because the likelihood of having to meet the terms of the guarantee is possible (but not probable), details of the contingent liability will be given in the notes to the financial statements.

SSAP 17 – Accounting for post balance sheet events

This standard recognises that there may be

– events which occur, or

– information that becomes available

after the end of the financial year that need to be reflected in the financial statements. For example, if a debtor becomes insolvent after the year-end and the amount of the debt is material, it may be necessary to make changes in the financial statements for the year to reflect this.

Any such changes can only be made in the period

– after the end of the financial year, and

– before the financial statements are approved by the board of directors

Once the financial statements have been approved by the board of directors, they cannot be altered.

SSAP 17 distinguishes between

– adjusting events, and

– non-adjusting events

Adjusting events relate directly to something that existed at the balance sheet date. If material, changes should be made to the amounts shown in the financial statements. Examples of adjusting events include:

– fixed assets, the subsequent determination of the purchase price, or sale price, of assets bought or sold before the year-end

– property, where a valuation shows a permanent fall in value

– investments, where there has been a permanent fall in value

– stocks, where net realisable value falls below cost price

– debtors, where a customer has become insolvent

Non-adjusting events arise after the balance sheet date and have no direct link with something that existed at the balance sheet date. No adjustment is made to the financial statements; instead they are disclosed by way of notes in order to ensure that the financial statements are not misleading. Examples of non-adjusting events include:

- mergers and acquisitions
- issue of shares and debentures
- purchases and sales of fixed assets and investments
- losses of fixed assets and stocks caused by events such as fire or flood
- opening new, or extending existing, trading activities
- closing a significant part of the business
- changes in rates of foreign exchange
- strikes and labour disputes

PROFIT AND LOSS ACCOUNT

In this section we look at accounting standards that affect mainly the profit and loss account:

FRS 15	– Tangible fixed assets
FRS 3	– Reporting financial performance
FRS 14	– Earnings per share
SSAP 25	– Segmental reporting
SSAP 20	– Foreign currency translation
FRS 17	– Retirement benefits
FRS 8	– Related party disclosures

Note that these standards often also have an effect on the balance sheet – affecting either assets or liabilities.

FRS 15 – Tangible fixed assets

We have already seen – in Chapter 4 – how this standard sets out the principles of accounting for tangible fixed assets. Thus the standard affects both balance sheet and profit and loss account.

Profit and loss account is mainly affected by the depreciation charge, where the objective of depreciation is to reflect in operating profit the cost of the use of the tangible fixed assets in the period.

All tangible fixed assets having a known useful economic life are to be depreciated (the most common exception is land).

Further details of FRS 15 are given on pages 103 - 105.

FRS 3 – Reporting financial performance

The accounting requirements of FRS 3 have already been considered in Chapter 3 (pages 58 - 62).

The standard distinguishes between three categories of non-recurring profits and losses:

- exceptional items
- extraordinary items
- prior period adjustments

FRS 3 requires that the profit and loss account must distinguish between:

- results of continuing operations (including acquisitions – shown as a separate figure)
- results of discontinued operations
- exceptional items
- extraordinary items

The standard also requires that a statement of total recognised gains and losses is included in the year-end financial statements.

In addition to the accounting requirements of FRS 3 which we have already seen in Chapter 3, the standard requires two notes to the accounts to be shown:

- the reconciliation of movements in shareholders' funds
- the note of historical cost profit and losses

reconciliation of movements in shareholders' funds

This statement explains how shareholders' funds have changed from the beginning of the financial year to the end. Note that the term 'shareholders' funds' means the issued share capital (including preference shares, if any), plus all the reserves (capital reserves, eg share premium account, revaluation reserve and revenue reserves, eg profit and loss account, general reserve).

At its most simple, the statement will show (using example figures):

	£
Profit for the financial year (after tax)	50,000
Dividends	(30,000)
Addition to shareholders' funds	20,000
Opening shareholders' funds	150,000
Closing shareholders' funds	170,000

The statement, therefore, shows the link between profit and loss account and the shareholders' stake recorded on the balance sheet.

A more complex statement will also include:

- items from the statement of total recognised gains and losses
- other changes to shareholders' funds, such as a new issue of shares, or the repayment of shares

A further statement (using example figures) shows:

	£
Profit for the financial year (after tax)	50,000
Dividends	(30,000)
	20,000
Other recognised gains and losses (from the statement of total recognised gains and losses)	10,000
New share capital	25,000
Net addition to shareholders' funds	55,000
Opening shareholders' funds	150,000
Closing shareholders' funds	205,000

note of historical cost profit and losses

- This note is required only where there is a material difference between:
  - profit or loss figure shown in profit and loss account, and
  - historical cost profit or loss (prepared on the basis that no asset revaluations have taken place)

- Where this note is required, it commences with the reported profit on ordinary activities before tax and, after adjustments, concludes with the historical cost profit on ordinary activities before tax. The two most common adjustments shown in the note are:
  - the difference between depreciation charges based on the historical cost of fixed assets and those based on revalued amounts (note that where fixed assets have been revalued upwards, the depreciation charge will be higher than that based on historical cost)
  - gains which have been recognised in the statement of total recognised gains and losses in previous years, but which have been realised (ie the asset has been sold) in the current year (note that, if the assets had been kept at historical cost, then the full amount of the gain would be shown in the current year's profit and loss account)

- The note will appear as follows (using example figures):

	£
Reported profit on ordinary activities before taxation	90,000
Difference between historical cost depreciation charge and actual depreciation charge of the year calculated on the revalued amount	*10,000
Realisation of property revaluation gains of previous years	*18,000
Historical cost profit on ordinary activities before taxation	118,000
Historical cost profit for the year retained after taxation, minority interests, extraordinary items and dividends	70,000

* Both of these are added because:

– historical cost depreciation is lower than that based on revalued (upwards) amounts, ie historical cost will be higher as a result of a lower depreciation figure

– under historical cost accounting the full amount of realised gains is reported through profit and loss account, ie no part of the gain would be recognised in earlier years through the statement of total recognised gains and losses

The note requires the historical cost profit figure to be stated both before tax and after tax, minority interests (see Chapter 8), extraordinary items and dividends.

The main reason why FRS 3 requires this note is to enable comparison of the historical cost profit figures of similar companies. It would be almost impossible to make meaningful comparison if one company had kept fixed assets at historical costs whilst the other was using revaluations.

FRS 14 – Earnings per share

Earnings per share (EPS) is an accounting ratio that is widely used by investors to measure the performance of a company (see Chapter 7, page 196). The figure is given in all published accounts of public limited companies and is widely quoted in the financial press – the *Financial Times*, for example, quotes the EPS figure for those companies listed on its share prices pages.

The main method of calculating earnings per share allowed by FRS 14 is the *basic method* which is calculated as follows:

$$\frac{\text{net profit after tax and preference dividends}}{\text{number of issued ordinary shares}}$$

Note that the profit used in the calculation is the amount that is attributable to ordinary shareholders, ie after deducting:

– taxation

- minority interests (see Chapter 8)
- preference dividends

As well as stating a figure for EPS calculated using the basic method, other methods can be used by companies (eg the exclusion of extraordinary items, if any) but they have to:

- explain the method of calculation
- apply the method on a consistent basis
- provide a reconciliation of their method with the basic method

It is important to note that EPS is affected by the issue of additional ordinary shares during a financial year:

- when the issue has been at full market price, EPS is calculated on the basis of the average number of shares in issue during the period, using the weighted average; for example:

start of year (1 January)	100,000	ordinary shares
new issue (1 July)	50,000	ordinary shares
average number of shares in issue	*125,000	

* 100,000 + (50,000 ÷ 2 [ie half a year])

- when a bonus issue (see page 77) has been made during the year, EPS is calculated on the basis of the number of shares in issue *after* the bonus issue (this is done because, with a bonus issue, there is no inflow of cash to the company – it has the same net assets before and after the bonus issue)

Case Study

MARTLEY SERVICES: CALCULATING EARNINGS PER SHARE

situation

The profit and loss account (extract) of Martley Services Ltd for 2004 is as follows:

Profit and loss account (extract) for the year ended 31 December 2004

	£
Profit before taxation	8,200
Corporation tax	2,300
	5,900
Dividends:	
Ordinary shares	2,000
Preference shares	1,400
Retained profit for year	2,500

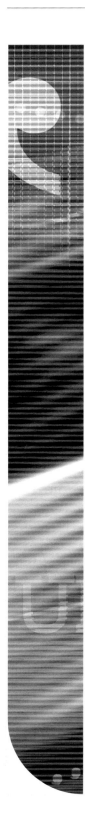

The 'financed by' section of the balance sheet at 31 December 2004 was:

Balance sheet (extract) as at 31 December 2004

FINANCED BY	£
Issued Share Capital	
Ordinary shares of £1 each	10,000
7% preference shares of £1 each	20,000
Retained profits	35,100
SHAREHOLDERS' FUNDS	65,100

(a) You are asked to calculate the basic earnings per share figure of Martley Services Limited for 2004 based on the information given above.

(b) What would the basic EPS figure be if Martley Services had made a new issue of 5,000 ordinary shares of £1 each at full market value on 1 October 2004?

(c) What would the basic EPS figure be if Martley Services had made, on 1 July 2004, a bonus issue of three fully paid ordinary shares for every ordinary share previously held?

Note: the ordinary dividend payable for 2004 will be the same for all three circumstances.

solution

(a) Basic earnings per share

$$\frac{\text{net profit after tax} - \text{preference dividend}}{\text{number of issued ordinary shares}} = \frac{£5,900 - £1,400}{10,000} = \text{45p per share}$$

(b) New issue at full market value

EPS is calculated on the basis of the weighted average number of shares in issue during the period:

$$\frac{£5,900 - £1,400}{10,000 + (5,000 \div 4)} = \frac{£4,500}{11,250} = \text{40p per share}$$

(c) Bonus issue

EPS is calculated on the basis of the number of shares in issue *after* the bonus issue:

$$\frac{£5,900 - £1,400}{10,000 + 30,000} = \frac{£4,500}{40,000} = \text{11.25p per share}$$

SSAP 25 – Segmental reporting

In order to help the user of accounts, SSAP 25 requires businesses to disclose information from their accounts in two principal ways:

- by class of business (eg hotels, pubs, clubs)
- by geographical segment (eg United Kingdom, European Union, North America)

A class of business is a distinguishable part of a business that provides a separate product or service.

A geographical segment is a geographical area comprising an individual country or group of countries.

SSAP 25 requires that, where a business has two or more classes of business, or operates in two or more geographical segments, it should disclose for each class of business and geographical segment:

- turnover
- profit
- net assets

An extract of the disclosure requirements from the accounts of Tesco PLC is shown below:

NOTE 2 Segmental analysis of sales, turnover, profit and net assets

The Group's operations of retailing and associated activities and property development are carried out in the UK, Republic of Ireland, France, Hungary, Poland, Czech Republic, Slovak Republic, Thailand, South Korea and Taiwan. The results for Thailand, South Korea, Taiwan and continental European operations are for the year ended 31 December 2001.

	Sales including VAT £m	Turnover excluding VAT £m	Operating profit £m	2002 Net operating assets £m	Sales including VAT £m	Turnover excluding VAT £m	Operating profit £m	2001 Net operating assets[†] £m
Continuing operations								
UK	21,685	20,052	1,213	7,131	19,884	18,372	1,100	6,348
Rest of Europe	2,475	2,203	90	1,079	1,970	1,756	70	925
Asia	1,494	1,398	29	916	919	860	4	545
	25,654	23,653	1,332		22,773	20,988	1,174	
Goodwill amortisation			(10)				(8)	
Operating profit			1,322				1,166	
Share of operating profit from joint ventures			42				21	
Net loss on disposal of fixed assets			(10)				(8)	
Net interest payable			(153)				(125)	
Profit on ordinary activities before taxation			1,201				1,054	
Operating margin (prior to goodwill amortisation)			5.6%				5.6%	
Capital employed				9,126				7,818
Net debt (note 20)				(3,560)				(2,804)
Net assets				5,566				5,014

Note that, for calculating segmental profits, common costs (ie those that relate to more than one segment) can be apportioned between segments – for example on the basis of turnover. If, however, such apportionment would be misleading, common costs should be deducted from the total of the segment results.

Segmental reporting enables the user of accounts to assess and compare the performance of the various segments of the business – especially in terms of turnover/assets and profit/assets.

SSAP 20 – Foreign currency translation

This standard applies:

- firstly, to companies which carry out business transactions denominated in foreign currencies

- secondly, where business is conducted through a foreign company, such as a subsidiary (see Chapter 8) which trades in its own currency

Currencies fluctuate against other currencies and the problem in accounting is to determine the rate of exchange to be used for transactions in foreign currencies.

The term **translation**, when used in connection with foreign currency transactions, means the process whereby financial data denominated in one currency are expressed in terms of another currency (**conversion** is the process of exchanging ownership of a sum of money in one currency for a sum of money in another currency).

SSAP 20 is concerned with the translation of assets, liabilities, revenues and costs denominated in foreign currencies.

The standard refers to two methods of translation:

- the closing rate method, which is based on the exchange rate at the balance sheet date

- the temporal method, which is based on historical exchange rates ruling at the date on which the amount recorded in the accounts was established

The closing rate method is referred to in the standard as 'closing rate/net investment'; it is the preferred method for translating the value of an investment in an overseas subsidiary company. The term '**net investment**' refers to the fact that such an investment is in the net worth of the foreign enterprise, rather than a direct investment in the separate assets and liabilities of that enterprise.

FRS 17 – Retirement benefits

When companies provide pension schemes as part of the remuneration package of their employees, it is necessary to have a standard accounting practice which deals with the accounting for, and the disclosure of, retirement benefit costs and obligations in the financial statements.

The objectives of FRS 17 are to ensure that:

- financial statements reflect fairly the assets and liabilities of an employer's retirement benefit obligations and any related funding

- the operating costs of providing retirement benefits to employees are recognised in the accounting periods in which the benefits are earned by the employees, and the related finance costs; any changes in value of the assets and liabilities are recognised in the accounting periods in which they arise

- the financial statements contain adequate disclosure of the cost of providing retirement benefits and the related gains, losses, assets and liabilities

There are two main retirement benefits schemes considered by the standard:

- **defined contribution scheme**, into which an employer pays regular contributions fixed as an amount or percentage of the employee's pay; the amount of retirement benefits payable to the employee is not guaranteed and will depend on the return achieved by the investments of the scheme

- **defined benefit scheme**, where the scheme rules define the benefits independently of the contributions payable, and the benefits are not directly related to the investments of the scheme

Profit and loss account is debited with the employer's pension costs for the accounting period.

With defined benefit schemes, because the pension benefits payable are independent of the value of the pension share investments, there has to be a regular valuation of the two, ie the pension scheme liabilities and the value of pension scheme assets. There may be a surplus (assets exceed liabilities) or a deficit (liabilities exceed assets).

For defined benefit schemes any surplus or deficit is shown in the accounts as follows:

- the statement of total recognised gains and losses is credited with the surplus, or debited with the deficit, of the scheme

- balance sheet shows the pension scheme surplus or deficit

An example of how a defined benefit pension scheme surplus will be reported in the balance sheet is shown on the next page.

BALANCE SHEET AS AT 31 DECEMBER 2004

Assets	£000s
Pension asset*	250
Reserves	
Pension reserve**	250

---

* Pension scheme investments (valued at market values, eg current share price of investment), less pension scheme liabilities (valued by an actuary – at least every three years – to reflect the retirement benefits that the employer will have to provide).

** The amount of the pension scheme surplus at the balance sheet date, any changes having been reported through the statement of total recognised gains and losses.

When a defined benefit scheme has a surplus, the employer will usually reduce contributions in the future. With a deficit, the employer may have a legal obligation (under the terms of the pension scheme trust deed) to make good the shortfall – such a liability must be recognised in the financial statements.

FRS 8 – Related party disclosures

As we saw in Chapter 1, many different parties have an interest in the financial statements of limited companies. Where such an interest extends to the ability to control or influence the financial or operating policies then such a party is known as a **related party**.

The objective of FRS 8 is to ensure that financial statements contain the disclosures necessary to draw attention to the existence of related parties, and material transactions with them. Such transactions may have an effect on the results shown by the financial statements.

Related parties exist under any one of the following circumstances:

– one party has direct or indirect control of another party

– the parties are subject to common control from the same source

– one party has influence over the financial or operating policies of the other party to an extent that the other party might be inhibited from pursuing at all times its own separate interests

- the parties, in entering a transaction, are subject to influence from the same source to such an extent that one of the parties to the transaction has subordinated its own separate interests (ie has put its own interests below that of the other)

Some parties are always related parties of the reporting entity. These include companies within the same group (see Chapter 8), associated companies, the entity's directors (and directors of the entity's parent company), pension funds and those who control 20 per cent or more of the voting rights.

Certain parties are presumed to be related parties of the reporting entity unless it can be demonstrated that neither party has influenced the financial and operating policies of the other in such a way as to inhibit the pursuit of separate interests. Examples include the key management of the reporting entity and the key management of its parent undertaking.

FRS 8 requires disclosure of:

- all material related party transactions
- the name of the party controlling the reporting entity

CONFIDENTIALITY PROCEDURES

The Companies Act requires that all large companies (together with some small and medium-sized companies):

- disclose whether the accounts have been prepared in accordance with applicable accounting standards

- give particulars of any material departure from the standards and the reasons for the departure

Thus, such information is readily available to users of accounts. However, other information (which may be available to those involved in the preparation of accounts) is subject to confidentiality procedures which must be observed at all times; for example:

- details of any discussion about accounting standards with the directors

- the application of standards to a particular set of financial statements

- details of any workings used, but not disclosed in the accounts, such as in the calculation of deferred tax, provisions, depreciation, etc

- discussion of whether to treat an item one way rather than another, such as deciding whether to classify something as a provision to be recognised in the financial statements, or as a contingent liability to be disclosed as a note

- **FRS 16** 'Current tax' requires that current tax is to be recognised in profit and loss account. However, where a gain (or loss) has been recognised directly in the statement of total recognised gains and losses, the tax relating to the gain (or loss) is recognised directly in that statement.

- **FRS 19** 'Deferred tax' requires deferred tax to be recognised on most types of timing differences.

- **SSAP 5** 'Accounting for value added tax' requires that:

  - the turnover figure in profit and loss account is to be shown net of VAT

  - irrecoverable VAT on fixed assets is to be included in their cost

  - the net amount due to, or from, HM Customs and Excise is to be included in the figures for creditors and debtors respectively, and need not be disclosed separately

- **SSAP 21** 'Leases and hire purchase contracts' requires to be shown, on the liabilities side of the balance sheet, the amount due to the finance company for the capital amount – split between long-term and current liabilities, as appropriate. See also pages 108-109.

- **FRS 4** 'Capital instruments' states how capital instruments – shares, debentures, loans and debt instruments – are to be treated in the financial statements.

- **FRS 12** 'Provisions, contingent liabilities and contingent assets' ensures that appropriate recognition criteria and measurement bases are applied to these three types of uncertainties. It requires that sufficient information is disclosed in the notes to financial statements to enable users to understand their nature, timing and amount.

- **SSAP 17** 'Accounting for post balance sheet events' allows for events which may occur, or information that becomes available, in the period between the end of the financial year and the approval of financial statements by the board of directors to be reflected in the financial statements. The standard distinguishes between adjusting events and non-adjusting events.

- **FRS 15** 'Tangible fixed assets' (see also pages 103-105) requires that all tangible fixed assets having a known useful economic life are to be depreciated.

- **FRS 3** 'Reporting financial performance' (see also pages 58-62):

  - distinguishes between three categories of non-recurring profits and losses: exceptional items, extraordinary items and prior period adjustments

- requires that the profit and loss account distinguishes between: results of continuing operations, results of discontinued operations, exceptional items, extraordinary items

- requires that a statement of total recognised gains and losses is included in the year-end financial statements

- requires two notes to the accounts to be shown: reconciliation of movements in shareholders' funds, and a note of historical cost profit and losses

- **FRS 14** 'Earnings per share' requires the EPS figure to be given in the published accounts of public limited companies. The main method of calculating EPS allowed by the standard is called the basic method.

- **SSAP 25** 'Segmental reporting' requires businesses to disclose information from their accounts in two principal ways:

  - by class of business

  - by geographical segment

- **SSAP 20** 'Foreign currency translation' is concerned with the translation of assets, liabilities, revenues and costs denominated in foreign currencies. The standard refers to two methods of translation:

  - the closing rate method

  - the temporal method

  The 'closing rate/net investment' method is seen as the preferred method for translating the value of an investment in an overseas subsidiary company.

- **FRS 17** 'Retirement benefits' distinguishes between two main retirement benefits schemes:

  - defined contribution scheme

  - defined benefit scheme

  The objectives of the standard are to ensure that the financial statements reflect fairly the assets and liabilities, operating costs, and changes in value of assets and liabilities, of an employer's retirement benefit obligations and any related funding.

- **FRS 8** 'Related party disclosures' ensures that financial statements contain the disclosures necessary to draw attention to the existence of related parties, and material transactions with them.

Key Terms		
	current tax	the amount of tax estimated to be due on the profits of the accounting period
	deferred tax	'estimated future tax consequences of transactions and events recognised in the financial statements of the current and previous periods' (FRS 19)
	Value Added Tax	a tax on the supply of goods and services, which is eventually borne by the final consumer, but is collected at each stage of the production and distribution chain
	capital instruments	'all instruments that are issued by reporting entities as a means of raising finance, including shares, debentures, loans and debt instruments, options and warrants that give the holder the right to subscribe for or obtain capital instruments' (FRS 4)
	provision	a liability of uncertain timing or amount, to be settled by the transfer of economic benefits
	contingent liability	*either* a possible obligation arising from past events whose existence will be confirmed only by the occurrence of one or more uncertain future events not wholly within the entity's control;
		or a present obligation that arises from past events but is not recognised because:
		– it is not probable that a transfer of economic benefits will be required to settle the obligation; or
		– the obligation cannot be measured with sufficient reliability
	contingent asset	a possible asset arising from past events whose existence will be confirmed only by the occurrence of one or more uncertain future events not wholly within the entity's control
	adjusting event	a post balance sheet event that relates directly to something that existed at the balance sheet date; if material, changes should be made to the amounts shown in the financial statements
	non-adjusting event	an event that arises after the balance sheet date and has no direct link with something that existed at the balance sheet date; no adjustment is made to the financial statements, but it is disclosed by way of a note in order to ensure that the financial statements are not misleading

earnings per share

basic method:

$$\frac{\text{net profit after tax and preference dividends}}{\text{number of issued ordinary shares}}$$

class of business

a distinguishable part of a business that provides a separate product or service

geographical segment

a geographical area comprising an individual country or group of countries

foreign currency translation

the process whereby financial data denominated in one currency are expressed in terms of another currency; there are two main methods of translation:

- the closing rate method (based on the exchange rate at the balance sheet date)

- the temporal method (based on historical exchange rates ruling at the date on which the amount recorded in the accounts was established)

defined contribution scheme

pension scheme into which an employer pays regular contributions fixed as an amount or percentage of the employee's pay; the amount of retirement benefits payable to the employee is not guaranteed and will depend on the return achieved by the investments of the scheme

defined benefit scheme

pension scheme where the scheme rules define the benefits independently of the contributions payable, and the benefits are not directly related to the investments of the scheme

related parties

exist under any one of the following:

- one party has direct or indirect control of another party

- the parties are subject to common control from the same source

- one party has influence over the financial or operating policies of the other party to an extent that the other party might be inhibited from pursuing at all times its own separate interests

- the parties, in entering a transaction, are subject to influence from the same source to such an extent that one of the parties to the transaction has subordinated its own separate interests

Student Activities

5.1   Which of the following could be charged to the profit and loss account as an expense?

(a)   a non-adjusting post balance sheet event.

(b)   a possible contingent liability

(c)   non-purchased (inherent) goodwill

(d)   research and development expenditure

5.2   FRS 12 Provisions, contingent liabilities and contingent assets, states that a contingent liability at the balance sheet date should be provided for in the accounts for that year, if:

(a)   its occurrence is probable and the loss can be estimated with reasonable certainty.

(b)   its occurrence is possible.

(c)   its occurrence is remote.

(d)   its occurrence is neither probable, possible or remote.

5.3   According to SSAP 17 *Accounting for post balance sheet events*, which one of the following is an adjusting event?

(a)   a flash flood which occurred after the year end ruining a certain amount of stock.

(b)   the signing of a major export contract with Japan on the last day of the financial year.

(c)   a strike by the workforce after the year end, which threatens the profitability of the company.

(d)   a customer who was forced into liquidation, after the year end, but the amount due is recorded in the balance sheet as at the actual year end.

5.4   When dealing with current tax (FRS 16) which of the following best describes the amount due to be paid in the accounts?

(a)   debit profit and loss account   credit cash

(b)   debit profit and loss account   credit corporation tax payable

(c)   debit cash   credit corporation tax payable

(d)   debit cash   credit profit and loss account

5.5 Which one of the following statements is correct when dealing with deferred taxation, according to FRS 19?

(a) the taxable profit and the business profit are one and the same, allowances being based upon depreciation

(b) the taxable profit is the same as the bank account balance, ensuring that there is enough cash to pay the tax payable

(c) the taxable profit is the same as the NBV of the tangible fixed assets, after adjusting for depreciation

(d) the taxable profit is different to the business profit due to the fact that depreciation is replaced by a system of capital allowances

5.6 Define adjusting and non-adjusting events, giving an example of each.

5.7 State how a material contingent loss and a material contingent gain should be treated and accounted for in financial statements.

5.8 Explain the main purpose of a statement of recognised gains and losses.

5.9 What is the main purpose for issuing SSAP 25 segmental reporting?

5.10 What are the main differences between a defined contribution pension scheme and a defined benefit pension scheme?

5.11 When a company deals abroad in a foreign currency what are the differences as you understand them, between conversion and translation?

6 Cash flow statements

this chapter covers . . .

In this chapter we study the cash flow statement, which links profit from the profit and loss account with changes in assets and liabilities in the balance sheet, and the effect on the cash of the company.

We will cover:

- *an appreciation of the need for a cash flow statement*

- *the cash flows for the main sections of the statement*

- *how the cash flows relate to the main areas of business activity*

- *the interpretation of cash flow statements*

NVQ PERFORMANCE CRITERIA COVERED

unit 11: DRAFTING FINANCIAL STATEMENTS

element 11.1

draft limited company financial statements

A   draft limited company financial statements from the appropriate information

B   correctly identify and implement subsequent adjustments and ensure that discrepancies, unusual features or queries are identified and either resolved or referred to the appropriate person

C   ensure that limited company financial statements comply with relevant accounting standards and domestic legislation and with the organisation's policies, regulations and procedures

D   prepare and interpret a limited company cash flow statement

E   ensure that confidentiality procedures are followed at all times

INTRODUCTION

The profit and loss account shows profitability, and the balance sheet shows asset strength. While these two financial statements give us a great deal of information on the progress of a company during an accounting period, profit does not equal cash, and strength in assets does not necessarily mean a large bank balance.

The **cash flow statement** links profit with changes in assets and liabilities, and the effect on the cash of the company.

A cash flow statement uses information from the accounting records (including profit and loss account and balance sheet) to show an overall view of money flowing in and out of a company during an accounting period.

Such a statement explains to the shareholders why, after a year of good profits for example, there is a reduced balance at the bank or a larger bank overdraft at the year-end than there was at the beginning of the year. The cash flow statement concentrates on the liquidity of the business: it is often a lack of cash (a lack of liquidity) that causes most businesses to fail. The importance of the cash flow statement is such that all but small limited companies must include the statement as a part of their accounts.

The format used in this chapter for the cash flow statement follows the guidelines set out in FRS 1 *Cash Flow Statements*.

FORMAT OF THE CASH FLOW STATEMENT

FRS 1 provides a format for cash flow statements which is divided into eight sections:

1   Operating activities

2   Returns on investments and servicing of finance

3   Taxation

4   Capital expenditure and financial investment

5   Acquisitions and disposals

6   Equity dividends paid

7   Management of liquid resources

8   Financing

The cash flows for the year affecting each of these main areas of business activity are shown in the statement, although not every company will have cash flows under each of the eight sections. The final figure at the bottom of the cash flow statement shows the net cash inflow or outflow for the period.

The diagram on the next page shows the main cash inflows and outflows under each heading, and indicates the content of the cash flow statement. The first section – operating activities – needs a word of further explanation, particularly as it is the main source of cash inflow for most companies.

operating activities

The net cash inflow from operating activities is calculated by using figures from the profit and loss account and balance sheet as follows:

operating profit (ie net profit, before deduction of interest)

add   depreciation for the year

add   loss on sale of fixed assets (or *deduct* profit on sale of fixed assets) – see page 168

add   decrease in stock (or *deduct* increase in stock)

add   decrease in debtors (or *deduct* increase in debtors)

add   increase in creditors (or *deduct* decrease in creditors)

Note that depreciation is added to profit because depreciation is a non-cash expense, that is, no money is paid out by the company in respect of depreciation charged to profit and loss account.

LAYOUT OF A CASH FLOW STATEMENT

A cash flow statement uses a common layout which can be amended to suit the particular needs of the company for which it is being prepared. The example layout shown on page 164 (with specimen figures included) is commonly used – see also the cash flow statement for Tesco PLC shown on page 65.

CASH FLOW STATEMENT

Operating activities

- Operating profit (ie net profit, before deduction of interest)
- Depreciation charge for the year (see page 168 for treatment of a profit or a loss on sale of fixed assets)
- Changes in stock, debtors and creditors

Returns on investments and servicing of finance

- Inflows: interest received, dividends received
- Outflows: interest paid, dividends paid on preference shares (but not ordinary shares – see below)

Taxation

- Outflow: corporation tax paid by limited companies during the year

Capital expenditure and financial investment

- Inflows: sale proceeds from fixed assets and investments
- Outflows: purchase cost of fixed assets and investments

Acquisitions and disposals

- Inflows: sale proceeds from investments and interests in
  - subsidiary companies (where more than 50 per cent of the shares in another company is owned)
  - associated companies (where between 20 per cent and 50 per cent of the shares in another company is owned)
  - joint ventures (where a project is undertaken jointly with another company)
- Outflows: purchase cost of investments in subsidiary companies, associated companies, and of interests in joint ventures

Equity dividends paid

- Outflow: the amount of dividends paid to equity (ordinary) shareholders during the year

Management of liquid resources

- Inflows: sale proceeds from short-term investments that are almost as good as cash – such as treasury bills (a form of government debt), and term deposits of up to a year with a bank
- Outflows: purchase of short-term liquid investments

Financing

- Inflows: receipts from increase in share capital, raising/increase of loans (note: no cash inflow from a bonus issue of shares – see page 77)
- Outflows: repayment of share capital/loans

Contents of a cash flow statement

ABC LIMITED
CASH FLOW STATEMENT FOR THE YEAR ENDED 31 DECEMBER 2004

	£	£
Net cash inflow from operating activities		89,000
Returns on investments and servicing of finance:		
Interest received	10,000	
Interest paid	(5,000)	
		5,000
Taxation:		
Corporation tax paid (note: amount paid during year)		(6,000)
Capital expenditure and financial investment:		
Payments to acquire fixed assets	(125,000)	
Receipts from sales of fixed assets	15,000	
		(110,000)
Acquisitions and disposals:		
Purchase of subsidiary undertakings	(–)	
Sale of a business	–	
		–
Equity dividends paid: (note: amount paid during year)		(22,000)
Cash outflow before use of liquid resources and financing		(44,000)
Management of liquid resources:		
Purchase of treasury bills	(250,000)	
Sale of treasury bills	200,000	
		(50,000)
Financing:		
Issue of share capital	275,000	
Repayment of capital/share capital	(–)	
Increase in loans	–	
Repayment of loans	(90,000)	
		185,000
Increase in cash		91,000

Reconciliation of operating profit to net cash inflow from operating activities

Operating profit (note: before tax and interest)	75,000
Depreciation for year	10,000
Decrease in stock	2,000
Increase in debtors	(5,000)
Increase in creditors	7,000
Net cash inflow from operating activities	89,000

notes on the cash flow statement

- The separate amounts shown for each section can, if preferred, be detailed in a note to the cash flow statement. The operating activities section is invariably set out in detail as a note below the cash flow statement (see example opposite), with just the figure for net cash flow from operating activities being shown on the statement (see grey line).

- Money amounts shown in brackets indicate a deduction or, where the figure is a sub-total, a negative figure.

- The changes in the main working capital items of stock, debtors and creditors have an effect on cash balances. For example, a decrease in stock increases cash, while an increase in debtors reduces cash.

- The cash flow statement concludes with a figure for the increase or decrease in cash for the period. This is calculated from the subtotals of each of the eight sections of the statement.

Case Study

NEWTOWN TRADING COMPANY LIMITED: CASH FLOW STATEMENT

situation

The balance sheets of Newtown Trading Company Limited for 2003 and 2004 are shown on the next page.

Prepare a cash flow statement for the year ended 31 December 2004 and comment on the main points highlighted by the statement. Note the following points:

- Extract from the profit and loss account for 2004:

	£
Operating profit	9,400
Interest paid	400
Net profit	9,000
Less: Corporation tax	1,500
Proposed ordinary dividend	2,500
Retained profit for year	5,000

- During 2004 the land was revalued at £125,000.

Tutorial note

When preparing a cash flow statement from financial statements, take a moment or two to establish which is the earlier year and which is the later year. In this Case Study they are set out from left to right, ie 2003 followed by 2004. In some Activities and Examinations, the later year is shown first, ie 2004 followed by 2003.

BALANCE SHEETS AS AT 31 DECEMBER

	2003 £ Cost	2003 £ Dep'n	2003 £ Net	2004 £ Cost or reval'n	2004 £ Dep'n	2004 £ Net
Fixed Assets						
Land	75,000	–	75,000	125,000	–	125,000
Vehicles	22,200	6,200	16,000	39,000	8,900	30,100
	97,200	6,200	91,000	164,000	8,900	155,100
Current Assets						
Stock		7,000			11,000	
Debtors		5,000			3,700	
Bank		1,000			500	
		13,000			15,200	
Less Current Liabilities						
Creditors	3,500			4,800		
Proposed dividends	2,000			2,500		
Corporation tax	1,000			1,500		
		6,500			8,800	
Working Capital			6,500			6,400
			97,500			161,500
Less Long-term Liabilities						
Debentures			5,000			3,000
NET ASSETS			92,500			158,500
FINANCED BY						
Ordinary share capital			80,000			90,000
Share premium account			1,500			2,500
Revaluation reserve			–			50,000
Retained profits			11,000			16,000
SHAREHOLDERS' FUNDS			92,500			158,500

solution

NEWTOWN TRADING COMPANY LIMITED
CASH FLOW STATEMENT FOR THE YEAR ENDED 31 DECEMBER 2004

	£	£
Net cash inflow from operating activities		10,700
Returns on investments and servicing of finance:		
Interest paid		(400)
Taxation:		
Corporation tax paid		(1,000)
Capital expenditure and financial investment:		
Payments to acquire fixed assets (vehicles)		(16,800)
Equity dividends paid:		(2,000)
Cash outflow before use of liquid resources and financing		(9,500)
Financing:		
Issue of ordinary shares at a premium		
ie £10,000 + £1,000 =	11,000	
Repayment of debentures	(2,000)	
		9,000
Decrease in cash**		(500)

Reconciliation of operating profit to net cash inflow from operating activities	
Operating profit (before interest)	9,400
Depreciation for year*	2,700
Increase in stock	(4,000)
Decrease in debtors	1,300
Increase in creditors	1,300
Net cash inflow from operating activities	10,700

notes on the cash flow statement

*   Depreciation charged: £8,900 – £6,200 = £2,700

** Decrease in cash: from £1,000 to £500 = £500

Both proposed dividends and corporation tax – which are current liabilities at 31 December 2003 – are paid in 2004. Likewise, the current liabilities for dividends and tax at 31 December 2004 will be paid in 2005 (and will appear on that year's cash flow statement).

The revaluation of the land (increase in the value of the fixed asset, and revaluation reserve recorded in the 'financed by' section) does not feature in the cash flow statement because it is a non-cash transaction.

how useful is the cash flow statement?

The following points are highlighted by the statement on the previous page:

• net cash inflow from operating activities is £10,700

• a purchase of vehicles of £16,800 has been made, financed partly by operating activities, and partly by an issue of shares at a premium

• the bank balance during the year has fallen by £500, ie from £1,000 to £500

In conclusion, the picture shown by the cash flow statement is that of a business which is generating cash from its operating activities and using them to build for the future.

PROFIT OR LOSS ON SALE OF FIXED ASSETS

a difference between book value and sale proceeds

When a company sells fixed assets it is most unlikely that the resultant sale proceeds will equal the net book value (cost price, less depreciation to date).

dealing with a profit or loss on sale

The accounting solution is to transfer any small profit or loss on sale – non-cash items – to profit and loss account. However, such a profit or loss on sale must be handled with care when preparing a cash flow statement because, in such a statement we have to adjust for non-cash items when calculating the net cash inflow from operating activities; at the same time we must separately identify the amount of the sale proceeds of fixed assets in the capital expenditure section.

Case Study

H & J WELLS LIMITED:
PROFIT OR LOSS ON SALE OF FIXED ASSETS

situation

H & J Wells Limited is an electrical contractor. For the year ended 30 June 2004 its profit and loss account is as follows:

	£	£
Gross profit		37,500
Less expenses:		
General expenses	23,000	
Provision for depreciation: machinery	2,000	
vehicles	3,000	
		28,000
Net profit		9,500

profit on sale

During the course of the year the company has sold the following fixed asset; the effects of the sale transaction have not yet been recorded in profit and loss account:

	£
Machine: cost price	1,000
depreciation to date	750
net book value	250
sale proceeds	350

As the machine has been sold for £100 more than book value, this sum is shown in profit and loss account, as follows:

	£	£
Gross profit		37,500
Profit on sale of fixed assets		100
		37,600
Less expenses:		
General expenses	23,000	
Provision for depreciation: machinery	2,000	
vehicles	3,000	
		28,000
Net profit		9,600

The cash flow statement, based on the amended profit and loss account, will include the following figures:

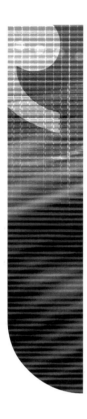

CASHFLOW STATEMENT (EXTRACT) OF H & J WELLS LIMITED
FOR THE YEAR ENDED 30 JUNE 2004

	£	£
Operating activities (this will be shown as a note)		
Operating profit (here, the same as net profit)	9,600	
Depreciation	5,000	
Profit on sale of fixed assets	(100)	
(Increase)/decrease in stock	. . .	
(Increase)/decrease in debtors	. . .	
Increase/(decrease) in creditors	. . .	
Net cash inflow from operating activities		14,500
Capital expenditure and financial investment:		
Payments to acquire fixed assets	(. . .)	
Receipts from sales of fixed assets	350	
		350

Note that profit on sale of fixed assets is deducted in the operating activities section because it is non-cash income. (Only the sections of the cash flow statement affected by the sale are shown above.)

loss on sale

If the machine in the Case Study had been sold for £150, this would have given a 'loss on sale' of £100. This amount would be debited to profit and loss account, to give an amended net profit of £9,400. The effect on the cash flow statement would be twofold:

1   In the operating activities section, loss on sale of fixed assets of £100 would be added; the net cash inflow from operating activities remains at £14,500 (which proves that both profit and loss on sale of fixed assets are non-cash items)

2   In the capital expenditure section, receipts from sales of fixed assets would be £150

conclusion: profit or a loss on sale of fixed assets

The rule for dealing with a profit or a loss on sale of fixed assets in cash flow statements is:

•   add the amount of the loss on sale, or deduct the amount of the profit on sale, to or from the operating profit when calculating the net cash flow from operating activities

•   show the total sale proceeds, ie the amount of the cheque received, as receipts from sales of fixed assets in the capital expenditure section

The Case Study of Retail News Limited (see below) incorporates calculations for both a profit and a loss on sale of fixed assets.

REVALUATION OF FIXED ASSETS

From time-to-time some fixed assets are revalued upwards and the amount of the revaluation is recorded in the balance sheet. The most common assets to be treated in this way are land and buildings. The value of the fixed asset is increased and the amount of the revaluation is placed to a revaluation reserve in the 'financed by' section of the balance sheet where it increases the value of the shareholders' investment in the company. As a revaluation is purely a 'book' adjustment, ie no cash has changed hands, it does not feature in a cash flow statement – see the Case Study of Newtown Trading Company Limited on pages 165 to 167.

Case Study

RETAIL NEWS LIMITED: PREPARING THE CASH FLOW STATEMENTS

Tutorial note

This is quite a complex example of cash flow statements which incorporates a number of points:

- profit on sale of fixed assets

- loss on sale of fixed assets

- issue of shares at a premium

- calculation of corporation tax paid and ordinary dividends paid

As there are two years' cash flow statements to produce, it is suggested that you work through the Case Study seeing how the figures have been prepared for the first year (year ended 2003); then attempt the second year (year ended 2004) yourself, checking against the Case Study.

situation

Martin Jackson is a shareholder in Retail News Limited, a company that operates newsagent shops in the town of Wyvern. Martin comments that, whilst the company is making reasonable profits, the bank balance has fallen quite considerably. He provides you with the following information for Retail News Limited:

Balance sheet as at 31 December

	2002		2003		2004	
	£000	£000	£000	£000	£000	£000
Fixed Assets at cost		274		298		324
Less depreciation		74		98		118
		200		200		206
Current Assets						
Stock	50		74		85	
Debtors	80		120		150	
Bank	10		–		–	
	140		194		235	
Less Current Liabilities						
Creditors	62		78		82	
Bank	–		15		46	
Final dividends	10		14		12	
Corporation tax	4		5		8	
	76		112		148	
Working Capital		64		82		87
NET ASSETS		264		282		293
FINANCED BY						
Ordinary share capital		200		210		210
Share premium account		–		5		5
Retained profits		64		67		78
SHAREHOLDERS' FUNDS		264		282		293

Profit and loss account extracts for the year ended 31 December

	2002 £000	2003 £000	2004 £000
Operating profit	25	31	50
Interest paid	–	3	15
Net profit	25	28	35
Corporation tax	5	7	10
Profit after tax	20	21	25
Ordinary dividends paid and proposed	15	18	14
Retained profit for year	5	3	11

Notes

• During the year to 31 December 2003, fixed assets were sold for £30,000, the cost of the fixed assets sold was £40,000 and depreciation was £20,000.

• During the year to 31 December 2004, fixed assets with an original cost of £35,000 were sold at a loss on sale of £5,000 below net book value; the depreciation on these fixed assets sold had amounted to £15,000.

REQUIRED: Prepare a cash flow statement for the years ended 2003 and 2004.

RETAIL NEWS LIMITED
CASH FLOW STATEMENT FOR THE YEAR ENDED 31 DECEMBER

	2003		2004	
	£000	£000	£000	£000
Net cash inflow from operating activities		17		53
Returns on investments and servicing of finance:				
Interest paid		(3)		(15)
Taxation:				
Corporation tax paid (see below)		(6)		(7)
Capital expenditure and financial investment:				
Payments to acquire fixed assets (see below)	(64)		(61)	
Receipts from sales of fixed assets	30		15	
		(34)		(46)
Equity dividends paid: (see below)		(14)		(16)
Cash outflow before use of liquid resources and financing		(40)		(31)
Financing:				
Issue of ordinary shares at a premium (see below)		15		–
Decrease in cash		(25)		(31)
Bank balance at start of year		10		(15)
Bank balance at end of year		(15)		(46)
Decrease in cash		(25)		(31)

Reconciliation of operating profit to net cash inflow from operating activities

	2003 (£000)	2004 (£000)
Operating profit	31	50
Depreciation for year (see below)	44	35
(Profit)/loss on sale of fixed assets (see below)	(10)	5
Increase in stock	(24)	(11)
Increase in debtors	(40)	(30)
Increase in creditors	16	4
Net cash inflow from operating activities	17	53

Points to note from the cash flow statement:
▪ **Depreciation for year**

	2003 £000	2004 £000
Depreciation at start of year*	74	98
Less depreciation on asset sold	20	15
	54	83
Depreciation at end of year*	98	118
Depreciation for year	44	35

* figures taken from balance sheet

■ **Profit/(loss) on sale of fixed assets**

	2003	2004
	£000	£000
Cost price of assets sold	40	35
Less depreciation to date	20	15
Net book value	20	20
Receipts from sale	30	*15
Profit/(loss) on sale	10	(5)

* Receipt from sale at £5,000 below net book value

Note that profit on sale is *deducted from*, and loss on sale is *added to*, operating profit because they are non-cash income; the receipts from sale are shown in the capital expenditure section

■ **Corporation tax paid**

From the information available we can calculate the amount of corporation tax in the year as follows:

Liability at start of year*	4	5
Profit and loss account transfer	7	10
	11	15
Less liability at end of year*	5	8
Amount paid in year	6	7

* figures taken from balance sheet

■ **Payments to acquire fixed assets**

Fixed assets at cost at start of year	274	298
Less cost price of asset sold	40	35
	234	263
Fixed assets at cost at end of year	298	324
Payments to acquire fixed assets	64	61

■ **Equity (ordinary) dividends paid**

From the information available we can calculate the amount of ordinary dividends paid in the year as follows:

Liability at start of year*	10	14
Profit and loss account transfer	18	14
	28	28
Less liability at end of year*	14	12
Amount paid in year	14	16

* figures taken from balance sheet

■ **Issue of ordinary shares at a premium**

Ordinary share capital at start of year	200
Share premium account at start of year	–
	200
Ordinary share capital at end of year	210
Share premium account at end of year	5
	215
Issue of ordinary shares at a premium	15

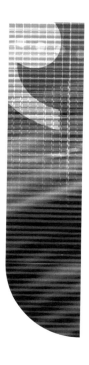

conclusion: how useful is the cash flow statement?

The following points are highlighted by the cash flow statements of Retail News Limited for 2003 and 2004:

- a good cash flow from operating profit in both years – well above the amounts paid for corporation tax and dividends

- stock, debtors and creditors have increased each year – in particular the debtors have increased significantly

- interest paid in 2004 is high because of the increasing bank overdraft (and will, most probably, be even higher in 2005)

- new fixed assets have been bought each year – £64,000 in 2003 and £61,000 in 2004. Apart from a share issue of £15,000 in 2003, these have been financed through the bank account

The company appears to be expanding quite rapidly, with large increases in fixed assets and the working capital items. As most of this expansion has been financed through the bank (apart from the share issue of £15,000 in 2003), there is much pressure on the bank account. It would be better to obtain long-term finance – either a loan or a new issue of shares – rather than using the bank overdraft.

LINKS TO OTHER FINANCIAL STATEMENTS

As the cash flow statement is one of the three financial statements prepared at the end of an accounting period, it needs to be read in conjunction with the profit and loss account and balance sheet. In order to provide links to the other financial statements, the accounting standard on cash flow statements, FRS1, requires that there should be two reconciliations – or formal notes – between:

- operating profit and the net cash flow from operating activities
- the increase or decrease in cash and the movement in net debt

operating profit with net cash flow from operating activities

We have already seen in the Case Studies how this reconciliation is prepared: the 'operating activities' section commences with the operating profit and, after adjustments for depreciation and the change in stocks, debtors and creditors, concludes with the net cash flow from operating activities. The figures making up the reconciliation are invariably shown as a note to the cash flow statement with just the figure for net cash flow from operating activities being shown on the face of the statement.

change in cash with movement in net debt

This reconciliation requires us to take the final figure on the cash flow statement – the increase or decrease in cash – and reconcile it with changes in net debt. (Note that net debt is the borrowing of the business – eg debentures, loans and overdrafts – less cash/bank balances and other liquid resources, such as treasury bills). Thus, for ABC Limited (see page 164) the reconciliation could be shown as follows, with specimen figures used:

Analysis of changes in net debt

	Net debt as at 1 Jan 2004	Cash flows year to 31 Dec 2004	Net debt as at 31 Dec 2004
	£	£	£
Cash at bank	(25,000)	91,000	66,000
Loans	(400,000)	90,000	(310,000)
Treasury bills	125,000	50,000	175,000
	(300,000)	231,000	(69,000)

The above indicates that ABC Limited has used a lot of cash this year both to reduce its loans by £90,000 and to increase its liquid resources (in the form of treasury bills) by £50,000. As a consequence, the bottom line of the analysis shows that its net debt has fallen from £300,000 at the start of the year to £69,000 at the end – a reduction of £231,000. (For businesses where borrowings are less than cash/bank balances and other liquid resources, the words 'net funds' are used in place of 'net debt'.)

INTERPRETING THE CASH FLOW STATEMENT

The cash flow statement is important because it identifies the sources of cash flowing into the company and shows how they have been used. To get an overall view of the company, we need to read the statement in conjunction with the other two financial statements – profit and loss account and balance sheet – and also in the context of the previous year's statements.

You could be asked to interpret a cash flow statement in the Examination. The following points should be borne in mind:

- Like the other financial statements, the cash flow statement uses the money measurement concept. This means that only items which can be recorded in money terms can be included; also we must be aware of the effect of inflation if comparing one year with the next.

- Look for a positive cash inflow from operating activities each year – this is the cash from the trading activities of the company.

- Make a comparison between the amount of operating profit and the cash inflow from operating activities. Identify the reasons for major differences between these figures – look at the changes in the working capital items of stock, debtors and creditors, and put them into context. For example, it would be a warning sign if there were large increases in these items in a company with a falling operating profit, and such a trend would put a strain on the liquidity of the business. Also consider the company's policies on debtor collection (and potential for bad debts), creditor payment (is the company paying creditors too quickly?) and stock control (are surplus stocks building up?).

- The statement will show the amount of investment made during the year (eg the purchase of fixed assets). In general there should be a link between the cost of the investment and an increase in loans and/or share capital – it isn't usual to finance fixed assets from short-term sources, such as a bank overdraft.

- Look at the amount of dividends paid – this is an outflow of cash that will directly affect the change in the bank balance. As a quick test, take the cash inflow from operating activities and deduct interest and taxation paid: the resultant figure should, in theory, be sufficient to cover dividends paid; if it doesn't, then it is likely that the level of dividends will have to be reduced in future years.

- In the Financing section of the statement, where there has been an increase in loans and/or share capital, look to see how the money has been used. Was it to buy fixed assets or other investments, or to finance stocks and debtors, or other purposes?

- The cash flow statement, as a whole, links profit with changes in cash. Both of these are important: without profits the company cannot generate cash (unless it sells fixed assets), and without cash it cannot pay bills as they fall due.

CONFIDENTIALITY PROCEDURES

The accounting standard FRS 1 requires that all but small companies produce a cash flow statement as a part of their financial statements. This means that cash flow statements are readily available to shareholders and interested parties either from the company itself or from Companies House (www.companieshouse.gov.uk). For small limited companies, as we have seen in this chapter, a cash flow statement provides useful information to the shareholders and other interested parties.

For those involved in the preparation of cash flow statements, confidentiality procedures must be observed at all times:

– during the preparation of published accounts

– during the period after the accounts have been prepared but before they are sent to shareholders, filed at Companies House, and disclosed to the public

– for detailed information that is needed in the preparation of cash flow statements (eg the calculation of profit or loss on sale of fixed assets, corporation tax paid, dividends paid) but is not disclosed

– for all information concerned with the cash flow statements of small companies

Chapter Summary

- The objective of a cash flow statement is to show an overall view of money flowing in and out of a company during an accounting period

- A cashflow statement is divided into eight sections:

  1 operating activities

  2 returns on investments and servicing of finance

  3 taxation

  4 capital expenditure and financial investment

  5 acquisitions and disposals

  6 equity dividends paid

  7 management of liquid resources

  8 financing

- FRS1 'Cash flow statements' provides a specimen layout.

- Larger limited companies are required to include a cash flow statement as a part of their published accounts. They are also useful statements for smaller limited companies.

Key Terms

cash flow statement	shows an overall view of money flowing in and out of a company during an accounting period
cash flow from operating activities	operating profit (before interest and tax), plus depreciation for the year, plus loss (or minus profit) on sale of fixed assets, together with changes in the working capital items (stock, debtors and creditors)

returns on investments and servicing of finance	interest received and paid; dividends received; dividends paid on preference shares
capital expenditure and financial investment	purchase and/or sale of fixed assets and investments
liquid resources	short term investments that are almost equal to cash
financing	issue or repayment of loans or share capital
net debt	borrowings (debentures, loans and overdrafts), less cash/bank balances and other liquid resources, such as treasury bills

 # Student Activities

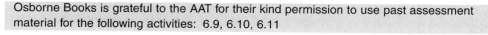
Osborne Books is grateful to the AAT for their kind permission to use past assessment material for the following activities: 6.9, 6.10, 6.11

6.1 The format, guidelines and layout for cash flow statements is set out in which Financial Reporting Statement?
   (a)   FRS 21
   (b)   FRS 11
   (c)   FRS 1
   (d)   FRS 10

6.2 Which of the following is **not** a standard heading for cash flow statements?
   (a)   taxation
   (b)   capital expenditure and financial investments
   (c)   equity dividends paid
   (d)   net profit for the year before taxation

6.3 In the reconciliation of operating activities, depreciation is added back because:
   (a)   it is not allowable for taxation purposes
   (b)   it is a non-cash expense
   (c)   it appears under the heading of capital expenditure and financial investment
   (d)   it is a financing activity

6.4   If a company's operating profit is £50,000 and there were the following movements in the year:

depreciation charges	£7,500
increase in stock	£5,000
decrease in debtors	£2,500
increase in creditors	£4,000

What is the net cash flow from operating activities for the year?
(a)   £59,000 inflow
(b)   £69,000 inflow
(c)   £36,000 inflow
(d)   £31,000 inflow

6.5   If a company's operating loss is £6,000 and there were the following movements in the year:

depreciation charges	£10,000
decrease in stock	£15,000
increase in debtors	£12,500
decrease in creditors	£14,000

What is the net cash flow from operating activities for the year?
(a)   £7,500 inflow
(b)   £1,500 outflow
(c)   £1,500 inflow
(d)   £7,500 outflow

6.6   What are the advantages to a company in producing a cash flow statement in accordance with FRS 1? Why might the creditors of a company be interested in this statement?

6.7   The book-keeper of Cashedin Limited has asked for your assistance in producing a cash flow statement for the company for the year ended 30 September 20-5 in accordance with FRS 1.

He has derived the information which is required to be included in the cash flow statement, but is not sure of the format in which it should be presented. The information is set out below:

	£000s
Operating profit before interest and tax	24
Depreciation charge for the year	318
Proceeds from sale of fixed assets	132
Issue of shares for cash	150
Cash received from new loan	200
Purchase of fixed assets for cash	358
Interest paid	218
Taxation paid	75
Dividends paid	280
Increase in stocks	251
Increase in debtors	152
Increase in creditors	165
Decrease in cash	345

REQUIRED

Using the information provided by the book-keeper, prepare a cash flow statement for Cashedin Limited for the year ended 30 September 20-5 in accordance with the requirements of FRS 1.

Show clearly your reconciliation between operating profit and net cash inflow from operating activities.

6.8   Radion plc's profit and loss account for the year ended 31 December 20-3 and balance sheets for 20-2 and 20-3 were as follows:

Radion plc Profit and Loss Account for the year to 31 December 20-3

	£000	£000
Sales turnover		652
Cost of sales		349
GROSS PROFIT		303
Wages and salaries	107	
Depreciation charges	30	
Administrative expenses	62	199
OPERATING PROFIT		104
Interest payable		5
PROFIT BEFORE TAX		99
Taxation		22
PROFIT AFTER TAX		77
Dividends		30
RETAINED PROFIT FOR THE YEAR		47

Radion plc Balance Sheets as at 31 December

	20-3		20-2	
	£000	£000	£000	£000
FIXED ASSETS				
Tangibles at net book value		570		600
CURRENT ASSETS				
Stock	203		175	
Debtors	141		127	
Cash in hand/ bank	6			
	350		302	
CURRENT LIABILITIES				
Creditors	142		118	
Taxation	22		19	
Bank overdraft			16	
Dividends proposed	30		20	
	194		173	
NET CURRENT ASSETS		156		129
		726		729
LONG-TERM LIABILITIES				
Loans and debentures				50
		726		679
CAPITAL AND RESERVES				
Called up share capital		300		300
Share premium account		60		60
Profit and loss account		366		319
		726		679

Notes to the accounts

During the year there were no purchases or sales of fixed assets made.

REQUIRED

Prepare a reconciliation statement between the cash flows from operating activities and operating profit for the year ended 31 December 20-3

Note: you are not required to prepare an actual cash flow statement.

6.9 Pratt plc has supplied you with the following abridged profit and loss account for the year to 31 October 20-3.

	£000
Operating profit	2,520
Interest payable	168
Taxation	750
Dividends payable	540
RETAINED PROFIT FOR THE YEAR	1,062

Balance Sheets as at 31 October

	20-3		20-2	
	£000	£000	£000	£000
FIXED ASSETS				
At cost	9,000		8,400	
Depreciation to date	1,800	7,200	1,500	6,900
CURRENT ASSETS				
Stock	84		69	
Debtors	255		270	
Bank	48		30	
	387		369	
CURRENT LIABILITIES				
Trade creditors	108		81	
Taxation	606		285	
Dividends	225		144	
	939		510	
NET CURRENT LIABILITIES		552		141
		6,648		6,759
LONG-TERM LIABILITIES				
Loans		600		2,400
		6,048		4,359
CAPITAL AND RESERVES				
Called up share capital		3,000		2,550
Share premium		177		
Profit and loss account		2,871		1,809
		6,048		4,359

Additional Information

During the year the company sold a vehicle for £8,000 cash. The vehicle had originally cost £29,000 and had been depreciated by £18,000 at the time of sale.

REQUIRED

Task 1

Prepare a statement to show the net cash flow derived from trading operations for the year to 31 October 20-3.

Task 2

Prepare a cash flow statement complying with FRS1, to highlight the change in the bank balance during the year.

6.10 Sadler plc's profit and loss account for the year to 30 June 20-3 and balance sheets for 20-2 and 20-3 were as follows:

Sadler plc abridged Profit and Loss Account for the year to 30 June 20-3

	£000
OPERATING PROFIT	1,100
Interest payable	(100)
PROFIT BEFORE TAX	1,000
Taxation	(200)
PROFIT AFTER TAX	800
Dividends	(400)
RETAINED PROFIT FOR THE YEAR	400

Sadler PLC Balance Sheets as at 30 June

	20-2		20-3	
FIXED ASSETS	£000	£000	£000	£000
At cost	13,600		16,300	
Depreciation to date	(8,160)	5,440	(9,660)	6,640
CURRENT ASSETS				
Stock	300		340	
Debtors	1,200		1,300	
Prepayments	100		80	
Cash in hand/ bank	40		20	
	1,640		1,740	
CURRENT LIABILITIES				
Creditors	660		800	
Accruals	60		120	
Taxation	360		260	
Dividends proposed	400		200	
	1,480		1,380	

NET CURRENT ASSETS		160			360
		5,600			7,000
LONG-TERM LIABILITIES					
20% Debentures		-			(1,000)
		5,600			6,000
CAPITAL AND RESERVES					
Called up share capital		4,000			4,000
Share premium account		600			600
Profit and loss account		1,000			1,400
		5,600			7,000

Notes to the accounts

During the year the company sold some machinery costing £1,600,000 on which there was accumulated depreciation totalling £400,000. The net proceeds from the sale amounted to £1,400,000.

REQUIRED

Prepare a cash flow statement for Sadler plc for the year to 30 June 20-3 together with the relevant formal notes, in accordance with FRS1.

6.11   You have been given the following information about George Limited for the year ending 31 March 20-5.

George Limited Profit and Loss Account for the year ended 31 March

	20-5		20-4	
	£000s	£000s	£000s	£000s
Turnover		2,500		1,775
Opening stock	200		100	
Purchases	1,500		1,000	
Closing stock	(210)		(200)	
Cost of sales		1,490		900
GROSS PROFIT		1,010		875
Depreciation		275		250
Other expenses		500		425
Profit on sales of fixed asset		2		–
OPERATING PROFIT		237		200
Interest paid		20		35
PROFIT BEFORE TAX		217		165
Taxation		25		21
PROFIT AFTER TAX		192		144
Proposed dividends		35		30
RETAINED PROFIT FOR THE YEAR		157		114

continued on the next page

George Limited Balance sheet as at 31 March

	20-5		20-4	
	£000s	£000s	£000s	£000s
FIXED ASSETS		330		500
CURRENT ASSETS				
Stocks	210		200	
Debtors	390		250	
Cash	–		10	
	600		460	
CURRENT LIABILITIES				
Trade creditors	150		160	
Dividends payable	35		30	
Taxation	25		21	
Bank overdraft	199		–	
	409		211	
NET CURRENT ASSETS		191		249
		521		749
LONG-TERM LIABILITIES				
Debentures				500
Long-term loan		200		100
		321		149
CAPITAL AND RESERVES				
Called up share capital		40		25
Profit and loss account		281		124
		321		149

Additional information

- In May 20-4 an asset was sold which originally cost £10,000 and was purchased when the company was started up two years ago. A new asset was bought for £110,000 in June 20-4. Fixed assets are depreciated at 25 per cent of cost. The policy is to charge a full year's depreciation in the year of purchase and none in the year of sale.

- Loan interest is charged at 10% p.a. The long-term loan was increased on 1 April 20-4.

- The 5% debentures were redeemed on 1 April 20-4.

- Sales and purchases were on credit. All other expenses, including interest due, were paid in cash.

- On 1 October 20-4 15,000 new ordinary £1 shares were issued at par.

REQUIRED

Task 1
Prepare a cash flow statement.

Task 2
Prepare a reconciliation between cash flows from operating activities and operating profit.

7 Interpretation of financial statements

this chapter covers . . .

The profit and loss accounts and balance sheets of limited companies are often interpreted by means of accounting ratios in order to assess strengths and weaknesses. Comparisons can be made between:

- *consecutive years for the same company*
- *similar companies in the same industry*
- *industry averages and the ratios for a particular company*

The accounts of a business can be interpreted in the areas of profitability, liquidity, efficient use of resources and financial position.

In this chapter we examine:

- *the importance of interpretation of financial statements*
- *the main accounting ratios and performance indicators*
- *a commentary on trends shown by the main accounting ratios*
- *how to report on the financial situation of a company*
- *limitations in the interpretation of accounts*

NVQ PERFORMANCE CRITERIA COVERED

unit 11: DRAFTING FINANCIAL STATEMENTS

element 11.2

interpret limited company financial statements

A   *identify the general purpose of financial statements used in limited companies*

B   *identify the elements of financial statements used in limited companies*

C   *identify the relationships between the elements within financial statements of limited companies*

D   *interpret the relationship between elements of limited company financial statements using ratio analysis*

E   *identify unusual features or significant issues within financial statements of limited companies*

F   *draw valid conclusions from the information contained within financial statements of limited companies*

G   *present issues, interpretations and conclusions clearly to the appropriate people*

INTERESTED PARTIES

Interpretation of financial statements is not always made by an accountant; interested parties – as we have seen in Chapter 1 (page 14) – include:

- **managers** of the company, who need to make financial decisions affecting the future development of the company

- **banks**, who are being asked to lend money to finance the company

- **creditors**, who wish to assess the likelihood of receiving payment

- **customers**, who wish to be assured of continuity of supplies in the future

- **shareholders**, who wish to be assured that their investment is sound

- prospective **investors**, who wish to compare relative strengths and weaknesses

- **employees** and **trade unions**, who wish to check on the financial prospects of the company

- **government** and **government agencies**, eg Inland Revenue, HM Customs and Excise, who wish to check they are receiving the amount due to them

We saw in Chapter 1 how *Statement of principles for financial reporting* requires that financial statements provide users with details of:

- financial performance

- financial position

From the financial statements the interested party will be able to calculate the main ratios, percentages and performance indicators. By doing this, the strengths and weaknesses of the company will be highlighted and appropriate conclusions can be drawn.

ACCOUNTING RATIOS AND THE ELEMENTS OF FINANCIAL STATEMENTS

The general term 'accounting ratios' is usually used to describe the calculations aspect of interpretation of financial statements. The term 'ratio' is, in fact, partly misleading because the performance indicators include percentages, time periods, as well as ratios in the strict sense of the word.

The main themes covered by the interpretation of accounts are:

- **profitability** – the relationship between profit and sales turnover, assets and capital employed
- **liquidity** – the stability of the company on a short-term basis
- **use of resources** – the effective and efficient use of assets and liabilities
- **financial position** – the way in which the company has been financed

In Chapter 1 we saw how the elements of financial statements are the building blocks from which financial statements are constructed. The elements are defined by *Statement of principles for financial reporting* and comprise (see also page 16):

- assets
- liabilities
- ownership interest
- income
- expenditure
- gains
- losses
- contributions from owners
- distributions to owners

Accounting ratios make use of the elements in the interpretation of accounts – the relationship between elements is what we are measuring, together with any changes from one year to the next, or between different companies in the same industry, or an industry average. The main themes of interpretation of accounts use the elements as follows:

- **profitability** – measures the relationship between income and expenditure and the gains or losses of the company; also the gains or losses measured against the ownership interest
- **liquidity** – focuses on the relationship between assets and liabilities
- **use of resources** – analyses the gains or losses in relation to the assets and liabilities used by the company
- **financial position** – compares the relationship between the ownership interest and the liabilities of the company

For example, one measure of the profitability of a company is to compare the gains or losses with the ownership interest, as follows:

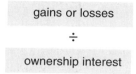

To illustrate this, the first two years' financial statements of a company show the relationship between the two elements to be:

Thus it can be seen that an increase in the gains in year two has had an effect on the profitability of the company because the relationship between gains and ownership interest has changed from year 1.

In interpretation of accounts we shall be using ratios to measure the relationships between the elements of financial statements.

MAKING USE OF ACCOUNTING RATIOS

It is important when examining a set of financial statements and calculating accounting ratios to relate them to reference points or standards. These points of reference might be to:

* establish trends from past years, to provide a standard of comparison
* benchmark against another similar company in the same industry
* compare against industry averages

Above all, it is important to understand the relationships between ratios: one ratio may give an indication of the state of the company, but this needs to be supported by other ratios. Ratios can indicate symptoms, but the cause will then need to be investigated.

Another use of ratios is to estimate forward the likely profit or balance sheet of a company. For example, it might be assumed that the same gross profit percentage as last year will also apply next year; thus, given an estimated increase in sales, it is a simple matter to estimate gross profit. In a similar way, by making use of ratios, net profit and the balance sheet can be forecast.

Whilst all of the ratios calculated in this chapter use figures from the profit and loss account and balance sheet, the cash flow statement is important too. It assists in confirming the views shown by the accounting ratios and provides further evidence of the position.

ACCOUNTING RATIOS FOR PROFITABILITY

■ Study the table and financial statements on the next two pages. They show the ways in which the profitability of a company is assessed.

■ Then read the section entitled 'Profitability' which follows.

■ Note that the accounting ratios from the financial statements of Wyvern Trading Company Limited are calculated and discussed in the Case Study on pages 207-212.

PROFITABILITY

One of the main objectives of a company is to make a profit. Profitability ratios examine the relationship between profit and sales turnover, assets and capital employed. Before calculating the profitability ratios, it is important to read the profit and loss account in order to review the figures.

The key profitability ratios are illustrated on the next page. We will be calculating and discussing the accounting ratios from these figures in the Case Study on pages 207-212.

gross profit percentage

$$\frac{Gross\ profit}{Sales} \quad x \ \frac{100}{1}$$

This expresses, as a percentage, the gross profit (sales minus cost of sales) in relation to sales. For example, a gross profit percentage of 20 per cent means that for every £100 of sales made, the gross profit is £20.

The gross profit percentage should be similar from year-to-year for the same company. It will vary between companies in different areas of business, eg the gross profit percentage on jewellery is considerably higher than that on

continued on page 193

PROFITABILITY

Gross profit/sales percentage $= \dfrac{\text{Gross profit}}{\text{Sales}} \times \dfrac{100}{1}$

Expense/sales percentage $= \dfrac{\text{Specified expense}}{\text{Sales}} \times \dfrac{100}{1}$

Operating profit/sales percentage $= \dfrac{\text{Operating profit*}}{\text{Sales}} \times \dfrac{100}{1}$

* profit before interest and tax

Net profit/sales percentage $= \dfrac{\text{Net profit}}{\text{Sales}} \times \dfrac{100}{1}$

Return on capital employed $= \dfrac{\text{Operating profit}}{\text{Capital employed*}} \times \dfrac{100}{1}$

* share capital + reserves + long-term liabilities

Return on equity $= \dfrac{\text{Profit after tax} - \text{preference dividend (if any)}}{\text{Equity*}} \times \dfrac{100}{1}$

* ordinary share capital + reserves

Earnings per share $= \dfrac{\text{Profit after tax} - \text{preference dividend (if any)}}{\text{Number of issued ordinary shares}}$

Wyvern Trading Company Limited
TRADING AND PROFIT AND LOSS ACCOUNT
for the year ended 31 December 2004

	£000s	£000s
Sales		1,430
Opening stock	200	
Purchases	1,000	
	1,200	
Less Closing stock	240	
Cost of sales		960
Gross profit		470
Less overheads:		
Selling expenses	150	
Administration expenses	140	
		290
Operating profit		180
Less: Debenture interest		10
Net profit for year before taxation		170
Less: Corporation tax		50
Profit for year after taxation		120
Less:		
preference dividend paid	25	
ordinary dividend proposed	75	
		100
Retained profit for the year		20
Add balance of retained profits at beginning of year		180
Balance of retained profits at end of year		200

BALANCE SHEET (extract)

Capital employed (share capital + reserves + long-term liabilities)	1,550
Equity (ordinary share capital + reserves)	1,200
Number of issued ordinary shares (000s)	1,000

Note: Items used in the ratios on the previous page are shown in bold type on a grey background

food. A significant change from one year to the next, particularly a fall in the percentage, requires investigation into the buying and selling prices.

Gross profit percentage, and also net profit percentage (see next page), need to be considered in context. For example, a supermarket may well have a lower gross profit percentage than a small corner shop but, because of the supermarket's much higher turnover, the amount of profit will be much higher. Whatever the type of business, gross profit – both as an amount and a percentage – needs to be sufficient to cover the overheads (expenses), and then to give an acceptable return on capital.

expense/sales percentage

$$\frac{Specified\ expense}{Sales} \quad x \quad \frac{100}{1}$$

A large expense or overhead item can be expressed as a percentage of sales: for example, the relationship between advertising and sales might be found to be 10 per cent in one year, but 20 per cent the next year. This could indicate that an increase in advertising had failed to produce a proportionate increase in sales.

Note that each expense falls into one of three categories of cost:

1   fixed costs, or

2   variable costs, or

3   semi-variable costs

Fixed costs remain constant despite other changes. Variable costs alter with changed circumstances, such as increased output or sales. Semi-variable costs combine both a fixed and a variable element, eg hire of a car at a basic (fixed) cost, with a (variable) cost per mile.

It is important to appreciate the nature of costs when interpreting accounts: for example, if sales this year are twice last year's figure, not all expenses will have doubled.

operating profit percentage

$$\frac{Operating\ profit^*}{Sales} \quad x \quad \frac{100}{1}$$

profit before interest and tax

Net profit is calculated after loan and bank interest has been charged to profit and loss account. Thus it may be distorted when comparisons are made between two different companies where one is heavily financed by means of loans, and the other is financed entirely by ordinary share capital. The solution is to calculate the operating profit percentage which uses profit before interest and tax. Note that, in accounting terminology, operating profit is often referred to as 'net profit' – however, strictly speaking, it should be 'net profit before interest.'

net profit percentage

$$\frac{Net\ profit}{Sales} \times \frac{100}{1}$$

As with gross profit percentage, the net profit percentage should be similar from year-to-year for the same company, and should also be comparable with other companies in the same line of business. Net profit percentage should, ideally, increase from year-to-year, which indicates that the profit and loss account costs are being kept under control. Any significant fall should be investigated to see if it has been caused by:

• a fall in gross profit percentage

• and/or an increase in one particular expense, eg wages and salaries, advertising, etc

Tutorial note: Net profit percentage is not as good an indicator of business performance as operating profit percentage. This is because net profit may be distorted – as mentioned above – by loan and bank interest. If there is a choice between the two ratios in Examinations, always calculate and comment upon operating profit percentage in preference to net profit percentage.

return on capital employed (ROCE)

Return on capital employed expresses the profit of a company in relation to the capital employed. The percentage return is best thought of in relation to other investments, eg a bank or building society might offer a return of five per cent. A person setting up a company is investing a sum of money in that company, and the profit is the return that is achieved on that investment. However, it should be noted that the risks in running a company are considerably greater than depositing the money with a bank or building society, and an additional return to allow for the extra risk is needed.

The calculation of return on capital employed for limited companies must take note of their different methods of financing. It is necessary to distinguish between the ordinary shareholders' investment (the equity) and the capital employed by the company, which includes preference shares and debentures/long-term loans.

The calculation for capital employed is:

> *Ordinary share capital*
>
> *add*   *Reserves (capital and revenue)*
>
> *equals*   *Equity*
>
> *add*   *Preference share capital*
>
> *add*   *Debentures/long-term loans*
>
> *equals*   *Capital Employed*

The reason for including preference shares and debentures/long-term loans in the capital employed is that the company has the use of the money from these contributors for the foreseeable future, or certainly for a fixed time period.

The calculation of return on capital employed is:

$$\frac{\text{Operating profit*}}{\text{Capital employed**}} \quad x \quad \frac{100}{1}$$

    *   profit before interest and tax

    **   ordinary share capital + reserves + preference share capital + debentures/long-term loans

Return on capital employed is also known as the *primary ratio* – see page 203.

return on equity

$$\frac{\text{Profit after tax – preference dividend (if any)}}{\text{Equity*}} \quad x \quad \frac{100}{1}$$

* ordinary share capital + reserves

Whilst return on capital employed looks at the overall return on the long-term sources of finance (the capital employed), return on equity focuses on the return for the ordinary shareholders. Also known as 'return on ordinary shareholders' equity', return on equity indicates the return the company is making on their funds, ie ordinary shares and reserves. The decision as to whether they remain as ordinary shareholders is primarily whether they could get a better return elsewhere.

Note that, when calculating return on equity, use the profit after tax and preference dividends (if any), ie the amount of profit available to the ordinary shareholders after all other parties (corporation tax, preference share dividend) have been deducted.

earnings per share

$$\frac{\textit{Profit after tax} - \textit{preference dividend (if any)}}{\textit{Number of issued ordinary shares}}$$

Earnings per share (or EPS) measures the amount of profit – usually expressed in pence – earned by each ordinary share, after corporation tax and preference dividends. Comparisons can be made with previous years to provide a basis for assessing the company's performance.

See also FRS 14 'Earnings per share' on page 146.

ACCOUNTING RATIOS FOR LIQUIDITY, USE OF RESOURCES AND FINANCIAL POSITION

■ Study the ratios table and financial statements on the next two pages. They show the ways in which the liquidity, use of resources, and financial position of a company are assessed.

■ Then read the sections which follow.

■ Note that the accounting ratios from the financial statements of Wyvern Trading Company Limited are calculated and discussed in the Case Study on pages 207-212.

LIQUIDITY

Liquidity ratios measure the financial stability of a company, ie the ability of a company to pay its way on a short-term basis. Here we focus our attention on the current assets and current liabilities sections of the balance sheet.

The key liquidity ratios are shown on the next page; these are linked to the balance sheet of Wyvern Trading Company Limited. The ratios are calculated and discussed in the Case Study on pages 207-212.

continued on page 199

LIQUIDITY

Working capital ratio =
(or current ratio)
$$\frac{\text{Current assets}}{\text{Current liabilities}}$$

Liquid capital ratio =
(or quick ratio/acid test)
$$\frac{\text{Current assets} - \text{stock}}{\text{Current liabilities}}$$

USE OF RESOURCES

Stock turnover (days) =
$$\frac{\text{Stock}}{\text{Cost of sales}} \times 365 \text{ days}$$

Debtors' collection period (days) =
$$\frac{\text{Debtors}}{\text{Sales}} \times 365 \text{ days}$$

Creditors' payment period (days) =
$$\frac{\text{Creditors}}{\text{Purchases}} \times 365 \text{ days}$$

Asset turnover ratio =
$$\frac{\text{Sales}}{\text{Net assets*}}$$

* fixed assets + current assets − current liabilities

FINANCIAL POSITION

Interest cover =
$$\frac{\text{Operating profit}}{\text{Interest paid}}$$

Gearing =
$$\frac{\text{Debt (long-term loans, including preference shares)}}{\text{Capital employed*}} \times \frac{100}{1}$$

* ordinary share capital + reserves + preference share capital + long-term loans

alternative calculation:
$$\frac{\text{Debt}}{\text{Equity*}} \times \frac{100}{1}$$

* ordinary share capital + reserves

Wyvern Trading Company Limited
BALANCE SHEET
as at 31 December 2004

Fixed Assets	Cost	Dep'n to date	Net
	£000s	£000s	£000s
Premises	1,100	250	850
Fixtures and fittings	300	120	180
Vehicles	350	100	250
	1,750	470	1,280

Current Assets		
Stock		240
Debtors		150
Bank/cash		135
		525

Less Current Liabilities		
Creditors	130	
Proposed ordinary dividend	75	
Corporation tax	50	
		255

Net Current Assets		270
		1,550

Less Long-term Liabilities		
10% Debentures		100
NET ASSETS		1,450

FINANCED BY
Authorised and Issued Share Capital

1,000,000 ordinary shares of £1 each, fully paid		1,000
250,000 10% preference shares of £1 each, fully paid		250
		1,250

Revenue Reserve		
Profit and loss account		200
SHAREHOLDERS' FUNDS		1,450

PROFIT AND LOSS ACCOUNT (extract)

Cost of sales	960
Sales	1,430
Purchases	1,000

Note: Items used in ratios are shown in bold type with a grey background.

working capital

Working capital = Current assets – Current liabilities

Working capital (often called *net current assets*) is needed by all companies in order to finance day-to-day trading activities. Sufficient working capital enables a company to hold adequate stocks, allow a measure of credit to its customers (debtors), and to pay its suppliers (creditors) as payments fall due.

working capital ratio (or current ratio)

Working capital ratio = Current assets : Current liabilities

Working capital ratio uses figures from the balance sheet and measures the relationship between current assets and current liabilities. Although there is no ideal working capital ratio, an acceptable ratio is about 2:1, ie £2 of current assets to every £1 of current liabilities. However, a company in the retail trade may be able to work with a lower ratio, eg 1.5:1 or even less, because it deals mainly in sales for cash and so does not have a large figure for debtors. A working capital ratio can be too high: if it is above 3:1 an investigation of the make-up of current assets and current liabilities is needed: eg the company may have too much stock, too many debtors, or too much cash at the bank, or even too few creditors.

Note that the current ratio can also be expressed as a percentage. For example, a current ratio of 2:1 is the same as 200 per cent.

liquid capital ratio (or quick ratio, or acid test)

$$Liquid\ capital\ ratio = \frac{Current\ assets\ -\ stock}{Current\ liabilities}$$

The liquid capital ratio uses the current assets and current liabilities from the balance sheet, but stock is omitted. This is because stock is the least liquid current asset: it has to be sold, turned into debtors, and then the cash has to be collected from the debtors. Also, some of the stock included in the balance sheet figure may be unsaleable or obsolete. Thus the liquid ratio provides a direct comparison between debtors/cash/bank and short-term liabilities. The balance between liquid assets, that is debtors and cash/bank, and current liabilities should, ideally, be about 1:1, ie £1 of liquid assets to each £1 of current liabilities. At this ratio a company is expected to be able to pay its current liabilities from its liquid assets; a figure below 1:1, eg 0.75:1, indicates that the company would have difficulty in meeting pressing demands from creditors. However, as with the working capital ratio, some companies are able to operate with a lower liquid ratio than others.

The liquid capital ratio can also be expressed as a percentage, eg 1:1 is the same as 100%.

USE OF RESOURCES

Use of resources measures how efficiently the management controls the current aspects of the company – principally stock, debtors and creditors. Like all accounting ratios, comparison needs to be made either with figures for the previous year, or with a similar company.

stock turnover

$$\frac{Stock}{Cost\ of\ sales} \quad x \quad 365\ days$$

Stock turnover is the number of days' stock held on average. This figure will depend on the type of goods sold by the company. For example, a market trader selling fresh flowers, who finishes each day when sold out, will have a stock turnover of one day. By contrast, a jewellery shop – because it may hold large stocks of jewellery – will have a much slower stock turnover, perhaps sixty or ninety days, or longer. Nevertheless, it is important for a company to keep its stock days as short as possible, subject to being able to meet the needs of most of its customers. A company which is improving in efficiency will generally have a quicker stock turnover comparing one year with the previous one, or with the stock turnover of similar companies.

Stock turnover can also be expressed as number of times per year:

$$Stock\ turnover\ (times\ per\ year) \quad = \quad \frac{Cost\ of\ sales}{Stock}$$

A stock turnover of, say, twelve times a year means that about thirty days' stock is held. Note that stock turnover can only be calculated where a company buys and sells goods; it cannot be used for a company that provides a service.

debtors' collection period

$$\frac{Debtors}{Sales} \quad x \quad 365\ days$$

This calculation shows how many days, on average, debtors take to pay for goods sold to them by the company. The debt collection time can be compared with that for the previous year, or with that of a similar company. In the UK, most debtors should make payment within about 30 days; however, sales made abroad will take longer for the proceeds to be received. A comparison from year-to-year of the collection period is a measure of the company's efficiency at collecting the money that is due to it and we are looking for some reduction in debtor days over time. Ideally debtor days should be shorter than creditor days (see the next page): this indicates that money is being received from debtors before it is paid out to creditors.

creditors' payment period

$$\frac{Creditors}{Purchases} \quad x \quad 365 \; days$$

This calculation is the opposite aspect to that of debtors: here we are measuring the speed it takes to pay creditors. While creditors can be a useful temporary source of finance, delaying payment too long may cause problems. This ratio is most appropriate for companies that buy and sell goods; it cannot be used for a company that provides a service; it is also difficult to interpret when a company buys in some goods and, at the same time, provides a service, eg an hotel. Generally, though, we would expect to see the creditor days period longer than the debtor days, ie money is being received from debtors before it is paid out to creditors. We would also be looking for a similar figure for creditor days from one year to the next: this would indicate a stable company.

Note that there is invariably an inconsistency in calculating both debtors' collection and creditors' payment periods: the figures for debtors and creditors on the balance sheet include VAT, while sales and purchases from the trading account exclude VAT. Strictly, therefore, we are not comparing like with like; however, the comparison should be made with reference to the previous year, or a similar company, calculated on the same basis from year-to-year.

asset turnover ratio

$$\frac{Sales}{Net \; assets^*}$$

* fixed assets + current assets − current liabilities

This ratio measures the efficiency of the use of net assets in generating sales. An increasing ratio from one year to the next indicates greater efficiency. A fall in the ratio may be caused either by a decrease in sales, or an increase in net assets – perhaps caused by the purchase or revaluation of fixed assets, or increased stockholding, or increased debtors as a result of poor credit control.

Different types of businesses will have very different asset turnover ratios. For example a supermarket, with high sales and relatively few assets, will have a very high figure; by contrast, an engineering company, with lower sales and a substantial investment in fixed and current assets, will have a much lower figure.

Note that for the purpose of ratio analysis, net assets is defined as:

fixed assets + current assets − current liabilities

FINANCIAL POSITION

Financial position measures the strength and long-term financing of the company. Two ratios are calculated – interest cover and gearing. Interest cover considers the ability of the company to meet (or cover) its interest payments from its operating profit; gearing focuses on the balance in the long-term funding of the company between monies from loan providers and monies from ordinary shareholders.

Both ratios look at aspects of loan finance and it is important to remember that both interest and loan repayments must be made on time; if they are not the loan provider may well be able to seek payment by forcing the company to sell assets and, in the worst case, may well be able to force the company into liquidation.

interest cover

$$\frac{Operating\ profit}{Interest}$$

The interest cover ratio, linked closely to gearing, considers the safety margin (or cover) of profit over the interest payable by a company. For example, if the operating profit of a company was £10,000, and interest payable was £5,000, this would give interest cover of two times, which is a low figure. If the interest was £1,000, this would give interest cover of ten times which is a higher and much more acceptable figure. Thus, the conclusion to draw is that the higher the interest cover, the better (although there is an argument for having some debt).

gearing

$$\frac{Debt\ (long\text{-}term\ loans\ including\ any\ preference\ shares)}{Capital\ employed^*} \times \frac{100}{1}$$

* ordinary share capital + reserves + preference share capital + long-term loans

Whilst the liquidity ratios seen earlier focus on whether the company can pay its way in the short-term, gearing is concerned with long-term financial stability. Here we measure how much of the company is financed by debt (including any preference shares) against capital employed (debt + equity), defined above. The higher the gearing percentage, the less secure will be the financing of the company and, therefore, the future of the company. This is because debt is costly in terms of interest payments (particularly if interest rates are variable). It is difficult to set a standard for an acceptable gearing ratio: in general terms, most investors (or lenders) would not wish to see a gearing percentage of greater than 50%.

Gearing can also be expressed as a ratio, ie debt:equity. Thus a gearing percentage of 50% is a ratio of 0.5:1.

An alternative calculation for gearing is to measure debt in relation to the equity of the company:

$$\frac{Debt}{Equity^*} \quad x \quad \frac{100}{1}$$

* ordinary share capital + reserves

Usually in Examinations, either calculation is acceptable; both methods use similar components:

either $\dfrac{Debt}{Capital\ employed}$ or $\dfrac{Debt}{Equity}$

The first calculation will always give a lower gearing percentage than the second when using the same figures. For example:

$$\frac{£50,000\ (debt)}{£50,000\ (debt) + £100,000\ (equity)} \quad = 33\%$$

$$\frac{£50,000\ (debt)}{£100,000\ (equity)} \quad = 50\%$$

When making comparisons from one year to the next, or between different companies, it is important to be consistent in the way in which gearing is calculated in order for appropriate conclusions to be drawn.

USE OF THE PRIMARY RATIO

Return on capital employed (see page 194) is perhaps the most effective ratio used in the interpretation of accounts. This is because it expresses profit in relation to the capital employed and so is a direct measure of the efficiency of a company in using the capital available to it in order to generate profits.

Return on capital employed is often referred to as the primary ratio, since it can be broken down into the two secondary factors of:

- net or operating profit percentage (see pages 193-194)
- asset turnover ratio (see page 201)

The relationship between the three can be expressed in the form of a 'pryamid of ratios' (where the ratio at the top of the pyramid is formed from and relates arithmetically to the other two ratios):

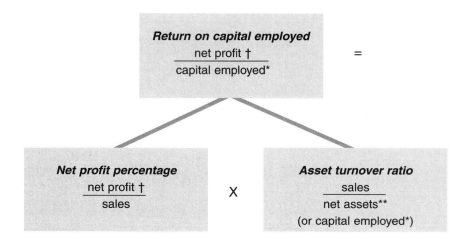

† net profit or, preferably, operating profit (ie profit before interest)
* capital employed, ie share capital + reserves + long-term liabilities
** net assets, ie fixed assets + current assets – current liabilities

examples

- **Company Aye** has sales of £500,000, a net profit of £50,000, and net assets/capital employed of £250,000. The pyramid of ratios is:

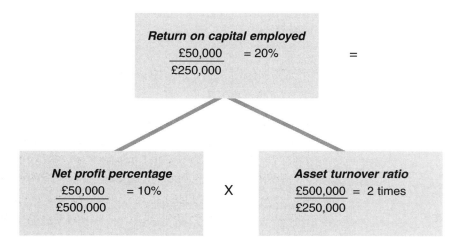

Thus it can be seen that, when the net profit percentage is multiplied by the asset turnover ratio, the answer is return on capital employed (the primary ratio):

$$10\% \times 2 \text{ times} = 20\% \text{ (primary ratio)}$$

- **Company Bee** has sales of £1,000,000, a net profit of £20,000, and net assets/capital employed of £100,000. The pyramid of ratios is:

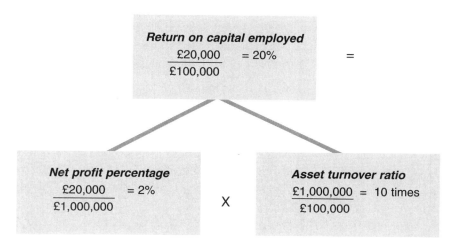

Here the primary ratio is made up of:

$$2\% \times 10 \text{ times} = 20\% \text{ (primary ratio)}$$

By using the pyramid of ratios, we can get a better idea of how ratios relate one to another rather than considering them in isolation. Thus the primary ratio shows how the same return on capital employed can be achieved in different ways, depending on the type of business. It demonstrates the different ways of running a business – eg the supermarket (with low profit margins and high turnover) and the specialist shop (with higher profit margins, but lower turnover) – and how each achieves its return on capital employed.

INTERPRETATION OF ACCOUNTS

Interpretation of accounts is much more than a mechanical process of calculating a number of ratios. It involves the analysis of the relationships between the elements within financial statements and the presentation of the information gathered in a meaningful way to interested parties.

It is important that a logical approach is adopted to the process of interpreting accounts. The needs of the user – the person who has requested the information – must be the starting point. These needs are linked to the main themes of interpretation: profitability, liquidity, use of resources, and financial position. In recent AAT Examinations for *Drafting Financial Statements* the users have included:

- potential investors – mainly concerned about the profitability of an investment in a company

- potential lenders – concerned with a borrower's liquidity, use of resources, and financial position

- potential buyers – investigating financial statements to assess a proposed supplier's profitability, liquidity, and financial position

From the financial statements – usually profit and loss account and balance sheet of a company – it is necessary to calculate a number of appropriate accounting ratios. In Examinations, often you will be given two years' financial statements and will be told which ratios to calculate (but the formulae will not be given). Sometimes you may be asked to compare the ratios calculated with industry average figures (which will be given). In addition, you may be asked to indicate – but not required to calculate – other appropriate ratios.

The way in which the interpretation of accounts is presented to the user must be appropriate to the needs of the user. Thus a letter is most appropriate for a potential investor, a report for a potential lender, and a memorandum for a potential buyer (where both the buyer and the writer of the report work for the same company). Whichever form of presentation is used, take care over the layout and make sure that there are plenty of sub-sections to guide the user.

The form of the presentation to the user will usually include the following:

- calculation of ratios from financial statements (an Examination question will normally state which ratios are to be calculated and for how many years)

- an explanation of the meaning of each ratio (try to use language that can be understood by users with a non-financial background)

- comment on the financial position of the company as shown by the ratios (making comparisons against guideline standards where applicable – eg 2:1 for the working capital ratio – and against industry averages, if they are given in the question)

- a statement of how the financial position of the company has changed over the period covered by the financial statements – usually two years (look for trends in the ratios and comment on what these mean and whether they show an improving or a worsening financial position; include comparisons against industry averages, if they are given in the question)

- a conclusion which links back to the needs of the user (to invest in, or to lend to, the company, or to use as a supplier) and summarises against the themes of interpretation relevant to the user: profitability, liquidity, use of resources, and financial position

Two Case Studies which now follow put into practice the analytical approach explained earlier in this chapter:

1 **Wyvern Trading Company Limited**

In the first we look at limited company financial statements from the point of view of a potential investor (for clarity, one year's statements are given although, in practice, more than one year would be used to establish a trend). The comments given indicate what should be looked for when analysing and interpreting a set of financial statements.

2 **Surgdressings Limited**

In the second we consider financial statements from the point of view of a potential buyer of products from the company. The interpretation seeks to assess the risk of switching to the supplier, and to make comparisons with industry average figures.

Case Study

WYVERN TRADING COMPANY LIMITED: ACCOUNTING RATIOS

situation

The following are the financial statements of Wyvern Trading Company Limited. The business trades in office supplies and sells to the public through its three retail shops in the Wyvern area; it also delivers direct to businesses in the area from its modern warehouse on a local business park.

The financial statements and accounting ratios are to be considered from the viewpoint of a potential investor.

solution

We will now analyse the accounts from the point of view of a potential investor. All figures shown are in £000s. The analysis starts on page 210.

Wyvern Trading Company Limited
TRADING AND PROFIT AND LOSS ACCOUNT
for the year ended 31 December 2004

	£000s	£000s
Sales		1,430
Opening stock	200	
Purchases	1,000	
	1,200	
Less Closing stock	240	
Cost of sales		960
Gross profit		470
Less overheads:		
Selling expenses	150	
Administration expenses	140	
		290
Operating profit		180
Less: Debenture interest		10
Net profit for year before taxation		170
Less: Corporation tax		50
Profit for year after taxation		120
Less:		
preference dividend paid	25	
ordinary dividend proposed	75	
		100
Retained profit for the year		20
Add balance of retained profits at beginning of year		180
Balance of retained profits at end of year		200

Wyvern Trading Company Limited
BALANCE SHEET as at 31 December 2004

Fixed Assets	Cost	Dep'n to date	Net
	£000s	£000s	£000s
Premises	1,100	250	850
Fixtures and fittings	300	120	180
Vehicles	350	100	250
	1,750	470	1,280

Current Assets			
Stock		240	
Debtors		150	
Bank/cash		135	
		525	

Less Current Liabilities			
Creditors	130		
Proposed ordinary dividend	75		
Corporation tax	50		
		255	

Net Current Assets			270
			1,550

Less Long-term Liabilities			
10% debentures			100
NET ASSETS			1,450

FINANCED BY

Authorised and Issued Share Capital

1,000,000 ordinary shares of £1 each, fully paid	1,000
250,000 10% preference shares of £1 each, fully paid	250
	1,250

Revenue Reserve

Profit and loss account	200
SHAREHOLDERS' FUNDS	1,450

PROFITABILITY

Gross profit/sales percentage

$$\frac{£470}{£1,430} \quad \times \quad \frac{100}{1} \qquad = \quad 32.87\%$$

Selling expenses to sales

$$\frac{£150}{£1,430} \quad \times \quad \frac{100}{1} \qquad = \quad 10.49\%$$

Operating profit/sales percentage

$$\frac{£180}{£1,430} \quad \times \quad \frac{100}{1} \qquad = \quad 12.59\%$$

Net profit/sales percentage

$$\frac{£170}{£1,430} \quad \times \quad \frac{100}{1} \qquad = \quad 11.89\%$$

Return on capital employed

$$\frac{£180}{£1,000 + £250 + £200 + £100} \quad \times \quad \frac{100}{1} \qquad = \quad 11.61\%$$

Return on equity

$$\frac{£120 - £25}{£1,000 + £200} \quad \times \quad \frac{100}{1} \qquad = \quad 7.92\%$$

Earnings per share

$$\frac{£120 - £25}{1,000} \qquad\qquad\qquad = \text{9.5p per ordinary share}$$

The gross and net profit percentages seem to be acceptable figures for the type of business, although comparisons should be made with those of the previous accounting period. A company should always aim at least to hold its percentages and, ideally, to make a small improvement. A significant fall in the percentages may indicate a poor buying policy, poor pricing (perhaps caused by competition), and the causes should be investigated.

Selling expenses seem to be quite a high percentage of sales. As these are likely to be a relatively fixed cost, it would seem that the company could increase sales turnover without a corresponding increase in sales expenses.

The small difference between net profit percentage and operating profit percentage indicates that finance costs are relatively low.

Return on capital employed is satisfactory, but could be better. At 11.61% it is less than two percentage points above the ten per cent cost of the preference shares and debentures (ignoring the taxation advantages of issuing debentures). Return on equity is 7.92%, but a potential shareholder needs to compare this with the returns available elsewhere.

The figure for earnings per share indicates that the company is not highly

profitable for its shareholders; potential shareholders will be looking for increases in this figure.

LIQUIDITY
Working capital (or current) ratio

$$\frac{£525}{£255} \qquad = 2.06:1$$

Liquid capital ratio (or quick ratio/acid test)

$$\frac{(£525 - £240)}{£255} \qquad = 1.12:1$$

The working capital and liquid capital ratios are excellent: they are slightly higher than the expected 'norms' of 2:1 and 1:1 respectively (although many companies operate successfully with lower ratios); however, they are not too high which would be an indication of inefficient use of assets.

These two ratios indicate that the company is very solvent, with no short-term liquidity problems.

USE OF RESOURCES
Stock turnover

$$\frac{£240 \times 365}{£960} \qquad = \ 91 \text{ days (or 4 times per year)}$$

Debtors' collection period

$$\frac{£150 \times 365}{£1,430} \qquad = 38 \text{ days}$$

Creditors' payment period

$$\frac{£130 \times 365}{£1,000} \qquad = 47 \text{ days}$$

Asset turnover ratio

$$\frac{£1,430}{£1,550^*} \qquad = \ 0.92:1$$

* fixed assets + current assets – current liabilities

This group of ratios shows the main weakness of the company: not enough business is passing through for the size of the company.

Stock turnover is very low for an office supplies business: the stock is turning over only every 91 days – surely it should be faster than this?

Debtors' collection period is acceptable on the face of it – 30 days would be better – but quite a volume of the sales will be made through the retail outlets in cash. This amount should, if known, be deducted from the sales turnover before calculating the debtors' collection period: thus the collection period is, in reality, longer than that calculated.

Creditors' payment period is quite leisurely for this type of business – long delays

could cause problems with suppliers in the future.

The asset turnover ratio says it all: this type of business should be able to obtain a much better figure:

- either, sales need to be increased using the same net assets
- or, sales need to be maintained, but net assets reduced

FINANCIAL POSITION

Interest cover

$$\frac{£180}{£10} = 18 \text{ times}$$

Gearing

$$\frac{£250 + £100}{£1,000 + £200 + £250 + £100} \times \frac{100}{1} = 23\% \text{ or } 0.23:1$$

The interest cover figure of 18 is very high and shows that the company has no problems in paying interest.

The gearing percentage is low: anything up to 50% (0.5:1) could be seen. With a low figure of 23% this indicates that the company could borrow more money if it wished to finance, say, expansion plans (there are plenty of fixed assets for a lender – such as a bank – to take as security for a loan). At the present level of gearing there is only a low risk to potential investors.

Note that the alternative calculation for gearing is:

$$\frac{£250 + £100}{£1,000 + £200} \times \frac{100}{1} = 29\% \text{ or } 0.29:1$$

CONCLUSION

This appears to be a profitable company, although there may be some scope for cutting down somewhat on the profit and loss account selling expenses (administration expenses could be looked at too). The company offers a reasonable return on capital, although things could be improved.

The company is solvent and has good working capital and liquid capital ratios. Interest cover is high and gearing is low – a good sign during times of variable interest rates.

The main area of weakness is in asset utilisation. It appears that the company could do much to reduce the days for stock turnover and the debtors' collection period; at the same time creditors could be paid faster. Asset turnover is very low for this type of business and it does seem that there is much scope for expansion within the structure of the existing company. As the benefits of expansion flow through to the financial statements, the earnings per share figure should show an improvement from its present modest amount. However, a potential investor will need to consider if the directors have the ability to focus on the weaknesses shown by the ratio analysis and to take steps to improve the company.

Case Study

ASSESSING A SUPPLIER – SURGDRESSINGS LIMITED: ACCOUNTING RATIOS

situation

You work for the Wyvern Private Hospital plc. The company has been approached by a supplier of surgical dressings, Surgdressings Limited, which is offering its products at advantageous prices.

The Surgical Director of Wyvern Private Hospital is satisfied with the quality and suitability of the products offered and the Finance Director, your boss, has obtained the latest financial statements from the company which are set out on the next page.

You have been asked to prepare a report for the Finance Director recommending whether or not to use Surgdressings Limited as a supplier of surgical dressings to the Hospital. You are to use the information contained in the financial statements of Surgdressings Limited and the industry averages supplied. Included in your report should be:

- comments on the company's
  - profitability
  - liquidity
  - financial position

- consideration of how the company has changed over the two years

- comparison with the industry as a whole

The report should include calculation of the following ratios for the two years:
  - return on capital employed
  - net profit percentage
  - quick ratio/acid test
  - gearing

The relevant industry average ratios are as follows:

	2003	2002
Return on capital employed	11.3%	11.1%
Net profit percentage	16.4%	16.2%
Quick ratio/acid test	1.0:1	0.9:1
Gearing (debt/capital employed)	33%	35%

SURGDRESSINGS LIMITED
Summary profit and loss accounts for the year ended 31 December

	2003	2002
	£000s	£000s
Turnover	4,600	4,300
Cost of sales	2,245	2,135
Gross profit	2,355	2,165
Overheads	1,582	1,491
Net profit before tax	773	674

Summary balance sheets as at 31 December

	2003		2002	
	£000s	£000s	£000s	£000s
Fixed Assets		5,534		6,347
Current Assets				
Stock	566		544	
Debtors	655		597	
Bank	228		104	
	1,449		1,245	
Current Liabilities				
Trade creditors	572		504	
Taxation	242		288	
	814		792	
Net Current Assets		635		453
Long-term loan		(1,824)		(3,210)
NET ASSETS		4,345		3,590
Share capital (ordinary shares)		2,300		2,000
Share premium		670		450
Profit and loss account		1,375		1,140
SHAREHOLDERS' FUNDS		4,345		3,590

solution

REPORT

To: Finance Director, Wyvern Private Hospital plc

From: A Student

Date: today's date

Re: Analysis of Surgdressings Limited's financial statements 2002/2003

Introduction

The purpose of this report is to analyse the financial statements of Surgdressings Limited for 2002 and 2003 to determine whether the Hospital should use the company as a supplier of surgical dressings.

Calculation of ratios

The following ratios have been calculated:

	2003			2002	
	company	*industry average*		*company*	*industry average*
Return on capital employed	$\frac{773}{6,169}$ =12.5%	11.3%		$\frac{674}{6,800}$ = 9.9%	11.1%
Net profit percentage	$\frac{773}{4,600}$ =16.8%	16.4%		$\frac{674}{4,300}$ = 15.7%	16.2%
Quick ratio/acid test	$\frac{883}{814}$ = 1.1:1	1.0:1		$\frac{701}{792}$ = 0.9:1	0.9:1
Gearing	$\frac{1,824}{6,169}$ = 30%	33%		$\frac{3,210}{6,800}$ = 47%	35%

Comment and analysis

▪ In terms of profitability, the company has improved from 2002 to 2003.

▪ Return on capital employed has increased from 15.7% to 16.8% – this means that the company is generating more profit in 2003 from the available capital employed than it did in 2002. The company has gone from being below the industry average in 2002 to being better than the average in 2003.

▪ Net profit percentage has also improved, increasing from 15.7% in 2002 to 16.8% in 2003. This means that the company is generating more profit from sales in 2003 than it did in the previous year. In 2002 the company was below the industry average but in 2003 it is better than the average. As it is now performing better than the average, this suggests that it may continue to be successful in the future.

- The liquidity of the company has improved during the year.

- The quick ratio (or acid test) has gone up from 0.9:1 to 1.1:1. This indicates that the liquid assets, ie debtors and stock, are greater than current liabilities in 2003. The company has gone from being the same as the industry average in 2002 to better than average in 2003. Thus, in 2003, Surgdressings Limited is more liquid than the average business in the industry.

- The financial position of the company has improved considerably during the year.

- In 2002 the gearing ratio was a high 47%. In 2003 the percentage of debt finance to capital employed declined to 30%. A high gearing ratio is often seen as a risk to a company's long-term survival: in times of economic downturn, when profits fall, a high-geared company will have increasing difficulty in making interest payments on debt – in extreme cases, a company could be forced into liquidation. In 2002, the gearing ratio of Surgdressings Limited was much higher than the industry average, making it relatively more risky than the average of companies in the industry. The much improved ratio in 2003 is now below the industry average, making it less risky than the average of other companies in the industry.

CONCLUSION

- Based solely on the information provided in the financial statements of Surgdressings Limited and the ratios calculated, it is recommended that the company is used by Wyvern Private Hospital as a supplier of surgical dressings.

- The company has increasing profitability, liquidity and financial position in 2003 when compared with 2002. It also compares favourably with other companies in the same industry and appears to present a lower risk than the average of the sector.

LIMITATIONS IN THE INTERPRETATION OF ACCOUNTS

Although accounting ratios can usefully highlight strengths and weaknesses, they should always be considered as a part of the overall assessment of a company, rather than as a whole. We have already seen the need to place ratios in context and relate them to a reference point or standard. The limitations of ratio analysis should always be borne in mind.

retrospective nature of accounting ratios

Accounting ratios are usually retrospective, based on previous performance and conditions prevailing in the past. They may not necessarily be valid for making forward projections: for example, a large customer may become insolvent, so threatening the company with a bad debt, and also reducing sales in the future.

differences in accounting policies

When the financial statements of a company are compared, either with previous years' figures, or with figures from a similar company, there is a danger that the comparative statements are not drawn up on the same basis as those currently being worked on. Different accounting policies, in respect of depreciation and stock valuation for instance, may well result in distortion and invalid comparisons.

inflation

Inflation may prove a problem, as most financial statements are prepared on an historic cost basis, that is, assets and liabilities are recorded at their original cost. As a result, comparison of figures from one year to the next may be difficult. In countries where inflation is running at high levels any form of comparison becomes practically meaningless.

reliance on standards

We have already mentioned guideline standards for some accounting ratios, for instance 2:1 for the working capital ratio. There is a danger of relying too heavily on such suggested standards, and ignoring other factors in the balance sheet. An example of this would be to criticise a company for having a low current ratio when the company sells the majority of its goods for cash and consequently has a very low debtors figure: this would in fact be the case with many well-known and successful retail companies.

other considerations

Economic: The general economic climate and the effect this may have on the nature of the business, eg in an economic downturn retailers are usually the first to suffer, whereas manufacturers feel the effects later.

State of the business: The chairman's report of the company should be read in conjunction with the financial statements (including the cash flow statement) to ascertain an overall view of the state of the company. Of great importance are the products of the company and their stage in the product life cycle, eg is a car manufacturer relying on old models, or is there an up-to-date product range which appeals to buyers?

Comparing like with like: Before making comparisons between 'similar' companies, we need to ensure that we are comparing 'like with like'. Differences, such as the acquisition of assets – renting premises compared with ownership, leasing vehicles compared with ownership – will affect the profitability of the company and the structure of the balance sheet; likewise, the long-term financing of a company – the balance between debt finance and equity finance – will also have an effect.

Chapter Summary

- Accounting ratios are numerical values (percentages, time periods, ratios) extracted from the financial statements. They can be used to measure:
  - profitability
  - liquidity
  - use of resources
  - financial position

- Comparisons need to be made with previous financial statements, or those of similar companies.

- There are a number of limitations to be borne in mind when drawing conclusions from accounting ratios:
  - retrospective nature, based on past performance
  - differences in accounting policies
  - effects of inflation when comparing year-to-year
  - reliance on standards
  - economic and other factors

Key Terms

profitability	measures the relationship between profit and sales turnover, assets and capital employed; ratios include: • gross profit percentage • expenses/sales percentage • operating profit percentage • net profit percentage • return on capital employed • return on equity • earnings per share
liquidity	measures the financial stability of a company, ie the ability of a company to pay its way on a short-term basis; ratios include: • working capital (current) ratio • liquid capital ratio (or quick ratio/acid test)
use of resources	measures how efficiently the management controls the current aspects of the company – principally stock, debtors and creditors; ratios include: • stock turnover • debtors' collection period • creditors' payment period • asset turnover ratio
financial position	measures the strength and long-term financing of the company; ratios include: • gearing • interest cover

Student Activities

Osborne Books is grateful to the AAT for their kind permission to use past assessment material for the following activities: 7.8, 7.9, 7.10

7.1 The net profit/sales percentage measures which one of the following?
  (a)   liquidity
  (b)   return on investment
  (c)   risk
  (d)   profitability ✓

7.2 The working capital ratio measures which one of the following?
  (a)   profitability
  (b)   use of assets
  (c)   liquidity ✓
  (d)   return on investment

7.3 The rate of stock turnover in a trading period, is best described by which one of the following definitions?
  (a)   value of stock at the start of the year
  (b)   value of stock at the end of the year
  (c)   number of times that the average level of stock has been sold
  (d) ✓ average amount of time that stock has been held throughout the year

7.4 Which one of the following headings best describes and measures gearing?
  (a)   financial position (risk) ✓
  (b)   liquidity
  (c)   profitability
  (d)   performance/efficiency

7.5 Below is the balance sheet of Matlock plc for the year ended 30 September 20-3

	£000	£000
FIXED ASSETS		
At NBV		500
CURRENT ASSETS		
Stock	150	
Debtors	95	
Cash in hand	5	
	250	

CREDITORS: Amounts falling due within one year

Creditors	175
Bank overdraft	25
	200

NET CURRENT ASSETS	50
Total assets less current liabilities	550

CREDITORS: Amounts falling due after more than one year

Bank loan	100
	450

CAPITAL AND RESERVES	
Called up ordinary share capital	300
Share premium account	50
Profit and loss account	100
	450

1   What is the acid test ratio for Matlock plc?
    (a)   1.25:1
    (b)   0.5:1
    (c)   1:1
    (d)   5:1

2   The gearing ratio for Matlock plc should be calculated as follows:
    (a)   300/450 x 100
    (b)   350/450 x 100
    (c)   125/550 x 100
    (d)   100/550 x 100

3   If Matlock plc's sales for the year (all on credit) were £405,000, what is the asset turnover ratio?
    (a)   0.9:1
    (b)   0.74:1
    (c)   0.81:1
    (d)   1.11:1

4   What is the debtor collection period in days if the credit sales of the business are £405,000 as in 3 above? (You will need to round up to whole days)
    (a)   86 days
    (b)   68 days
    (c)   158 days
    (d)   61 days

5   Which of the following is the correct calculation for interest cover?
    (a)   total debt/interest payable
    (b)   interest payable/total debt
    (c)   operating profit/interest payable
    (d)   interest payable/ perating profit

7.6 Study the financial statements of the two public limited companies listed below and then calculate the accounting ratios in the questions which follow.

PROFIT AND LOSS ACCOUNTS	Hanadi plc		Abeer plc	
	£000	£000	£000	£000
Sales		350		300
Less Cost of sales				
Opening stock	40		20	
Purchases	170		150	
	210		170	
Closing stock	(110)	(100)	(70)	(100)
GROSS PROFIT		250		200
Expenses		(100)		(50)
NET PROFIT BEFORE TAXATION		150		150
Taxation		(35)		(30)
NET PROFIT AFTER TAXATION		115		120
Dividends		(60)		(45)
RETAINED PROFIT FOR THE YEAR		55		75

BALANCE SHEETS	Hanadi plc		Abeer plc	
	£000	£000	£000	£000
FIXED ASSETS AT NBV		465		325
CURRENT ASSETS				
Stock	110		70	
Debtors	95		60	
Bank	15		30	
	220		160	
CURRENT LIABILITIES				
Creditors	120		60	
Dividends payable	60		45	
Taxation payable	35		30	
	215		135	
NET CURRENT ASSETS		5		25
		470		350
Represented by				
CAPITAL AND RESERVES				
Ordinary shares £1 each		300		200
Share premium account		50		50
		350		250
Profit and loss account		120		100
		470		350

REQUIRED

Task 1

Calculate the following ratios for both businesses:

(a)   Gross profit as a percentage of sales
(b)   Net profit as a percentage of sales
(c)   Net profit as a percentage return on capital employed (ROCE)
(d)   Current ratio
(e)   Acid test ratio

Task 2

Comment upon what the ratios reveal, and make recommendations as to which business offers the better return from a profitability, efficiency and investment point of view.

7.7   Ratio analysis is a useful way for a business to compare one year's results with another and to highlight trends. It can also be a useful tool when comparing the results of a business with the results of a competitor. However the limitations of ratio analysis should always be kept in mind, when making any realistic judgement concerning the overall performance of any business.

REQUIRED

Discuss the limitations of ratio analysis when assessing and comparing company performance.

7.8   Jake Matease plans to invest in Fauve Limited. This is a chain of retail outlets. He is going to meet the Managing Director of Fauve Limited to discuss the profitability of the company. To prepare for the meeting he has asked you to comment on the change in profitability and the return on capital of the company. He has given you the profit and loss accounts of Fauve Limited and the summarised balance sheets for the last two years. These are set out below:

Fauve Limited
Summary profit and loss accounts for the year ended 30 September

	2001	2000
	£000	£000
Turnover	4,315	2,973
Cost of sales	1,510	1,189
Gross profit	2,805	1,784
Distribution costs	983	780
Administrative expenses	571	380
Operating profit	1,251	624
Interest paid and similar charges	45	27
Profit on ordinary activities before taxation	1,206	597
Tax on profit on ordinary activities	338	167
Profit for the financial year	868	430
Dividends	340	300
Retained profit for the financial year	528	130

Fauve Limited
Balance sheets as at 30 September

	2001		2000	
	£000	£000	£000	£000
Fixed assets		6,663		4,761
Current assets			2,031	
Current liabilities			1,387	
Net current assets		1,767		644
		8,430		5,405
Called up share capital:				
ordinary shares of £1 each		4,000		1,703
Profit and loss account		3,930		3,402
Long-term loan		500		300
		8,430		5,405

REQUIRED

Prepare a report for Jake Matease tha   llowing:

(a)   a calculation of the following ra   ited for each of the two years:
   • return on capital employed
   • net profit percentage
   • gross profit percentage
   • asset turnover

(b)   an explanation of the meaning of each ratio and a comment on the performance of Fauve Limited as shown by each of the ratios

(c)   a conclusion on how the overall performance has changed over the two years

7.9   The directors of Dowango Ltd have asked to have a meeting with you. They are intending to ask the bank for a further long-term loan to enable them to purchase a company which has retail outlets. The directors have identified two possible companies to take over and they intend to purchase the whole of the share capital of one of the two targeted companies.

The directors have obtained the latest financial statements of the two companies, in summary form and these are set out below:

Summary profit and loss accounts

	Company A	Company B
	£000	£000
Turnover	800	2,100
Cost of sales	440	1,050
Gross profit	360	1,050
Expenses	160	630
Net profit before interest and tax	200	420

Summary balance sheets

	Company A	Company B
	£000	£000
Fixed assets	620	1,640
Net current assets	380	1,160
Long-term loan	(400)	(1,100)
	600	1,700
Share capital and reserves	600	1,700

REQUIRED

Advise the directors as to which of the two companies targeted for takeover is the more profitable and which one provides the higher return on capital. Your answer should include calculation of the following ratios:

- return on capital employed
- net profit margin
- asset turnover

You should also calculate and comment on at least *one* further ratio of your choice, for which you have sufficient information, which would be relevant to determining which of the companies is more profitable or provides the greater return on capital.

7.10 Rowan Healthcare plc is a private hospital group which has just lost its supplier of bandages. The company that has been supplying it for the last five years has gone into liquidation. The directors of Rowan Healthcare are concerned to select a new supplier which can be relied upon to supply the group with its needs for the foreseeable future. You have been asked by the finance director to analyse the financial statements of a potential supplier of bandages. You have obtained the latest financial statements of the company, in summary form, which are set out below.

Patch Limited
Summary profit and loss accounts for the year ended 30 September

	20-8	20-7
	£000	£000
Turnover	2,300	2,100
Cost of sales	1,035	945
Gross profit	1,265	1,155
Expenses	713	693
Net profit before interest and tax	552	462

Patch Limited
Summary Balance sheets as at 30 September

	20-8		20-7	
	£000	£000	£000	£000
Fixed assets		4,764		5,418

continued on next page

Current assets				
Stocks	522		419	
Debtors	406		356	
Cash	117		62	
	1,045		837	
Current liabilities				
Trade creditors	305		254	
Taxation	170		211	
	475		465	
Net current assets		570		372
Long-term loan		(1,654)		(2,490)
		3,680		3,300
Share capital		1,100		1,000
Share premium		282		227
Profit and loss account		2,298		2,073
		3,680		3,300

You have also obtained the relevant industry average ratios which are as follows:

	20-8	20-7
Return on capital employed	9.6%	9.4%
Net profit percentage	21.4%	21.3%
Quick ratio/acid test	1.0:1	0.9:1
Gearing (Debt/Capital Employed)	36%	37%

REQUIRED

Prepare a report for the finance director of Rowan Healthcare plc recommending whether or not to use Patch Ltd as a supplier of bandages. Use the information contained in the financial statements of Patch Ltd and the industry averages supplied.

Your answer should:

- comment on the company's profitability, liquidity and financial position;
- consider how the company has changed over the two years;
- include a comparison with the industry as a whole.

The report should include calculation of the following ratios for the two years:

(a)   Return on capital employed

(b)   Net profit percentage

(c)   Quick ratio/acid test

(d)   Gearing

8 Consolidated accounts

This chapter examines the financial statements of groups of companies. The final accounts for a group comprise consolidated profit and loss account and consolidated balance sheet. Such consolidated accounts show the position of the group as if it was a single entity. The chapter covers:

- definitions of parent and subsidiary companies
- accounting for goodwill, post-acquisition profits, and minority interests when using the acquisition method for preparing consolidated balance sheets
- the use of fair values in acquisition accounting
- inter-company adjustments and profits
- consolidated profit and loss accounts
- merger accounting

Towards the end of the chapter we look at incorporating the results of associated companies – where fewer than half of the shares are owned – into the financial statements of the investor company.

NVQ PERFORMANCE CRITERIA COVERED

unit 11: DRAFTING FINANCIAL STATEMENTS

element 11.1

draft limited company financial statements

A   draft limited company financial statements from the appropriate information

B   correctly identify and implement subsequent adjustments and ensure that discrepancies, unusual features or queries are identified and either resolved or referred to the appropriate person

C   ensure that limited company financial statements comply with relevant accounting standards and domestic legislation and with the organisation's policies, regulations and procedures

E   ensure that confidentiality procedures are followed at all times

THE ACCOUNTING SYSTEMS OF AN ORGANISATION

Throughout earlier studies of NVQ Accounting you will have been aware of how a business must adapt the accounting system to suit its particular needs. In the same way, in *Drafting Financial Statements* a company's accounting systems are affected by a number of factors – these include the role of the company, its organisational structure, its administrative systems and procedures, and the nature of its business transactions. Provided that a company complies with the requirements of the Companies Act and the accounting standards, it can arrange its accounting systems to suit its needs.

Up until now we have studied and prepared the financial statements of individual companies, eg Wyvern Trading Company Limited. Such financial statements are often referred to as *unitary* accounts – because they relate to one company only. In this chapter we will study the accounts of groups of companies – known as *consolidated* accounts – where one company (the parent company) owns or controls one or more other companies (subsidiary companies).

Before commencing our studies of consolidated accounts we will look at a Case Study which demonstrates two different ways of organising the accounting systems of large companies.

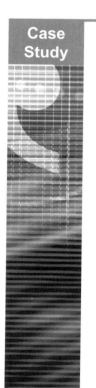

Case Study

CHOCOLAT LIMITED AND CHOC CABIN LIMITED: DIVISIONAL OR CONSOLIDATED?

situation

Both of these companies – Chocolat Limited and Choc Cabin Limited – manufacture high-quality chocolates and other confectionery which are sold through their own retail chains – shops on high streets and in shopping centres, and franchises located within department stores. Both companies also sell wholesale to major store chains, where the chocolates are boxed and branded under the name of the retailer.

The two companies are direct competitors, chasing the same market – their shops are to be found close to one another on many a high street or shopping centre. Despite their similarities, however, the way in which they organise their accounting systems is very different.

solution

Chocolat Limited – divisional accounting

This company uses a divisional approach to its accounting system, with a separate division for each of its main activities – manufacture, retail, and own-brand wholesale – illustrated as follows:

| CHOCOLAT LIMITED |
| finance director |
| chief accountant |

| **Manufacturing Division** | **Retail Division** | **Wholesale Division** |
| divisional accountant | divisional accountant | divisional accountant |

Each of the three divisions has a divisional accountant who is responsible for the accounting function and the submission of accounting information to the company's chief accountant. The financial statements of Chocolat Limited are presented in a unitary form by the company's finance director and contain a summary of the performance of each division.

Choc Cabin Limited – consolidated accounts

Each of the three main activities of this company is run by a separate company, which is wholly owned by Choc Cabin Limited. The accounting system is illustrated as follows:

| CHOC CABIN LIMITED |
| finance director |
| group accountant |

| **CHOC CABIN (MANUFACTURING) LIMITED** | **CHOC CABIN (RETAIL) LIMITED** | **CHOC CABIN (WHOLESALE) LIMITED** |
| company accountant | company accountant | company accountant |

Here, each company running one of the main activities maintains its own accounting system and is required to produce its own financial statements in accordance with the Companies Act and accounting standards – each has a company accountant to enable it to do so. As each company is wholly owned, it is a subsidiary company of Choc Cabin Limited, the parent company. In these circumstances, the Companies Act requires that consolidated – or group –

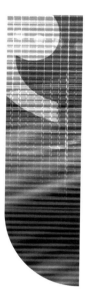

accounts are produced as the financial statements, in order to show a complete picture of the group. The parent company's group accountant will prepare the consolidated accounts for presentation by the company's finance director.

conclusion

This Case Study shows two different accounting systems – unitary financial statements with the reporting of divisional performance, and consolidated financial statements with subsidiary companies.

As an organisation grows, it must adapt its accounting systems to suit its needs – no one system is correct in all circumstances.

The divisional method often suits a company that grows organically where new divisions are set up to meet the requirements of the business, eg "we will set up a wholesale division". By contrast, subsidiary companies are often acquired as going concern businesses in order to expand rapidly, eg "we need to expand, let us buy an existing wholesale business".

While subsidiary companies often have more autonomy than divisions, the preparation of consolidated accounts is more complex – as we will see in this chapter – than that of unitary companies.

INTRODUCTION TO CONSOLIDATED ACCOUNTS

In recent years many companies have been taken over by other companies to form groups. Each company within a group maintains its separate legal entity, and so a group of companies may take the following form:

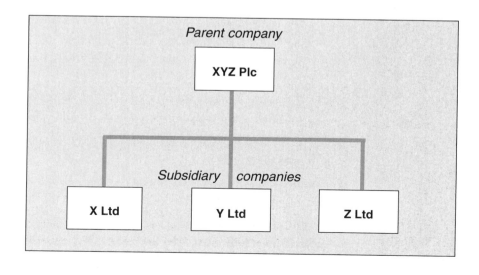

The Companies Act 1985 makes various provisions concerning groups of companies, including:

- A parent company and subsidiary company relationship generally exists where a parent company owns more than 50 per cent of another company's share capital, or controls the composition of its board of directors (see definitions below).

- Each subsidiary company produces its own financial statements in accordance with the Companies Act and accounting standards.

- A parent company is required to produce *group published accounts*.

- Group accounts must include a consolidated profit and loss account and a consolidated balance sheet. Such *consolidated accounts* are designed to show the position of the group as if it was a single entity.

- A parent company, which produces a consolidated profit and loss account, is not legally obliged to produce its own profit and loss account.

PARENT AND SUBSIDIARY COMPANIES DEFINED

FRS 2, *Accounting for subsidiary undertakings*, defines the parent/subsidiary company relationship as a situation where *any* of the following apply:

- the parent holds a majority of the voting rights in the subsidiary
- the parent is a shareholder of the subsidiary and has the right to appoint or remove directors holding a majority of the voting rights at meetings of the board on all, or substantially all, matters
- the parent has the right to exercise a *dominant influence* on the subsidiary either through the memorandum or articles of association, or through a control contract
- the parent is a shareholder of the subsidiary and controls alone, under an agreement with the other shareholders or members, a majority of the voting rights in the subsidiary
- the parent has a *participating interest* in the subsidiary and
  - either actually exercises a *dominant influence* over it
  - or both it and the subsidiary are *managed on a unified basis*
  as explained below . . .

Dominant influence is influence which can be exercised to achieve the operating and financial policies desired by the holder of the influence, notwithstanding the rights or influence of any other party.

Participating interest is an interest held by an undertaking in the shares of another undertaking which it holds on a long-term basis for the purpose of securing a contribution to its activities by the exercise of control or influence arising from or related to that interest. In this connection:

- a holding of 20 per cent or more of the shares of an undertaking is presumed to be a participating interest unless the contrary is shown

- an interest in shares includes an interest which is either convertible into shares, or includes an option to convert into shares

Managed on a unified basis occurs when the whole of the operations of two or more undertakings are integrated and they are managed as a single unit.

FRS 2 also covers the situation where a subsidiary is itself the parent of another undertaking, creating a parent, subsidiary and sub-subsidiary relationship:

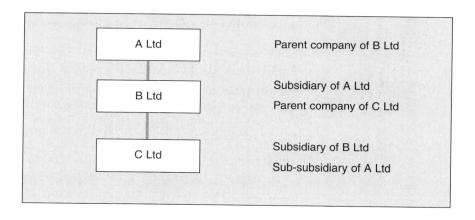

GROUP FINANCIAL STATEMENTS

A group is defined by FRS 2 as 'a parent undertaking and its subsidiary undertakings'. FRS 2 requires a parent undertaking to prepare consolidated financial statements for its group unless it uses one of the exceptions set out in the standard – for example, if the group is defined as being small or medium-sized.

We look firstly at the preparation of consolidated balance sheets, using the **acquisition method** (another method is the **merger method** – see page 255 – which can only be used when certain criteria are complied with).

We then look at the preparation of consolidated profit and loss accounts.

CONSOLIDATED BALANCE SHEETS: ACQUISITION METHOD

The objective of a consolidated balance sheet is to report the affairs of the group of companies as if it was a single entity.

The **acquisition method** regards the business combination as the acquisition of one company by another. Thus the identifiable assets of the company acquired are included in the consolidated balance sheet at the date of acquisition, and its results are included in the profit and loss account (see page 251) from the date of acquisition.

There are three major calculations in the preparation of a consolidated balance sheet under the acquisition method, each with a different relevant date:

1 goodwill – as at the date of acquisition of the subsidiary

2 post-acquisition profits – since the date of acquisition of the shares in the subsidiary

3 minority interests – the stake of the other shareholders in the subsidiary at the date of the consolidated balance sheet

In the Case Studies which follow, we look at the preparation of consolidated balance sheets – starting with simple groups, and then incorporating calculations for goodwill, post-acquisition profits and minority interests. Included in the Case Studies are tutorial notes which explain the calculations.

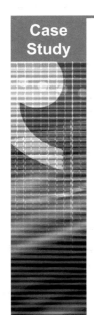

Case Study

ACCOUNTING FOR SIMPLE GROUPS OF COMPANIES

situation

The summary balance sheets of Pam Limited, a parent company, and Sam Limited, the subsidiary of Pam, are shown below as at 31 December 2004. Sam Limited was acquired by Pam Limited as a subsidiary company on 31 December 2004.

	Pam Ltd £000	Sam Ltd £000
Investment in Sam:		
20,000 £1 ordinary shares at cost	40	–
Other net assets	40	40
	80	40
Share capital (£1 ordinary shares)	60	20
Reserves: retained profits	20	20
	80	40

solution

The first thing to look at is the percentage of shares owned in the subsidiary by the parent company. Here Pam Limited owns all 20,000 shares of Sam Limited, so the subsidiary is 100 per cent owned. Note that the shares have been bought at the financial year-end, ie the date of the consolidated balance sheet.

The method of preparing the consolidated balance sheet of Pam Limited and its subsidiary Sam Limited is as follows:

1 the £40,000 cost of the investment in Sam (shown on Pam's balance sheet) cancels out directly against the share capital (£20,000) and reserves (£20,000) of Sam and is not shown on the consolidated balance sheet

2 add together the net assets of the two companies

3 show only the share capital and reserves of the parent company

The consolidated balance sheet (CBS) is shown in the far right column:

	Pam Ltd £000	Sam Ltd £000	CBS £000
Investment in Sam:			
20,000 £1 ordinary shares at cost	~~40~~	–	
Other net assets	40	40	80
	80	40	80
Share capital (£1 ordinary shares)	60	~~20~~	60
Reserves: retained profits	20	~~20~~	20
	80	40	80

Tutorial Note

The reason for cancelling out the amount of the investment against the share capital and reserves of the subsidiary is because the amounts record a transaction that has taken place within the group. It does not need reporting because the balance sheet shows the group as if it was a single entity.

Case Study

GOODWILL – POSITIVE AND NEGATIVE

situation

The summary balance sheets of Peeble Limited, a parent company, and Singh Limited and Salvo Limited, its two subsidiaries, as at 31 December 2004 appear below. The investments in Singh Limited and Salvo Limited were bought on 31 December 2004.

	Peeble Ltd £000	Singh Ltd £000	Salvo Ltd £000
Fixed assets	30	25	20
Investment in Singh:			
20,000 £1 ordinary shares at cost	50		
Investment in Salvo:			
24,000 £1 ordinary shares at cost	25		
Net current assets	10	15	10
	115	40	30
Share capital (£1 ordinary shares)	70	20	24
Reserves: retained profits	45	20	6
	115	40	30

solution

Peeble Limited owns all the shares of Singh Limited and Salvo Limited – the subsidiaries are 100 per cent owned. The investments have been bought at the financial year-end – the date of the consolidated balance sheet.

As the cost price of the investment in the subsidiaries does not cancel out directly against the share capital and reserves, the difference represents goodwill:

	Singh £000	Salvo £000
cost of investment	50	25
value* of subsidiary at date of acquisition	40	30
goodwill	10	(5)

* share capital + reserves

positive goodwill	**negative goodwill**
cost of investment is higher than value acquired in subsidiary	cost of investment is lower than value acquired in subsidiary

The consolidated balance sheet of Peeble Limited and its subsidiaries can now be prepared following the principles outlined in the previous Case Study. Note that positive goodwill is shown on the assets side of the consolidated balance sheet, with negative goodwill also shown on the assets side, but deducted.

PEEBLE LIMITED AND ITS SUBSIDIARIES
Consolidated balance sheet as at 31 December 2004

	£000
Fixed Assets	
Intangible assets:	
Goodwill	10
Negative goodwill	(5)
Tangible assets 30 + 25 + 20	75
Net Current Assets 10 + 15 + 10	35
	115
Share Capital	70
Reserves	
Retained profits	45
	115

Tutorial Note

In future years goodwill – both positive and negative – will most probably be amortised through profit and loss account over its estimated useful economic life, although there are alternative ways of accounting for goodwill (see FRS 10, pages 99-100).

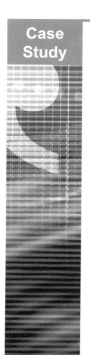

Case Study

PRE-ACQUISITION AND POST-ACQUISITION PROFITS

situation

The summarised balance sheets of Peat Limited, a parent company, and Stone Limited, its subsidiary, as at 31 December 2004 appear as follows:

	Peat Ltd	Stone Ltd
	£000	£000
Fixed assets	80	25
Investment in Stone:		
20,000 £1 ordinary shares at cost	35	
Current assets	25	10
Current liabilities	(10)	(8)
	130	27
Share capital (£1 ordinary shares)	100	20
Reserves: retained profits	30	7
	130	27

Stone Limited was bought by Peat Ltd on 31 December 2003, when Stone's retained profit was £5,000 (note that Stone has earned £2,000 of retained profits since the date of acquisition).

The accounting policy of Peat is to amortise goodwill over an estimated useful economic life of ten years.

Tutorial Note

The reserves held by the subsidiary at the date of acquisition are those that have been earned pre-acquisition: they are included in the goodwill calculation.

The reserves earned by the subsidiary after acquisition – post-acquisition profits – are earned while it is part of the group and are, therefore, part of the consolidated reserves shown on the consolidated balance sheet. Such consolidated reserves are available for distribution as dividends to shareholders – provided that there is sufficient cash in the bank to pay the dividends.

---

solution

1   Peat Limited owns all the shares of Stone Limited, ie the subsidiary is 100% owned.

2   The calculation of goodwill in Stone is as follows:

	£000
cost of investment	35
value of subsidiary at date of acquisition 20 + 5	*25
positive goodwill	10

* £20,000 of share capital, plus £5,000 of retained profits at date of acquisition (ie pre-acquisition profits)

3   As Peat's accounting policy is to amortise goodwill over an estimated useful economic life of ten years, £1,000 will be written off to profit and loss account in 2004, leaving £9,000 of goodwill to be shown in the balance sheet.

4   The post-acquisition profits of Stone for the consolidated balance sheet are:

	£000
reserves at date of consolidated balance sheet	7
reserves at date of acquisition of Stone	5
post-acquisition profits	2

PEAT LIMITED AND ITS SUBSIDIARY
Consolidated balance sheet as at 31 December 2004

	£000
Fixed Assets	
Intangible asset: goodwill 10 – 1	9
Tangible assets 80 + 25	105
Current Assets 25 + 10	35
Current Liabilities (10) + (8)	(18)
	131
Share Capital	100
Reserves	
Retained profits 30 + 2 – 1*	31
	131

* goodwill amortised

<table>
<tr><td>**Case Study**</td><td colspan="2"># MINORITY INTERESTS</td></tr>
</table>

Tutorial Note

Minority interests occur where the parent company does not own all the shares in the subsidiary company, eg a subsidiary is 75 per cent owned by a parent company; the 25 per cent of shares not owned by the parent is the minority interests.

The amount shown for minority interests on the consolidated balance sheet reflects the value of the subsidiary held by them, and is shown as a liability of the group on the 'financed by' side of the consolidated balance sheet.

situation

The summarised balance sheets of Pine Limited, a parent company, and Spruce Limited, its subsidiary, as at 31 December 2004 are shown below.

The investment in Spruce was bought on 31 December 2003, when Spruce's retained profit was £8,000.

The accounting policy of Pine is to amortise goodwill over an estimated useful economic life of five years.

	Pine Ltd	Spruce Ltd
	£000	£000
Fixed assets	80	25
Investment in Spruce:		
15,000 £1 ordinary shares at cost	26	
Current assets	25	12
Current liabilities	(10)	(5)
	121	32
Share capital (£1 ordinary shares)	100	20
Reserves: retained profits	21	12
	121	32

solution

1   Pine Limited owns 75 per cent of the shares of Spruce Limited, ie 15,000 shares out of 20,000 shares. Thus minority shareholders own 25 per cent of Spruce.

2   The calculation of goodwill in Spruce is as follows:

	£000
cost of investment	26
value of subsidiary at date of acquisition	
20 + 8 = 28 x 75% owned =	21
positive goodwill	5

Note that, for the goodwill calculation, the value of the subsidiary at date of acquisition is reduced to the percentage of shares owned, here 75 per cent.

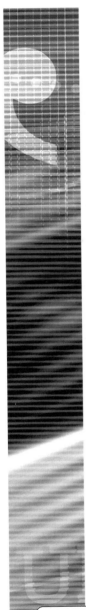

3 As Pine's accounting policy is to amortise goodwill over an estimated useful economic life of five years, £1,000 will be written off to profit and loss account in 2004, leaving £4,000 of goodwill to be shown in the balance sheet.

4 The post-acquisition profits of Spruce for the consolidated balance sheet are:

	£000
reserves at date of consolidated balance sheet	12
reserves at date of acquisition of Spruce	8
post-acquisition profits	4
75% owned	3

Note that, for the calculation of post-acquisition profits, the amount is reduced to the percentage of shares owned, here 75 per cent.

5 The minority interests of Spruce are:

	£000
value at date of consolidated balance sheet	32
25% minority interests	8

Note that, for the calculation of minority interests, the amount is reduced to the percentage of shares owned by the minority shareholders, here 25 per cent.

PINE LIMITED AND ITS SUBSIDIARY
Consolidated balance sheet as at 31 December 2004

	£000
Fixed Assets	
Intangible asset: goodwill 5 − 1	4
Tangible assets 80 + 25	105
Current Assets 25 + 12	37
Current Liabilities (10) + (5)	(15)
	131
Share Capital	100
Reserves	
Retained profits 21 + 3 − 1*	23
	123
Minority Interests	8
	131

* goodwill amortised

Tutorial Note

When there are minority interests, note that we do not reduce the value of the subsidiary's assets and liabilities in the consolidated balance sheet to allow for minority shareholders – what we are saying is that the parent company has *control* over the subsidiary's assets and liabilities.

The amount shown for minority interests on the consolidated balance sheet is the value of the subsidiary held by them *at the date of the consolidated balance sheet*.

Minority interests are included on the 'financed by' side of the consolidated balance sheet in order to show the overall view of the group.

FAIR VALUES IN ACQUISITION ACCOUNTING

When a parent company acquires a majority holding of shares in a subsidiary company, it acquires both control of the subsidiary and also control of the subsidiary's assets and liabilities. The objective of FRS 7, *Fair values in acquisition accounting*, is to ensure that when a business entity is acquired by another:

- all the assets and liabilities that existed in the acquired entity at the date of acquisition are recorded at fair values reflecting their condition at that date

- all changes to the acquired assets and liabilities, and the resulting gains and losses, that arise after control of the acquired entity has passed to the acquirer are reported as part of the post-acquisition financial performance of the acquiring group

Fair value is defined by the standard as 'the amount at which an asset or liability could be exchanged in an arm's length transaction between informed and willing parties, other than in a forced or liquidation sale'.

FRS 7 gives guidance on valuing individual categories of assets:

- tangible fixed assets – the fair value should be based on either their market value or their depreciated replacement cost

- intangible assets – the fair value should be based on their replacement cost, which is normally their estimated market value

- stocks and work-in-progress – should be valued at the lower of replacement cost and net realisable value

- quoted investments – should be valued at market price

- monetary assets and liabilities (eg debtors and creditors) – should be valued at the amounts expected to be received or paid

Fair value has an effect on the calculations for goodwill, minority interests (where applicable), and sometimes on post-acquisition profits:

- goodwill is the cost of the investment in the subsidiary, less the fair value of the subsidiary's assets and liabilities

- minority interests is the proportion of the subsidiary owned, based on the fair value of the subsidiary's assets and liabilities

- post-acquisition profits will be affected where the use of fair value for fixed assets leads to a different depreciation charge from that based on historic costs

The procedure for dealing with fair values is to restate the subsidiary's balance sheet using fair values. Increases in the valuation of fixed assets and current assets are credited to revaluation reserve; decreases in fixed assets and current assets are debited to revaluation reserve. Any changes to the value of liabilities are also passed through revaluation reserve. The Case Study which follows shows how fair values affect the calculations for the consolidated balance sheet.

One further aspect of FRS 7 to note is that the standard does not allow the liabilities of the acquired company to be increased by the inclusion of provisions for future re-organisation costs and for future operating losses. Such costs are to be dealt with post-acquisition and will be charged to the profit and loss account of the year in which they are incurred. For example, if the acquiring company considers that it will have to spend money on upgrading the computer systems of the subsidiary, it cannot make a provision for this – against which future costs can be charged – at the date of acquisition. Instead, the costs will be charged against post-acquisition profits as they are incurred.

Case Study

FAIR VALUES IN ACQUISITION ACCOUNTING

situation

On 31 December 2004, Pipe Limited bought 75 per cent of the share capital of Soil Limited at a cost of £37,000. At that date the two companies' balance sheets were as follows:

	Pipe Ltd £000	Soil Ltd £000
Fixed assets	60	18
Investment in Soil:		
9,000 £1 ordinary shares at cost	37	
Current assets	20	16
Current liabilities	(13)	(6)
	104	28
Share capital (£1 ordinary shares)	80	12
Reserves: retained profits	24	16
	104	28

At the date of acquisition

– the fair value of Soil's fixed assets was £30,000

– the fair value of Soil's current assets was £12,000

The accounting policy of Pipe is to amortise goodwill over an estimated useful economic life of ten years.

solution

1   We must incorporate the fair values into Soil's balance sheet as follows:

Fixed assets (increase in value)	£000	£000
debit fixed assets account	12	
credit revaluation reserve		12

Current assets (reduction in value)		
debit revaluation reserve	4	
credit current assets		4

2   Thus Soil's balance sheet is:

	before	adjustment	after
	£000	£000	£000
Fixed assets	18	+ 12	30
Current assets	16	− 4	12
Current liabilities	(6)	−	(6)
	28	+ 8	36
Share capital	12	−	12
Reserves: revaluation	−	+ 12 }	8
		− 4	
retained profits	16	−	16
	28	+ 8	36

3   Goodwill is:

	£000
cost of investment	37
value of subsidiary at date of acquisition	
fair value of 36 (see above) x 75% owned	27
positive goodwill	10

4   Minority interests are:

	£000
value at date of consolidated balance sheet	36
25% minority interests	9

5   There will be no post-acquisition profits at 31 December 2004, as this is the date at which the investment in the subsidiary is being made.

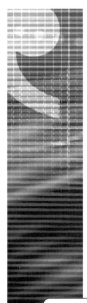

PIPE LIMITED AND ITS SUBSIDIARY
Consolidated balance sheet as at 31 December 2004

	£000
Fixed Assets	
Intangible asset: goodwill	10
Tangible assets 60 + 30 (at fair value)	90
Current Assets 20 + 12 (at fair value)	32
Current Liabilities (13) + (6)	(19)
	113
Share Capital	80
Reserves	
Retained profits	24
	104
Minority Interests	9
	113

Tutorial Note

Goodwill will be amortised over ten years at £1,000 per year through profit and loss account.

There may be an adjustment each year to post-acquisition profits if the use of fair values leads to an additional depreciation charge.

INTER-COMPANY ADJUSTMENTS

We have already seen the need to cancel out the inter-company balances of investment in the subsidiary company (shown in the parent company's balance sheet) against the share capital and reserves (shown in the subsidiary company's balance sheet). Other inter-company amounts also have to be cancelled out or adjusted against each other when preparing consolidated balance sheets.

debtors, creditors and loans

Where there are debtors, creditors and loans between companies that are part of the same group, they cancel out against each other and do not show on the consolidated balance sheet.

Example 1

Beech Limited has sold goods to Cedar Limited for £5,000. Both Beech and Cedar are subsidiaries of Ash Limited. At the date of the consolidated balance sheet Cedar has not yet paid Beech for the goods, so:

- Beech has an asset of debtors, including the £5,000 due from Cedar
- Cedar has a liability of creditors, including the £5,000 due to Beech

For the consolidated balance sheet of Ash Limited and its subsidiaries, the inter-company balance of debtors and creditors will not be shown because it is between group companies.

Example 2

Ash Limited has made a loan to Beech Limited of £10,000. The loan shows:

- as an asset on Ash's balance sheet
- as a liability on Beech's balance sheet

For the consolidated balance sheet, the loan will not be shown because it is an inter-company balance within the group.

dividends proposed

When a dividend is proposed by a subsidiary company, the amount is shown as a current liability on its balance sheet. In the parent company's balance sheet, the amount of the dividend is shown as a current asset (dividend receivable), having been credited to the parent company's profit and loss account (provided that the dividend represents a distribution of post-acquisition profits). Such inter-company balances will cancel each other out when the consolidated balance sheet is prepared.

Note that, if the subsidiary is partly owned, then the proportion of the proposed dividend that does not belong to the parent company is shown as a current liability due to the minority shareholders.

inter-company profits

Inter-company profits occur when one group company sells goods to another company within the group. If the goods have then been sold to buyers outside the group, then no adjustment to the consolidated balance sheet is necessary as the profit has been realised. However, when some or all of the goods remain in the stock of a group company at the date of the consolidated balance sheet, then an adjustment for unrealised inter-company profits must be made.

For example, Able Limited and Baker Limited are parent company and subsidiary company respectively. Able sells goods which cost it £1,000 to Baker for £1,500. A consolidated balance sheet is prepared before Baker sells any of the stock. The £500 profit made by Able is included in its profit and loss account, whilst the value of the stock held by Baker includes Able's profit. For the consolidated balance sheet:

- the profit and loss account of Able is reduced by £500
- the stock of Baker is reduced by £500

This accounting adjustment ensures that the stocks of the group are stated in the consolidated balance sheet at cost to the group (or net realisable value, if lower) and that no unrealised profit is shown in the group accounts. Note that, if some of the goods had been sold by Baker, then only the profit on the proportion remaining in the group would be adjusted.

When a partly-owned subsidiary has sold goods to another group company and there are unrealised inter-company profits at the date of the consolidated balance sheet, minority interests need to be adjusted for their share of the unrealised profits. This is a requirement of FRS 2, and is illustrated in the Case Study which follows.

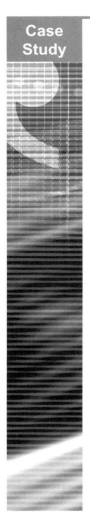

Case Study

INTER-COMPANY ADJUSTMENTS

situation

The summary balance sheets of Pearl Limited, a parent company, and Sea Limited, its subsidiary, as at 31 December 2004 are shown below.

The investment in Sea Limited was bought on 31 December 2003, when Sea's retained profit was £10,000. At that date there were no material differences between the book value and fair value of any of the assets of Sea.

The accounting policy of Pearl is to amortise goodwill over an estimated useful economic life of ten years.

In November 2004, Sea sold goods costing £5,000 to Pearl at a price of £7,000. At 31 December 2004 half of those goods were unsold by Pearl.

	Pearl Ltd £000	Sea Ltd £000
Investment in Sea:		
12,000 £1 ordinary shares at cost	28	
Loan to Sea	10	
Net current assets	42	46
Loan from Pearl		(10)
	80	36
Share capital (£1 ordinary shares)	60	20
Reserves: retained profits	20	16
	80	36

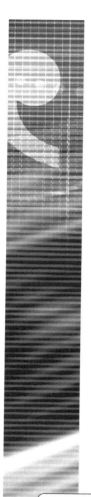

solution

1   Pearl Limited owns 60 per cent of the shares in Sea Limited.

2   The calculation of goodwill is as follows:

	£000
cost of investment	28
value of subsidiary at date of acquisition	
20 + 10 = 30 x 60% owned =	18
positive goodwill	10

As Pearl's accounting policy is to amortise goodwill over an estimated useful economic life of ten years, £1,000 will be written off to profit and loss account in 2002, leaving £9,000 of goodwill to be shown in the balance sheet.

3   *Inter-company adjustments:*

Loan

The £10,000 loan from Pearl to Sea cancels out for the consolidated balance sheet, ie the asset on Pearl's balance sheet cancels out against the liability on Sea's balance sheet.

Inter-company profits:

Of the £2,000 profit made when Sea sold goods to Pearl at the date of the consolidated balance sheet, £1,000 is unrealised (because the goods remain in Pearl's stock). For the consolidated balance sheet:

- the profit and loss account of Sea is reduced by £1,000
- the stock of Pearl is reduced by £1,000

Tutorial note

It is always advisable to make the inter-company adjustments before calculating post-acquisition profits and minority interests. By doing this, minority shareholders (if any) will be charged or credited with their share of adjustments which affect the subsidiary company, as required by FRS 2.

---

4   The post-acquisition profits of Sea are:

	£000
reserves at date of consolidated balance sheet:	
16 – 1 unrealised profit	15
reserves at date of acquisition	10
post-acquisition profits	5
60% owned	3

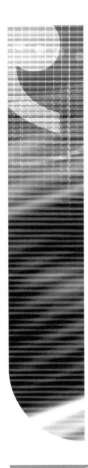

5   The minority interests of Sea are:

	£000
value at date of consolidated balance sheet:	
36 – 1 unrealised profit	35
40% minority interests	14

PEARL LIMITED AND ITS SUBSIDIARY
Consolidated balance sheet as at 31 December 2004

	£000
Fixed Assets	
Intangible asset: goodwill 10 – 1 (amortisation)	9
Net Current Assets 42 – 1 (stock) + 46	87
	96
Share Capital	60
Reserves	
Retained profits 20 – 1 (goodwill amortised) + 3	22
	82
Minority Interests	14
	96

Case Study

PREPARING FOR ASSESSMENT:
THE CONSOLIDATED BALANCE SHEET

Tutorial note

The task which follows is taken from the December 2001 AAT Examination; it is reproduced by kind permission of AAT. We will use it to demonstrate how the calculations for goodwill, post-acquisition profits and minority interests can be presented in a tabular format, which can be used for the calculations.

situation

You have been asked to assist in the preparation of the consolidated accounts of the Jake Group.

Set out on the next page are the balance sheets of Jake Limited and Dinos Limited for the year ended 30 September 2001:

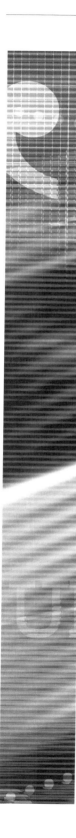

Balance sheets as at 30 September 2001				
	Jake Ltd		**Dinos Ltd**	
	£000	£000	£000	£000
Tangible fixed assets		18,104		6,802
Investment in Dinos Limited		5,000		
Current assets	4,852		2,395	
Current liabilities	2,376		547	
Net current assets		2,476		1,848
Long-term loan		4,500		1,000
		21,080		7,650
Share capital		5,000		1,000
Share premium		3,000		400
Profit and loss account		13,080		6,250
		21,080		7,650

Further information:

- The share capital of both Jake Limited and Dinos Limited consists of ordinary shares of £1 each. There have been no changes to the balances of share capital and share premium during the year. No dividends were paid or proposed by Dinos Limited during the year.

- Jake Limited acquired 600,000 shares in Dinos Limited on 30 September 2000.

- At 30 September 2000 the balance on the profit and loss account of dinos Limited was £5,450,000.

- The fair value of the fixed assets of Dinos Limited at 30 September 2000 was £3,652,000 as compared with their book value of £3,052,000. The revaluation has not been reflected in the books of Dinos Limited (ignore any depreciation implications).

- Goodwill arising on consolidation is to be amortised using the straight-line method over a period of 10 years.

You are to prepare the consolidated balance sheet of Jake Limited and its subsidiary undertaking as at 30 September 2001.

(Note: an AAT Examination normally supplies a sample layout for this purpose).

solution

1 The percentage of shares owned by Jake Limited in Dinos Limited is:

$$\frac{600,000 \text{ shares}}{1,000,000 \text{ shares}} = \underline{60 \text{ per cent}}$$

2 The minority interests in Dinos are, therefore, 100% − 60% = <u>40 per cent.</u>

3 At the date of acquisition (30 September 2000), the fixed assets of Dinos had the following values:

	£000
fair value	3,652
book value	3,052
difference	600

4 As fair value is higher than book value, this increase must be recorded in Dinos' accounts:

	£000	£000
debit fixed assets account	600	
credit revaluation reserve		600

5 Goodwill on consolidation, post-acquisition profits, and minority interests are now calculated using a tabular layout. (Author's note: each of these figures can be calculated separately as demonstrated on previous pages; the answers will, of course, be the same!)

	total equity	attributable to Jake		minority interests
		at acquisition	after acquisition	
	100%	60%	60%	40%
	£000	£000	£000	£000
share capital	1,000	600		400
share premium	400	240		160
revaluation reserve				
(see above)	600	360		240
profit and loss account*				
at acquisition	5,450	3,270		2,180
after acquisition	800		480	320
	†8,250	4,470	480	3,300
price paid by Jake		5,000		
∴ positive goodwill		530		

* and † − see notes on the next page

Notes on the calculations on the previous page

	£000	
* profit and loss account:	5,450	at date of acquisition
	800	post-acquisition profits
	6,250	as shown by Dinos' balance sheet
† total equity:	7,650	as shown by Dinos' balance sheet
	600	revaluation reserve (to increase fixed assets to fair value)
	8,250	as shown above

Further calculations

6 The goodwill, an intangible asset, is to be amortised using the straight-line method over ten years:

530	goodwill on consolidation
53	amortisation for year to 30 September 2001 (ie date of consolidated balance sheet)
477	goodwill as at 30 September 2001

7 The amount of goodwill written off is debited to the consolidated profit and loss account as follows:

13,080	Jake's profit and loss account
480	post-acquisition profits of Dinos attributable to Jake (see above)
13,560	
53	less goodwill amortised
13,507	consolidated profit and loss account

8 The consolidated balance sheet can now be prepared as shown on the next page. Note that the workings figures (in £000s) are for guidance only and need not be detailed in the balance sheet.

JAKE LIMITED AND ITS SUBSIDIARY
Consolidated Balance Sheet as at 30 September 2001

	£000	£000
Fixed Assets		
Intangible assets 530 – 53 goodwill amortised	477	
Tangible assets 18,104 + 6,802 + 600 increase to fair value	25,506	
Investments	=	
		25,983
Current Assets		
Stock		
Debtors		
Investments		
Cash at bank and in hand		
4,852 + 2,395	7,247	
Creditors: amounts falling due within one year		
Trade creditors		
Proposed dividend		
Taxation		
2,376 + 547	2,923	
Net Current Assets		4,324
Total Assets *less* **Current Liabilities**		30,307
Creditors: amounts falling due after more than one year		
Long-term loan 4,500 + 1,000		5,500
Provisions for liabilities and charges		–
		24,807
Capital and Reserves		
Share capital		5,000
Share premium		3,000
Profit and loss account (see workings on page 249)		13,507
		21,507
Minority Interests (see tabulation on page 248)		3,300
		24,807

CONSOLIDATED PROFIT AND LOSS ACCOUNTS

The consolidated profit and loss account, like the consolidated balance sheet, is intended to show the position of the group as if it was a single entity. The consolidated profit and loss account shows the shareholders of the parent company how much profit has been earned by the parent company and the subsidiaries, with a deduction for the proportion of profit due to minority interests. The diagram below shows the format of a consolidated profit and loss account; as the diagram demonstrates, the figures are merged from the profit and loss accounts of the parent company and the subsidiaries.

Format of consolidated profit and loss account (for internal use)

Group turnover	parent + subsidiaries – inter-company sales
Cost of sales*	see below
Gross profit	parent + subsidiaries – inter-company unrealised profit
Distribution costs	parent + subsidiaries
Administrative expenses	parent + subsidiaries
Group operating profit	parent + subsidiaries
Interest receivable/payable	parent + subsidiaries
Profit on ordinary activities before tax	parent + subsidiaries
Tax on profit on ordinary activities	parent + subsidiaries
Profit on ordinary activities after tax	parent + subsidiaries
Minority interests	minority interests' share of subsidiaries' profit
Profit on ordinary activities after tax and minority interests	parent + profit of wholly-owned subsidiaries and/or + parent's share of profit of partly-owned subsidiaries
Dividends	parent
Retained profit/loss for group	to group reserves

* Cost of sales:	
opening stock	parent + subsidiaries
+ purchases	parent + subsidiaries – inter-company purchases
– closing stock	parent + subsidiaries – inter-company unrealised profit

notes on the profit and loss format

- the full profit of subsidiaries is shown, with a separate deduction for the proportion of the profit due to minority interests

- only the dividends paid and proposed of the parent company are shown

- inter-company transactions are deducted for
  - inter-company sales
  - inter-company purchases
  - inter-company unrealised profit

Two Case Studies follow which demonstrate the preparation of consolidated profit and loss accounts for internal use – firstly for a simple group, secondly incorporating inter-company transactions. The layout follows that shown in the diagram.

Case Study

PROFIT AND LOSS FOR SIMPLE GROUPS

situation

The summary profit and loss accounts of Pack Limited, a parent company, and Sack Limited, its subsidiary, for the year-ended 31 December 2004 are shown below.

Pack Limited bought 80 per cent of the ordinary shares of Sack Limited on 1 January 2004.

	Pack Ltd £000	Sack Ltd £000
Turnover (sales)	115	60
Cost of sales	65	28
Gross profit	50	32
Distribution costs	5	8
Administrative expenses	15	12
Profit before tax	30	12
Corporation tax	8	2
Profit after tax	22	10
Dividends	10	–
Retained profits	12	10

Note: ignore any write-off of goodwill for the period

solution

1 The figures from the profit and loss accounts are merged.

2 The after-tax profit of Sack is £10,000; of this 20 per cent, ie £2,000 is due to minority interests.

please see next page . . .

PACK LIMITED AND ITS SUBSIDIARY

Consolidated Profit and Loss Account for the year ended 31 December 2004

		£000
Group turnover	115 + 60	175
Cost of sales	65 + 28	93
Gross profit	50 + 32	82
Distribution costs	5 + 8	13
Administrative expenses	15 + 12	27
Group operating profit	30 + 12	42
Interest receivable/payable		–
Profit on ordinary activities before tax		42
Tax on profit on ordinary activities	8 + 2	10
Profit on ordinary activities after tax		32
Minority interests	20% x 10 (Sack's profit after tax)	2
Profit on ordinary activities after tax and minority interests		30
Dividends	Pack Limited	10
Retained profit for group		20

Case Study

GROUP PROFIT AND LOSS WITH ADJUSTMENTS

situation

The summary profit and loss accounts of Perch Limited, a parent company, and Sole Limited and Skate Limited, its subsidiaries for the year-ended 31 December 2004 are shown on the next page.

Perch Limited bought all of the shares of Sole Limited on 1 January 2002, and 75 per cent of the shares of Skate Limited on 1 January 2004.

During the year to 31 December 2004 the following inter-company trading took place:

– Perch sold goods costing £6,000 to Sole at a price of £10,000; all of these goods had been sold by the year-end for £12,000

– Perch sold goods costing £20,000 to Skate at a price of £40,000; at the year-end half of these goods were unsold by Skate

Perch's policy is to take credit for inter-company dividends.

Note: ignore any write-off of goodwill for the period

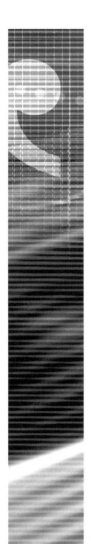

	Perch Ltd £000	Sole Ltd £000	Skate Ltd £000
Turnover (sales)	400	200	150
Opening stock	100	75	50
+ Purchases	300	150	100
– Closing stock	150	100	40
Cost of sales	250	125	110
Gross profit	150	75	40
Distribution costs	40	25	10
Administrative expenses	50	15	10
Dividends from subsidiaries:			
Sole	20		
Skate	9		
Net profit	89	35	20
Corporation tax	20	10	4
Profit after tax	69	25	16
Dividends	50	20	12
Retained profits	19	5	4

solution

Tutorial Note

Inter-company sales, purchases and unrealised profit are deducted from sales, purchases and closing stock respectively before the figures are shown in the consolidated profit and loss account.

Only the dividends of the parent company are shown. The dividends of subsidiary companies have been correctly recorded by Perch to show the proportion due to the parent company – these will not be shown on the consolidated profit and loss account because they are inter-company transactions.

The after-tax profit of Sole is £25,000; as this subsidiary is wholly owned, no deduction is made for minority interests.

The after-tax profit of Skate is £16,000; of this 25 per cent, ie £4,000, is due to minority interests.

please see next page for the consolidated profit and loss account . . .

PERCH LIMITED AND ITS SUBSIDIARIES

Consolidated Profit and Loss Account for the year ended 31 December 2004

		£000
Group turnover	400 + 200 + 150 − 10 − 40	700
Cost of sales*		445
Gross profit		255
Distribution costs	40 + 25 + 10	75
Administrative expenses	50 + 15 + 10	75
Group operating profit		105
Interest receivable/payable		–
Profit on ordinary activities before tax		105
Tax on profit on ordinary activities	20 + 10 + 4	34
Profit on ordinary activities after tax		71
Minority interests	25% x 16 (Skate's profit after tax)	4
Profit on ordinary activities after tax and minority interests		67
Dividends	Perch Limited	50
Retained profit for group		17
* cost of sales:		
opening stock	100 + 75 + 50	225
+ purchases	300 + 150 + 100 − 10 − 40	500
− closing stock	150 + 100 + 40 − 10 (unrealised profit)	280
		445

CONSOLIDATED BALANCE SHEETS: MERGER METHOD

In the consolidated balance sheets that we have seen earlier in this chapter we have used the **acquisition method** of consolidation. This method is where one company buys a majority of the shares in another, paying for the shares, usually in cash. Another method of consolidation is the **merger method** which can be used, under certain circumstances, when shares in the subsidiary are obtained on a share-for-share exchange basis, with no cash changing hands. For example:

- **acquisition method**

  The parent company buys all the shares in the subsidiary from existing shareholders at a cost of £2.50 per share paid in cash; note that there is a cash outflow.

- **merger method**

   The parent company's offer of one share in the parent for each share in the subsidiary is accepted by most of the subsidiary company's shareholders; note that no cash changes hands, and other criteria apply (see below).

FRS 6, *Acquisitions and mergers*, defines a merger as: 'a business combination that results in the creation of a new reporting entity formed from the combining parties, in which the shareholders of the combining entities come together in a partnership for the mutual sharing of the risks and benefits of the combined entity, and in which no party to the combination in substance obtains control over any other, or is otherwise seen to be dominant, whether by virtue of the proportion of its shareholders' rights in the combined entity, the influence of its directors or otherwise'.

An acquisition is defined by the FRS as 'a business combination that is not a merger.'

The standard states five criteria to determine whether a combination is a merger:

1 no party is portrayed as either acquirer or acquired

2 all parties participate in establishing the management structure for the combined entity

3 the relative sizes of the combining entities are not disparate (ie markedly different)

4 the consideration received by the equity (ordinary) shareholders of each party comprises primarily equity shares in the combined entity

5 no equity shareholders of any of the combined entities retain any material interest in the future performance of only part of the combined entity

Note that the fifth criterion fails if the holders of more than 10 per cent of the equity shares in one of the combining companies do not accept the terms of the merger; ie acceptance by 90 per cent, or more, is required.

All of the above five criteria must be satisfied for merger accounting to be used: if the criteria are met, then merger accounting must be used. If the criteria are not all satisfied, then acquisition accounting must be used.

merger method – accounting treatment

Merger accounting treats the two or more parties as combining on an equal footing, ie no party is seen as the acquirer or the acquired. The parties come together to share in the future risks and benefits of the combined entity. The diagram on the next page shows the main differences between the acquisition method and the merger method. The particular advantage of using the merger method is that all profits of the subsidiary – whenever they were earned – are available for distribution; this contrasts with the acquisition method where pre-acquisition profits are capitalised and go into the goodwill calculation, and only post-acquisition profits are available for distribution.

Acquisition method	Merger method
Parties seen as either the acquirer or the acquired	No party seen as the acquirer or the acquired
Shares in subsidiary bought from existing shareholders and paid for, usually, in cash	Shares in subsidiary obtained on a share-for-share exchange basis
If acquisition is financed by an issue of shares at a premium, a share premium account must be created	No share premium account is used – shares are accounted for at nominal value only
Fair values used to restate assets and liabilities at date of acquisition	Fair values not used – the emphasis is on the continuity of the parties to the combination
Goodwill – positive or negative – must be recognised	Difference on consolidation does not represent goodwill but is deducted from, or added to, reserves through a merger reserve
Pre-acquisition profits of the subsidiary are locked into the group and are no longer available for distribution	All profits of the subsidiary – whenever they were earned – are available for distribution
Minority interests can be a maximum of just under 50 per cent of the equity (ordinary) shares	Minority interests cannot exceed 10 per cent of the equity shares

Case Study

THE MERGER METHOD

Tutorial Note

AAT's Guidance Notes for this Unit state that the criteria for treating a business combination as an acquisition or a merger (see above) need to be known; the preparation of merger accounts will not be examined. Accordingly, this Case Study is provided to give an example – in simple terms – of how the merger method of consolidation is applied; however you will not be examined on the preparation of merger method consolidated balances sheets in this way.

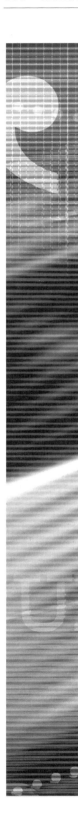

situation

The following are the summarised balance sheets of House Limited and Garden Limited before merger:

	House Ltd £000	Garden Ltd £000
Net assets	65	45
Share capital (£1 ordinary shares)	40	30
Reserves: retained profits	25	15
	65	45

House obtains shares in Garden, under the following circumstances, on a share-for-share exchange basis (each circumstance is to be treated separately):

1 House issues 35,000 £1 ordinary shares in exchange for the whole share capital of Garden

2 House issues 25,000 £1 ordinary shares in exchange for the whole share capital of Garden

3 House issues 35,000 £1 ordinary shares in exchange for 27,000 shares in Garden

Assume that the five criteria have been met for merger accounting to be used.

solution

circumstance 1

In merger accounting only the nominal value of shares issued and obtained is considered.

The difference between shares issued and shares obtained is a merger reserve which is
- deducted from reserves where shares issued are greater than shares obtained (as here)
- added to reserves where shares issued are fewer than shares obtained (see 2, below)

The consolidated balance is as follows:

	£000
Net assets 65 + 45	110
Share capital (£1 ordinary shares) 40 + 35	75
Reserves: retained profits	*35
	110
* House	25
Garden	15
	40

continued . . .

Less merger reserve

shares issued	35
shares obtained	30

5
35

circumstance 2

In this example, shares issued are fewer than shares obtained:

	£000
shares issued	25
shares obtained	30
merger reserve	5

Here, merger reserve is added to other reserves.

The consolidated balance sheet is as follows:

	£000
Net assets 65 + 45	110
Share capital (£1 ordinary shares) 40 + 25	*65
Reserves: retained profits 25 + 15	40
merger reserve (see above)	5
	110

* Note that all retained profits are available for distribution, this being a key feature of the merger method of consolidation.

circumstance 3

In this example, 27,000 out of 30,000 shares in Garden are being obtained, ie 90 per cent. Thus minority interests hold 10 per cent of the shares in Garden – the maximum permitted under the criteria for merger accounting.

Here, £35,000 of shares is being issued in order to obtain £27,000 of shares; this difference of £8,000 is deducted from reserves in the consolidated balance sheet.

The consolidated balance sheet is as follows:

	£000
Net assets 65 + 45	110
Share capital (£1 ordinary shares) 40 + 35	75
Reserves: retained profits	*30
	105
Minority interests 50 x 10%	5
	110

*	House	20
	Garden 20 x 90%	18
		38
	Less merger reserve (see above)	8
		30

ASSOCIATED COMPANIES

participating interest and significant influence

An associated company is defined by FRS 9, *Associates and joint ventures*, as: 'an entity (other than a subsidiary) in which another entity (the investor) has a participating interest and over whose operating and financial policies the investor exercises a significant influence'.

A **participating interest** is a long-term investment held for the purpose of contributing financial benefits to the investor's activities.

The **exercise of significant influence** is where the investor takes part in the process of making policy decisions, such as the expansion or contraction of the business, changes in products, markets, activities, etc.

As a general guideline, an associated company is where an investor owns between 20 per cent and 50 per cent of the ordinary shares of another company. However, ownership of shares by itself is not enough to establish an associated company relationship: ownership must be accompanied by a participating interest and the exercise of significant influence.

As we have seen earlier in this chapter, an ordinary share ownership above 50 per cent usually indicates a subsidiary company relationship; below 20 per cent is classed as a trade investment (see page 264). Thus an investment in an associated company is a substantial investment which is greater than a trade investment, but which is not as significant as a subsidiary company. The relationship is that of investor and investee (the associated company).

Note that FRS 9 also covers joint ventures – AAT's Guidance Notes for this Unit state that accounting for joint ventures will not be examined.

equity method of accounting

The equity method is the usual way of accounting for the results of associated companies. By this method we mean that the investor values its investment so as to reflect its interest in the net assets of the associated company. Initially the associated company is shown on the investor's balance sheet at cost (contrast this with subsidiary companies where assets and liabilities are included with those of the parent); the investor's share of subsequent profits or losses of the associated company are added to, or deducted from, the cost of the investment.

In the investor's financial statements, the key features of the equity method are:

- in the **profit and loss account** (see diagram below) show the investor's share of the associated company's:
  - operating profit (stated separately, immediately after group operating profit)
  - interest receivable/payable (include with amount for group)
  - corporation tax (include with amount for group)
- in the **balance sheet**
  - the investor's share of the net assets of the associated company should be included and separately disclosed
  - goodwill arising on the investor's acquisition of its associate – less any amortisation – should be included in the carrying amount of the associate but should be disclosed separately

---

Format of consolidated profit and loss account, incorporating share of associated companies

Note: this format is used for a group, ie parent + subsidiaries, together with associated companies

Group turnover	
Cost of sales	
Gross profit	no change to these figures: see page 251
Distribution costs	
Administrative expenses	
Group operating profit	
Share of operating profit in associates	share of associates – inter-company unrealised profit
Interest receivable/payable	group + share of associates
Profit on ordinary activities before tax	group + share of associates
Tax on profit on ordinary activities	group + share of associates
Profit on ordinary activities after tax	group + share of associates
Minority interests	minority interests' share of subsidiaries' profit
Profit on ordinary activities after tax and minority interests	parent + subsidiaries + share of associates
Dividends	parent
Retained profit/loss for group and share of associates	to group reserves

Case Study

ASSOCIATED COMPANIES

situation

On 31 December 2003, Icod Limited bought 25 per cent of the share capital of Arona Limited, its associated company, at a cost of £15,000. At that date the balance sheet of Arona was as follows:

	Arona Ltd £000
Fixed assets	28
Current assets	20
Current liabilities	(8)
	40
Share capital (£1 ordinary shares)	30
Reserves: retained profits	10
	40

At 31 December 2004, before including the results of Arona, the balance sheets of Icod and Arona were as follows:

	Icod Ltd £000	Arona Ltd £000
Fixed assets	100	35
Investment in associate at cost	15	–
Current assets	45	45
Current liabilities	(10)	(20)
	150	60
Share capital (£1 ordinary shares)	100	30
Reserves: retained profits at start of year	30	10
retained profits for 2004	20	20
	150	60

An extract from the profit and loss accounts of Icod and Arona for 2004 showed the following:

	Icod Ltd £000	Arona Ltd £000
Operating profit	75	28
Interest payable	5	4
Profit before tax	70	24
Corporation tax	20	4
Profit after tax	50	20
Dividends	30	–
Retained profits	20	20

Notes:

• At the date of acquisition there were no material differences between the book value and fair value of any of the assets of Arona

• The accounting policy of Icod is to amortise goodwill over an estimated useful economic life of five years

solution

Goodwill on acquisition

	£000
The calculation of goodwill in Arona is as follows:	
cost of investment	15
value of associate at date of acquisition	
40 (net assets) x 25% owned	10
goodwill	5

Tutorial note

For the goodwill calculation, the value of the associate – using net assets – at the date of acquisition is reduced to the percentage of shares owned, here 25 per cent.

As Icod's accounting policy is to amortise goodwill over an estimated useful economic life of five years, £1,000 will be written off to profit and loss account in 2004, leaving £4,000 of goodwill to be shown in the balance sheet.

Where fair values are different from book values, fair values are used in the calculation of goodwill.

Profit and loss account for 2004

Icod reports its share of the associated company's profits as follows:

	£000	£000	
Operating profit		75	
Share of operating profit in associate	7		28 x 25%
Less amortisation of goodwill on acquisition	1		see goodwill, above
		6	
		81	
Interest payable		6	5 + (4 x 25%)
Profit on ordinary activities before tax		75	
Tax on profit on ordinary activities		21	20 + (4 x 25%)
Profit on ordinary activities after tax		54	
Dividends		30	
Retained profits		24	

Tutorial note

The share of the operating profit of the associate has been shown separately, less the amount for amortisation of goodwill on acquisition.

The share of the associate's interest payable, and corporation tax have been included with the amounts of the investing company.

Balance sheet as at 31 December 2004

The value of Arona, the associated company, is calculated as:

				£000
net assets of associated company x investor's share				
£60,000	x	25%	=	15
plus goodwill, unamortised, £5,000 – £1,000			=	4
				19

The balance sheet of Icod, incorporating the results of Arona, is as follows (£000):

Fixed assets	100
Investment in associate	19
Current assets	45
Current liabilities	(10)
	154
Share capital (£1 ordinary shares)	100
Reserves: retained profits 30 + 24	54
	154

Tutorial note

	£000
An alternative way to calculate the value of Arona is:	
cost of investment	15
+ share of retained profits for year 20 x 25%	5
– amortisation of goodwill on acquisition	1
	19
Retained profits for the year are:	
Icod, the investing company	20
+ share of Arona, the associate	5
– amortisation of goodwill on acquisition	1
	24

TRADE INVESTMENTS

A trade investment is where a company holds shares in another company – either for its investment potential, or so as to take an interest in a major supplier or customer. Generally a trade investment is where the investor owns below 20 per cent of the ordinary shares of another company. At this level the percentage owned is not sufficient to make the investee an associated or subsidiary company – either because the investor has limited influence, or the interest is not long-term.

The accounting treatment for trade investments is very simple. The investor records the investment as either a fixed or a current asset – depending on how long the shares are to be held: if more than twelve months from the balance sheet date, the investment is a fixed asset; if less, it is a current asset. Fixed asset trade investments are valued at either cost or valuation; if there is impairment, the fixed asset should be written down to its recoverable amount. Current asset trade investments are valued at the lower of cost and net realisable value.

Income from trade investments – usually in the form of dividends received – is credited in profit and loss account as 'income from investments', while the dividend cheque is debited to bank account.

DISCLOSURE AND CONFIDENTIALITY

the extent of disclosure

The accounting standards FRS 2, *Accounting for subsidiary undertakings*, FRS 6, *Acquisitions and Mergers*, and FRS 7, *Fair values in acquisition accounting*, cover the techniques of consolidated accounting for parent and subsidiary companies and set out the detailed disclosures required in group accounts. FRS 9, *Associates and joint ventures*, deals with accounting for associated companies and joint ventures – note that the latter are not examined by AAT.

The published accounts of limited companies – which are readily available to shareholders and interested parties – include, where appropriate, group financial statements (profit and loss account, balance sheet and cash flow statement) which disclose the consolidated financial performance and financial position of the parent company and its subsidiary companies; the accounts also incorporate the results of associated companies. Thus the user is assured that the financial statements have been prepared in accordance with the Companies Acts and accounting standards. Nevertheless, only certain information is required to be disclosed in the published accounts; some details do not need to be disclosed.

confidentiality procedures

For those involved in the preparation of the accounts, confidentiality procedures must be observed at all times:

– with the detailed financial statements of subsidiary and associated companies

– with the detailed profit and loss account of the parent company (because, where a consolidated profit and loss account is produced, the parent company is not legally obliged to produce its own profit and loss account)

– during the preparation of published accounts which incorporate the figures from subsidiary and associated companies

– for detailed information that is needed in the preparation of the accounts but is not required to be disclosed under the Companies Acts and accounting standards

Chapter Summary

- Companies adapt their accounting systems to suit the needs of the organisation.

- Consolidated accounts are designed to show the position of a group – parent company and subsidiary companies – as if it was a single entity.

- There are two methods of preparing consolidated balance sheets: the acquisition method and the merger method.

- There are three major calculations in the preparation of a consolidated balance sheet under the acquisition method:
  - goodwill, calculated as at the date of acquisition of the subsidiary
  - post-acquisition profits, calculated since the date of acquisition of the shares in the subsidiary
  - minority interests, calculated at the date of the consolidated balance sheet

- The use of fair values in acquisition accounting affects:
  - goodwill, which is calculated as the cost of the investment in the subsidiary, less the fair value of the subsidiary's assets and liabilities
  - minority interests, which is the proportion of the subsidiary, based on the fair value of the subsidiary's assets and liabilities
  - post-acquisition profits, which will be affected where the use of fair value for fixed assets leads to a different depreciation charge from that based on historic costs

- Inter-company adjustments may have to be made when preparing consolidated balance sheets for:
  - debtors, creditors and loans, which cancel out between companies within the group
  - dividends proposed, which cancel out between group companies
  - inter-company profits, eg on sale of stock, which are unrealised at the date of the consolidated balance sheet

- When preparing a consolidated profit and loss account:
  - the full profit of subsidiaries is shown, with a separate deduction for the proportion of the profit due to minority interests
  - only the dividends paid and proposed of the parent company are shown
  - inter-company transactions are deducted for inter-company sales, inter-company purchases, and inter-company unrealised profit

- The five criteria to determine whether a combination is a merger:
  1   no party is portrayed as either acquirer or acquired

2   all parties participate in establishing the management structure for the combined entity

3   the relative sizes of the combining entities are not disparate

4   the consideration received by the equity shareholders of each party comprises primarily equity shares in the combined entity

5   no equity shareholders of any of the combined entities retain any material interest in the future performance of only part of the combined entity

Note: all of the above five criteria must be satisfied for merger accounting to be used.

- An associated company is where an investor owns generally between 20 per cent and 50 per cent of the ordinary shares of another company and has a participating interest and exercises significant influence over its operating and financial policies.

- The equity method is the usual way of accounting for the results of associated companies:

  - initially the investment in the associated company is shown at cost on the investor's balance sheet

  - the investor's share of subsequent profits or losses are added to, or deducted from, the cost of the investment

  - the investor's profit and loss account includes the share of the associated companies' operating profit, interest receivable/payable and corporation tax

Key Terms		
parent company/ subsidiary company	a parent company has a subsidiary where any of the following apply: • holds a majority of voting rights in subsidiary • controls composition of board of directors • has the right to exercise dominant influence • has a participating interest	
dominant influence	influence which can be exercised to achieve the operating and financial policies desired by the holder of the influence, notwithstanding the rights or influence of any other party	
participating interest	an interest held by an undertaking in the shares of another undertaking which it holds on a long-term basis for the purpose of securing a contribution to its activities by the exercise of control or influence arising from or related to that interest	

group

a parent undertaking and its subsidiary undertakings

acquisition method

the business combination is seen as the acquisition of one company by another; defined by FRS 6 as: 'a business combination that is not a merger'

merger method

the two or more parties are treated as combining on an equal footing; defined by FRS 6 as: 'a business combination that results in the creation of a new reporting entity formed from the combining parties, in which the shareholders of the combining entities come together in a partnership for the mutual sharing of the risks and benefits of the combined entity, and in which no party to the combination in substance obtains control over any other, or is otherwise seen to be dominant, whether by virtue of the proportion of its shareholders' rights in the combined entity, the influence of its directors or otherwise'

goodwill

the cost of the investment in the subsidiary, less the fair value of the subsidiary's assets and liabilities

fair value

'the amount at which an asset or liability could be exchanged in an arm's length transaction between informed and willing parties, other than in a forced or liquidation sale' (FRS 7)

post-acquisition profits

profits earned by a subsidiary since the date of acquisition

minority interests

the owners of shares which are not owned by the parent company

associated company

'an entity (other than a subsidiary) in which another entity (the investor) has a participating interest and over whose operating and financial policies the investor exercises a significant influence' (FRS 9)

significant influence

where the investor takes part in the process of making policy decisions, such as the expansion or contraction of the business, changes in products, markets, activities, etc

equity method of accounting

method of accounting for associated companies by which the investing company values its investment so as to reflect its interest in the net assets of the associated company

Student Activities

8.1 Sidney plc acquires 60% of the ordinary shares in Kidney Ltd on the 1 January 20-3. Kidney Ltd's net profit after tax for the year to 31 December 20-3 is £10,000.

What is the minority interest in the consolidated profit and loss account for the year ended 31 December 20-3?

(a) £6,000

(b) £4,000

(c) £2,000

(d) £10,000

8.2 The Takeover plc invested £305,000 in 800,000 ordinary shares of 10 pence each in the Subsidiary Co Ltd. The Subsidiary Co Ltd's issued share capital and reserves at the date of acquisition were £100,000 in shares and £200,000 in reserves (£300,000 in total).

What is the value for goodwill arising on the acquisition?

(a) £20,000

(b) £5,000

(c) £65,000

(d) £6,500

8.3 The issued share capital of the Landmark Co Ltd consists of 400,000 ordinary shares of 25 pence each. The reserves of the company currently total £120,000. Seaside plc currently owns 300,000 ordinary shares in Landmark.

What is the total value for minority interest?

(a) £55,000

(b) £130,000

(c) £165,000

(d) £25,000

8.4 Walkingman Ltd is a subsidiary company which is 80% owned. Its profits for the year after taxation to 31 December 20-3 are £200,000. Out of this profit it has provided its shareholders with a dividend of £60,000 for the year.

What figure will appear in the consolidated profit and loss account for minority interest?

(a) £160,000

(b) £40,000

(c) £28,000

(d) £52,000

8.5 What are group profits commonly referred to as when they are earned and generated whilst under the parent company's control?

   (a)   pre-acquisition profits

   (b)   post-acquisition profits

   (c)   ex-acquisition profits

   (d)   minority interest

8.6 As at 31 December 20-3 the parent company has on its balance sheet trade debtors totaling £85,000. Its subsidiary company on the same day shows trade debtors of £40,000, of which £10,000 is an inter-group debt due from the parent company.

On the consolidated balance sheet for the group what is the correct valuation for trade debtors?

   (a)   £125,000

   (b)   £45,000

   (c)   £135,000

   (d)   £115,000

8.7 Which Financial Reporting Statement (FRS) deals with the requirements of Associated Companies?

   (a)   FRS 2

   (b)   FRS 9

   (c)   FRS 10

   (d)   FRS 15

8.8 According to FRS 2, Accounting for subsidiary undertakings, what conditions are said to apply if an undertaking is deemed to be a parent undertaking of another undertaking (ie subsidiary undertaking)?

8.9 The directors of Phantom plc have been in negotiation with the directors/ shareholders of another company, Roover plc with regard to the purchasing of 80% of the share capital from them. Phantom will pay £2,900,000 for the shares based on the valuation of the company at 30 April 20-3, this being the agreed date for acquisition.

The fair value of the fixed assets in Roover plc at 30 April 20-3 is £4,200,000. All the other assets and liabilities of the company are stated at fair value (i.e. balance sheet valuation)

Roover plc Balance sheet as at 30 April 20-3 is as follows:

	£000	£000
FIXED ASSETS AT NBV		3,500
CURRENT ASSETS		
Stocks	450	
Debtors	300	
Cash at bank	100	
	850	
Creditors: amounts falling due within one year		
Trade creditors	250	
Dividends payable	150	
Taxation	200	
	600	
NET CURRENT ASSETS		250
		3,750
Creditors: amounts falling due after more than one year		
10% Debentures		1,000
		2,750

Represented by
CAPITAL AND RESERVES

Called up share capital	800
Share premium account	200
Profit and loss account	1,750
	2,750

REQUIRED

Calculate the goodwill on consolidation that would arise on acquisition if Phantom plc purchased an 80% stakeholding in Roover plc on 30 April 20-3.

What figure for minority interest would appear in the consolidated balance of Phantom plc as at 30 April 20-3?

8.10 You have been asked to assist in the preparation of the consolidated accounts of the Ringster Group of companies. Set out below are the balance sheets of Ringer plc and its subsidiary Sterling Ltd, as at 30 April 20-3.

	Ringer plc		Sterling Ltd	
	£000	£000	£000	£000
Fixed Assets at nbv		6,000		1,600
Investment in Sterling Limited		2,000		
Current Assets				
Stocks	1,900		800	
Debtors	1,500		500	
Cash at bank	600		100	
	4,000		1,400	

Creditors amounts falling due within one year

Creditors	1,500		400	
Taxation	400		100	
Dividends	1,000			
Net Current Assets		1,100		900
		9,100		2,500

Creditors: amounts falling due after more than one year

Long-term loans		2,000		500
		7,100		2,000

Capital and reserves

Called up share capital	2,000	1,000
Share premium account	1,000	500
Profit and loss account	4,100	500
	7,100	2,000

Additional information

The share capital of both companies consists of ordinary shares of £1 denomination.

Ringer plc acquired 600,000 shares in Sterling Ltd on 30 April 20-3.

The fair value of the fixed assets of Sterling Ltd at 30 April 20-3 was £1,900,000.

REQUIRED

Prepare a consolidated Balance Sheet for Ringer plc as at 30 April 20-3. Any goodwill arising on consolidation should be shown as an intangible asset.

8.11 Crispin plc purchased 25% of the ordinary share capital in Kingston Ltd for £320,000 on 1 April 20-2. Kingston Ltd is an associate company and the directors would like to know how Kingston Ltd would be included in the results of the Crispin group. Extracts from Kingston Ltd's accounts are listed below:

Profit and loss account for the year to 31 March 20-3

	£000
Net profit before taxation	420
Taxation	120
Net profit after taxation	300

Balance Sheet as at 31 March 20-3

	£000
Fixed Assets	900
Net Current Assets	200
	1,100
10% Debentures	100
	1,000
Capital and reserves	
Called up share capital	400
Share premium account	100
Profit and loss account	500
	1,000

Additional Information

Any goodwill is deemed to have an indefinite life and should not be amortised.

REQUIRED

What figures would appear in the consolidated profit and loss account and consolidated balance sheet of the Crispin Group for the year to 31 March 20-3 to account for the results of Kingston Ltd?

8.12 The following summarised balance sheets relate to the Winston group of companies as at 30 November 20-3.

		Winston plc £000		Churchill Ltd £000
Fixed Assets at NBV		5,000		600
Investment in Churchill Limited		900		
Current Assets				
Stock	150		30	
Debtors	80		35	
Cash at bank	10	240	5	70
Current liabilities				
Creditors		(160)		(120)
		5,980		550
CAPITAL AND RESERVES				
£1 Ordinary shares		4,000		400
Profit and loss account		1,980		150
		5,980		550

Additional Information

Winston plc purchased a 90% holding in Churchill Ltd on 1 December 20-1 when Churchill's profit and loss account balance was £50,000

During the year to 30 November 20-3 Churchill purchased goods from Winston for £60,000. Winston had invoiced these goods at cost plus 33.3%. A third of these goods were still in stock at the year end.

At 30 November 20-3 the following inter group debt was still outstanding: Churchill owed Winston £10,000.

Any goodwill arising upon consolidation is to be amortised over a 10 year period.

REQUIRED

Prepare the Winston group of companies consolidated balance sheet as at 30 November 20-3.

8.13 The summary profit and loss accounts of Tom Limited, a parent company, and Ben Limited and Sarah Limited, its subsidiaries for the year-ended 31 December 20-2 are as follows:

	Tom Ltd	Ben Ltd	Sarah Ltd
	£000	£000	£000
Turnover (sales)	800	400	300
Opening stock	200	150	100
+ Purchases	600	300	200
– Closing stock	300	200	80
Cost of sales	500	250	220
Gross profit	300	150	80
Distribution costs	80	50	20
Administration expenses	100	30	20
Dividends from subsidiaries:			
Ben	40		
Sarah	18		
Net profit	178	70	40
Corporation tax	40	20	8
Profit after tax	138	50	32
Dividends	100	40	24
Retained profits	38	10	8

Additional information

- Tom Limited bought all of the shares of Ben Limited on 1 January 20-0, and 75 per cent of the shares of Sarah Limited on 1 January 20-2.

- During the year to 31 December 20-2 the following inter-company trading took place:

  - Tom sold goods costing £12,000 to Ben at a price of £20,000; Ben had sold all of these goods by the year-end for £24,000.

  - Tom sold goods costing £40,000 to Sarah at a price of £80,000; by the year-end half of these goods were unsold by Sarah.

- Tom's policy is to take credit for inter-company dividends.

- Ignore any write-off of goodwill for the period.

REQUIRED

Prepare a consolidated profit and loss account for internal use of Tom Limited and its subsidiaries for the year ended 31 December 20-2.

8.14 The managing director of Perran plc has asked you to prepare the draft consolidated profit and loss account for the group. The company has one subsidiary undertaking, Porth Limited. The profit and loss accounts for the two companies prepared for internal purposes for the year ended 31 March 2004 are as follows:

Profit and loss accounts for the year ended 31 March 2004

	Perran plc	Porth Limited
	£000	£000
Turnover (sales)	36,450	10,200
Cost of sales	18,210	5,630
Gross profit	18,240	4,570
Distribution costs	5,735	1,210
Administration expenses	4,295	450
Operating profit	8,210	2,910
Dividends received from Porth Ltd	750	–
Profit on ordinary activities before interest	8,960	2,910
Interest payable and similar charges	1,720	300
Profit on ordinary activities before taxation	7,240	2,610
Tax on profit on ordinary activities	1,950	530
Profit on ordinary activities after taxation	5,290	2,080
Dividends	2,500	1,000
Retained profit for the financial year	2,790	1,080

Additional information

- Perran plc acquired 75% of the ordinary share capital of Porth Ltd on 1 April 2003.

- During the year Porth Limited sold stock which had cost £500,000 to Perran plc for £750,000. All of the stock had been sold by Perran plc by the end of the year.

- Ignore any write-off of goodwill for the period.

REQUIRED

Draft a consolidated profit and loss account for Perran plc and its subsidiary undertaking for the year ended 31 March 2004.

International accounting standards

This chapter covers the work of the International Accounting Standards Board. It shows how International Accounting Standards (IAS) compare with the UK Accounting Standards described elsewhere in this book.

The work of the International Accounting Standards Board is neatly summarised in an extract from its Mission Statement:

'The International Accounting Standards Board is an independent, privately-funded accounting standard setter based in London, UK. . . . The Board is committed to developing, in the public interest, a single set of high quality, understandable and enforceable global accounting standards that require transparent and comparable information in general purpose financial statements. In addition, the Board co-operates with national accounting standard setters to achieve convergence in accounting standards around the world.'

NVQ PERFORMANCE CRITERIA COVERED

The performance criteria for Unit 11 state that candidates may answer exam questions using either UK Accounting Standards or International Accounting Standards. While it is not expected that many candidates will at present answer using International Standards, candidates should be aware of their existence and importance.

INTRODUCTION – THE INTERNATIONAL DIMENSION

The UK has a comprehensive set of accounting standards as do most other developed countries. These sets of standards all differ in some key aspects. This means it is difficult to compare a set of accounts drawn up under UK accounting standards and (for example) German or French accounting standards. The ability to compare financial statements is one of the key qualities that makes financial statements useful (ASB Statement of Principles).

The development of global markets and the ability to speedily transmit information and money both increase the demand for comparability. In a European context, the introduction of the euro also means people will wish to compare the financial statements of companies from different countries because they use the same currency.

Many developing countries are looking to attract foreign investment but they do not have the infrastructure to develop their own accounting standards. Investors will want to know how their investments have performed in a way they can understand, so it makes sense to use an internationally recognised set of standards.

EU Regulation – International Accounting Standards

In 2002, the EU issued a mandatory regulation that the consolidated accounts of all EU stock exchange listed companies must be prepared using International Accounting Standards from 1 January 2005, at the latest. This covers the 7,000 largest European companies. In the UK this means all companies quoted on the London Stock Exchange. Numerically they are a small proportion of all companies, but their size and importance means that they dominate the business world and what they do strongly influences the rest.

So it is probably only a matter of time before it is extended to all limited companies and replaces UK standards. Member states of the EU may choose to do this. David Tweedie is the chairman of the International Accounting Standards Board and was previously chairman of the Accounting Standards Board. He has always recognised the importance of harmonising accounting standards so many recent UK Financial Reporting Standards are largely compatible with International Standards. This means the costs of adopting International Standards for all companies within the UK is relatively low.

the US dimension

The result will probably be two principal sets of accounting standards in the world: International Accounting Standards and Financial Accounting Standards (USA standards issued by the Financial Accounting Standards Board). It is unlikely the USA will wish to abandon their standards in favour of IAS, but there is an agreement to work together to narrow differences. Recently there has been a lot of questioning of US standards because of scandals like Enron, so it is possible there could eventually be a single set of accounting standards throughout the whole world.

International Accounting Standards Board (IASB)

The International Accounting Standards Committee (IASC) was created in 1973. This sought to build a consensus and get agreement between standard setters in many different countries. It was reorganised from 1 April 2001 and renamed the International Accounting Standards Board (IASB). It is based in London and is responsible for publishing International Exposure Drafts and International Financial Reporting Standards (IFRS). It is advised by the Standards Advisory Council, which forms a link between the national standard setters and the IASB. The structure is shown on the next page.

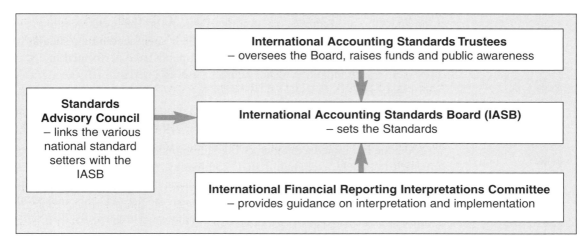

The Trustees appoint the chairman and the other members of the IASB. The Standards Advisory Council and the International Financial Reporting Interpretations Committee both act in an advisory role in the production of International Financial Reporting Standards (IFRS) – previously known as International Accounting Standards (IAS).

The process for introducing new standards is similar to that of the production of UK Accounting Standards. An international exposure draft (IED) is issued for discussion, followed by the accounting standard when all interested parties have had an opportunity to express their views.

when do international standards come into effect?

All companies covered by the EU Regulation have to use the international standards from 1 January 2005. They also have to provide prior year comparisons, so they will need to restate their accounts for 2004 using these standards. The Interpretations Committee provides guidance as to how to manage the change to the international standards. The main point is that standards should be applied as if they had always been applied.

IASB FRAMEWORK

The IASB 'Framework' is not itself an accounting standard. It sets out the concepts which underlie the preparation and presentation of financial statements. It helps the development of future International Financial Reporting Standards (IFRS) and the review of existing standards.

It deals with the objectives of financial statements, the qualitative characteristics of useful financial information and the definition, recognition and measurement of the elements of financial statements.

The framework identifies the main users of financial information as investors, employees, lenders, suppliers and other trade creditors, customers, government and the public.

the objective of financial statements

The framework states that the objective of financial statements is to provide information about the financial position, performance and changes in financial position that is useful to a wide range of users in making economic decisions.

Information on the financial position is provided by a balance sheet. The performance of an enterprise is usually presented in an income statement or profit and loss account. Changes in financial position are shown in a cash flow statement.

Financial statements do not provide all the information users may need since they only show the financial effects of what has happened in the past and exclude a lot of non-financial information. Users work with financial statements to assess the stewardship of management and make economic decisions.

underlying assumptions

When preparing financial statements, it is assumed they are prepared on an accrual basis and that they are a going concern. They must also exhibit the qualitative characteristics of useful information. These include understandability, relevance, materiality, reliability, faithful representation, substance over form, neutrality, prudence, completeness and comparability.

They must also consider any constraints on relevant and reliable information such as timeliness, benefits versus costs and any trade off between characteristics. The overall objective is to show a true and fair view of financial performance, position and changes in financial position.

financial position – balance sheet

The principal elements are assets, liabilities and equity.

An **asset** is a resource controlled by the enterprise as a result of past events from which future economic benefits are expected to flow.

A **liability** is a present obligation arising from past events which is expected to result in an outflow of resources.

Equity is the residual amount after deducting liabilities from assets. It includes funds contributed by shareholders, retained earnings, and reserves.

financial performance – the income statement

Profit is the measure for performance of an enterprise. It is the result of comparing income and expenses.

Income is an increase in economic benefits in the form of inflows or increases in assets that increase equity.

Expenses are decreases in economic benefits in the form of outflows or reductions in assets or the incurring of liabilities that decrease equity.

recognition in financial statements

Recognition is the process of including something in the balance sheet or income statement. An item should be recognised if it is probable that future economic benefits will flow to or from the enterprise and it has a cost or value that can be reliably measured. Assets and liabilities have traditionally been measured at their historic cost. Assets are recorded at the amount paid at the time of acquisition and liabilities are recorded at the amount expected to be paid.

comparison with ASB statement of principles

The IASB framework is similar to the UK Accounting Standards Board's Statement of Principles. The differences are minor. The IASB framework says that making economic decisions is the only objective whereas the Statement of Principles includes information for stewardship and making economic decisions. The IASB Framework says that assessing stewardship is only of value if it is used to make economic decisions.

We will now describe the main International Accounting Standards.

IAS 1 – PRESENTATION OF FINANCIAL STATEMENTS

The objective of this standard is to state how financial statements should be presented to ensure comparability with previous periods and other enterprises. A complete set of financial statements includes a balance sheet, income statement, a statement showing changes in equity, a cash flow statement and accounting policies and explanatory notes. Financial statements should present fairly the financial performance and position and cash flows of an enterprise.

Enterprises are encouraged to present a financial review by management to explain the main features of the financial statements.

Accounting policies are the specific principles, bases, conventions and rules adopted by an enterprise in preparing and presenting financial statements.

Managers should select and apply accounting policies so that financial statements comply with each International Accounting Standard.

the balance sheet

The balance sheet should show the following items:

- property, plant and equipment
- intangible assets
- financial assets (excluding investments, cash and receivables)
- investments accounted for using the equity method
- inventories (stock)
- cash and cash equivalents
- trade and other receivables
- trade and other payables
- tax liabilities
- provisions
- non-current interest-bearing liabilities
- minority interest
- issued capital and reserves

An enterprise should also disclose:

- the authorised, issued and fully paid number of shares for each class of share and state the nominal value per share
- a description of the nature and purpose of each reserve within owners' equity
- the amount of dividends proposed or declared after the balance sheet date but before the financial statements were authorised for issue

the income statement

The face of the income statement should present the following amounts:

- revenue
- the results of operating activities
- finance costs
- share of profits and losses of associates and joint ventures
- tax expenses
- profit or loss from ordinary activities
- extraordinary items
- minority interests
- net profit or loss for the period

IAS1 – comparison with Companies Act 1985

The presentation of the profit and loss account and balance sheet are determined in the UK by the Companies Act 1985. This defines the structure, layout and heading. IAS 1 does not prescribe a standard layout but states minimum disclosure. IAS 1 requires each enterprise to decide whether or not to present current and non current assets and liabilities as separate classifications on the face of the balance sheet. If it does not, assets and liabilities should be presented in order of liquidity.

If UK companies are to comply with international standards, it is important that there is no conflict with UK statute law. If this occurred there would need to be a change of law through Parliament which could take a long time. However, since the requirements of the Companies Act 1985 are more prescriptive, accounts prepared in the UK under the Companies Act 1985 will be acceptable under international standards.

comparison of IAS1 with FRS 3

The requirement to present a statement showing changes in equity is similar to a combined version of the statement of total recognised gains and losses and reconciliation of movements in shareholders' fund as required by FRS 3.

IAS 8 – NET PROFIT OR LOSS FOR THE PERIOD, FUNDAMENTAL ERRORS AND CHANGES IN ACCOUNTING POLICIES

Extraordinary items are income or expenses that arise from events or transactions that are distinct from ordinary activities and are not expected to recur frequently or regularly.

Ordinary activities are activities undertaken by an enterprise as part of its business.

Fundamental errors are errors discovered in the current period that are of such significance that the financial statements of one or more prior periods can no longer be considered to have been reliable at the date of their issue.

Accounting policies are the specific principles, bases, conventions, rules and practices adopted by an enterprise in preparing and presenting financial statements.

All items of income and expense recognised in a period should be included in the determination of net profit or loss for the period. The net profit or loss for the period includes the profit or loss from ordinary activities and any extraordinary items. The nature of any extraordinary items should be separately disclosed.

Any changes to accounting policies should be applied as if they had always been in use.

comparison of IAS 8 with FRS 3 and FRS 18

FRS 3 accepts the possibility of extraordinary items, but gives no examples. Its definition of operating activities is so all embracing that the likelihood of an extraordinary item is almost nil.

IAS 8 is consistent with FRS 18 in respect of the disclosure of the impact of changes in accounting policies.

IAS 35 – DISCONTINUING OPERATIONS

The objective of this standard is to provide users with information about discontinuing operations to help them estimate future cash flows.

A **discontinuing operation** is a part of an enterprise that can be separately identified and is being sold or demerged. The fact that an operation is being discontinued should be disclosed along with any pre-tax gain or loss on disposal.

comparison of IAS 35 with FRS 3

The requirements of IAS 35 are similar to the part of FRS 3 (reporting financial performance) which covers discontinuing operations.

IAS 33 – EARNINGS PER SHARE

An ordinary share is an equity instrument that is subordinate to all other classes of equity instruments. This means they will receive their money last in the event of winding up.

Basic earnings per share is calculated by dividing the net profit or loss for the period attributable to ordinary shareholders by the weighted average number of shares outstanding during the period.

The net profit or loss for the period attributable to ordinary shareholders should be the net profit or loss for the period after deducting preference dividends.

comparison of IAS 33 with FRS 14 – earnings per share

There are no significant differences between FRS 14 and IAS 33.

IAS 18 - REVENUE

The objective here is to ensure that revenue shown on the income statement is correctly stated.

Income is an increase in economic benefits as either inflows or enhancements of assets, or decreases in liabilities, that result in increases in equity. Income includes both revenue and other gains.

Revenue is income that arises in the course of ordinary activities of an enterprise and includes sales, fees, interest, dividends and royalties.

The main issue is when to recognise revenue. It is recognised when it is probable that future economic benefits will flow and the benefits can be measured reliably. Output VAT is therefore not included in revenue since economic benefits do not flow to the enterprise or result in an increase in equity.

Revenue from the sale of goods should be recognised when the significant risks and rewards of ownership have been transferred to the buyer.

comparison with SSAP 5 - accounting for VAT

There is no equivalent UK accounting standard on revenue, but IAS 18 requires the same treatment of VAT in respect of revenue and expenses as SSAP 5.

IAS 20 - ACCOUNTING FOR GOVERNMENT GRANTS AND DISCLOSURE OF GOVERNMENT ASSISTANCE

Government grants may take a number of formats and include payments to encourage an enterprise to embark on a course of action that it would not otherwise have done.

Grants of non-monetary assets should not be recognised until there is reasonable assurance that conditions attaching to them will be complied with and the grant will be received. They should be recognised as income over the periods necessary to match them with the related costs. They should not be credited to shareholders' funds. Disclosure should include accounting policies adopted, the nature and extent of government grants recognised and any unfulfilled conditions.

comparison with SSAP 4 - accounting for government grants

There are no significant differences between SSAP 4 and IAS 20.

IAS 7 – CASH FLOW STATEMENTS

Cash flow statements help users to assess the ability to generate cash and the demands on those cash flows. It also helps to evaluate changes in the net assets of an enterprise, its financial structure and its ability to adapt to changing circumstances. It also enhances comparability between enterprises because it eliminates the effects of different accounting policies for similar transactions and events.

Cash includes cash in hand and deposits on demand.

Cash flows are inflows and outflows of cash and cash equivalents.

Operating activities are the principal revenue producing activities of the enterprise and other activities that are not investing or financing activities. They include receipts from customers and payments to suppliers, employees, taxes and other expenses. It also includes the payment of taxes and dividends.

Investing activities are the acquisition and disposal of long-term assets and other investments not included in cash equivalents.

Financing activities include receipts from the issue of new shares or debentures or changes in other short or long term borrowings.

presentation of a cash flow statement

IAS 7 classifies cash flows into operating, investing and financing activities. Cash flows from operating activities indicate the cash generated to repay loans, maintain the operating capability of the enterprise, pay dividends and make new investments without external sources of finance. However the exact content of each section is open to some interpretation.

comparison of IAS 7 with FRS 1 – cash flow statements

IAS 7 is less prescriptive than FRS 1. The same item could appear in more than one category so it is important to be consistent from one year to another.

The table at the top of the next page illustrates where the sections of FRS 1 may appear in IAS 7.

FRS 1	IAS 7
Net cash inflow from operating activities	Operating activities
Dividends from joint ventures and associates	Operating, investing or financing activities
Returns on investment and servicing of finance	Operating, investing or financing activities
Taxation	Operating activities unless specifically identifiable with financing or investing activities
Capital expenditure and financial investment	Investing activities
Acquisitions and disposals	Investing activities
Equity dividends paid	Operating, investing or financing activities
Management of liquid resources	Financing activities/cash and cash equivalents
Financing	Financing activities

ASSETS AND LIABILITIES

The next group of International Accounting Standards covered in this chapter relate to the reporting of assets and liabilities.

IAS 16 – PROPERTY, PLANT AND EQUIPMENT

The objective of IAS 16 is to state the accounting treatment for property, plant and equipment.

Property, plant and equipment are tangible assets held for use in the production or supply of goods or services and expected to be used for more than one period.

Depreciation is the systematic allocation of the depreciable amount of an asset over its useful life.

Depreciable amount is the cost of an asset less any residual value.

Useful life is the length of time an asset is expected to be used.

Cost is the amount paid or the fair value given to acquire an asset.

Residual value is the net amount the enterprise expects to obtain for an asset at the end of its useful life after deducting the expected costs of disposal.

Fair value is the amount for which an asset could be exchanged between knowledgeable, willing parties in an arm's length transaction.

Carrying amount is the amount at which an asset is recognised in the balance sheet net of any accumulated depreciation or impairment losses.

An item of property, plant and equipment should be recognised as an asset when it is probable that future economic benefits will flow to the enterprise and the cost can be measured reliably. It should be recognised initially at cost, and subsequently shown at cost less accumulated depreciation or impairment losses.

If an asset is revalued, it should be carried at the revalued amount less any subsequent depreciation or impairment. It should also be revalued regularly.

On revaluation, any increase in value should be credited to equity under the heading of a revaluation surplus. Any decrease in value should be recognised as an expense.

The depreciable amount of an asset should be allocated on a systematic basis over its useful life. The depreciation method should reflect the pattern in which the asset's economic benefits are consumed. The depreciation charge for each period should be recognised as an expense.

Any gain or loss arising on disposal of an asset is the difference between estimated net disposal proceeds and its net book value. It should be recognised as income or expense in the income statement.

For each class of property, plant and equipment, the financial statements should disclose the measurement bases used, the depreciation methods used, the useful lives, and a reconciliation of the carrying amount at the beginning and end of the period showing additions and disposals.

comparison of IAS 16 with Companies Act 1985

The Companies Act 1985 requires a reconciliation of the movements on assets showing opening and closing cost and accumulated depreciation and any acquisitions and disposals during the year.

comparison of IAS 16 with FRS 15 – tangible fixed assets

There are no substantial differences between FRS 15 and IAS 16.

IAS 38 – INTANGIBLE ASSETS

IAS 38 defines the treatment of expenditure on acquiring, developing maintaining or enhancing intangible assets such as scientific or technical knowledge, licences, intellectual property, market knowledge and trademarks.

An **intangible asset** is an identifiable non-monetary asset without physical substance that is held for use in the business. This means an intangible asset must be able to be separately identified. It must be able to be rented, sold or exchanged without also disposing of the economic benefits of other assets.

Research is original and planned investigation undertaken with the prospect of gaining new scientific or technical knowledge and understanding.

Development is the application of research findings or other knowledge to a plan or design for the production of new or substantially improved materials, devices, products, systems or services.

Amortisation is the systematic allocation of the depreciable amount of an intangible asset over its useful life.

Depreciable amount is the cost of an asset less any residual value.

Useful life is the length of time an asset is expected to be used.

Cost is the amount paid or the fair value given to acquire an asset.

Residual value is the net amount the enterprise expects to obtain from an asset at the end of its useful life after deducting the expected costs of disposal.

Fair value is the amount for which an asset could be exchanged between knowledgeable, willing parties in an arm's length transaction.

An **impairment loss** is the amount by which the carrying amount of an asset exceeds its value.

The **carrying amount** is the amount at which an asset is recognised in the balance sheet net of any accumulated amortisation or impairment losses.

An intangible asset should be recognised if it is probable that economic benefits will flow to the enterprise and the cost of the asset can be measured reliably. It should be measured initially at cost.

Neither internally generated goodwill nor internally generated brands should be recognised as assets.

research

Expenditure on research should be recognised as an expense when it is incurred.

development

An intangible asset should be recognised only if an enterprise can demonstrate all of the following:

- the technical feasibility of completing the intangible asset so that it will be available for sale or use
- its intention to complete the intangible asset and use or sell it
- its ability to use or sell the intangible asset
- the way in which the intangible assets will generate probable future economic benefits
- it has the resources to complete the development and to use or sell the intangible asset
- its ability to measure the development expenditure reliably

The intangible asset should be amortised on a systematic basis over its useful life. It will be shown on the balance sheet at cost less accumulated amortisation and any accumulated impairment losses. The treatment of impairment losses is dealt with in IAS 36 Impairment of Assets. If the asset is revalued, valuations should be carried out regularly. If the revaluation results in an increase in value, it is credited to a revaluation reserve. Any reduction is treated as an expense.

For each class of intangible asset, disclosure should be made showing the useful life and amortisation rates, amortisation methods used and a reconciliation of the opening and closing balances. This should include all additions and disposals. The aggregate amount of research and development expenditure recognised as an expense during the period should also be disclosed.

comparison with SSAP13 – accounting for research and development

There is little difference between SSAP 13 and IAS 38.

IAS 36 – IMPAIRMENT OF ASSETS

The objective of this standard is to ensure that assets are included at no more than their value. It applies to assets that have been revalued under IAS 16, property, plant and equipment, but not to stocks, long term contracts, financial assets, deferred tax or employee benefits.

If the value of an asset is less than its carrying amount, the carrying amount should be reduced. This is an impairment loss and recognised as an expense in the income statement.

comparison with FRS11 – impairment of fixed assets and goodwill

There are no substantial differences between IAS 36 and FRS 11 in respect of impairment of fixed assets.

IAS 2 – INVENTORIES

Inventories include goods held for resale, work in progress and consumable materials and supplies. This does not include work in progress for construction contracts.

Net realisable value is the estimated selling price less any cost of completion and any selling costs.

Inventories should be measured at the lower of cost or net realisable value. The cost of inventories should include materials costs, labour costs and a fair share of fixed and variable overheads. The cost of inventories should be assessed on the basis of first-in, first-out (FIFO), or weighted average cost (AVCO). IAS 2 allows the use of last-in, first-out (LIFO) but this is not allowable in the UK.

comparison with SSAP 9 – stocks and long-term contracts

There are no substantial differences between IAS 2 and SSAP 9.

IAS 40 – INVESTMENT PROPERTY

Investment property is property held by a business to earn rent or for capital appreciation but not being used in the normal course of the business. It allows the business to choose to carry the property at cost or fair value. All changes (up and down) in fair value are recognised in the income statement. This is different to the normal treatment of crediting upward revaluations to a revaluation reserve.

comparison with SSAP 19 – accounting for investment properties

SSAP 19 requires that investment properties are carried at open market value, with revaluations shown in a property revaluation reserve and highlighted in the statement of total recognised gains and losses.

IAS 37 – PROVISIONS, CONTINGENT LIABILITIES AND CONTINGENT ASSETS

A **provision** is a liability where there is uncertainty about the timing or amount of the future expenditure required in settlement.

A **liability** is a present obligation arising from past events, which will result in an outflow of economic benefits.

An **obligating event** is an event that creates a legal obligation that results in an enterprise having to meet that obligation.

A **contingent liability** is a possible obligation that arises from past events and whose existence will be confirmed only by the occurrence or non-occurrence of one or more uncertain future events. It could also be a present obligation arising from past events not recognised because it is probable there will not be an outflow of resources or that the amount cannot be measured reliably.

A **contingent asset** is a possible asset that arises from past events and whose existence will be confirmed only by the occurrence or non-occurrence of one or more uncertain events not wholly within the control of the enterprise.

All provisions are contingent because they are uncertain in timing or amount, but the word 'contingent' is used for liabilities and assets that are not recognised because their existence will be confirmed only by the occurrence or non-occurrence of one or more uncertain future events not wholly within the control of the enterprise.

A provision should only be recognised when there is a present obligation as a result of past events, and it is probable that it will result in an outflow of resources and a reliable estimate can be made of the amount.

A contingent liability should not be recognised, but should be disclosed. A contingent asset should not be recognised, but disclosed where it is probable the benefits will be received.

comparison with FRS 12 – provisions, contingent liabilities and contingent assets

There are no substantial differences between FRS 12 and IAS 37.

IAS 17 – LEASES

The objective of this standard is to state the treatment of finance and operating leases.

A **lease** is an agreement whereby the lessee has the right to use an asset for an agreed period of time in return for payment.

A **finance lease** is a lease that transfers substantially all the risks and rewards associated with ownership of an asset. They should be shown in the balance sheet as an asset and a liability at an amount that represents their fair value or the present value of the lease payments. Lease payments should be apportioned between a finance charge (expense) and the reduction of the liability. There will be also be a depreciation charge.

An **operating lease** is any other lease. Payments made under an operating lease are treated as an expense.

comparison with SSAP 21 – accounting for leases and hire purchase contracts

There are no substantial differences between SSAP 21 and IAS 17.

CONSOLIDATED ACCOUNTS

The next group of International Accounting Standards covered in this chapter deals with the consolidation of accounts.

IAS 22 – BUSINESS COMBINATIONS AND IAS 27 – CONSOLIDATED FINANCIAL STATEMENTS AND ACCOUNTING FOR SUBSIDIARIES

The objective of these standards is to state the accounting treatment for business combinations. They cover the acquisition of one enterprise by another and the rare situation of the uniting of interests where an acquirer cannot be identified.

A **business combination** is the joining of separate enterprises into one economic entity when one enterprise obtains control over the net assets and operations of another or unites with it.

A **subsidiary** is an enterprise that is controlled by another company known as the parent.

A **parent** is an enterprise that has one or more subsidiaries.

A **group** is a parent and all its subsidiaries.

Consolidated financial statements are the financial statements of a group presented as a single enterprise.

Control is the power to govern the financial and operating policies of an enterprise to obtain benefits from its activities

An **acquisition** is where one enterprise obtains control over the net assets and operations of another enterprise in exchange for a transfer of assets or the incurring of a liability.

A **uniting of interests** is a business combination where the shareholders of both enterprises combine control over their net assets and operations to achieve a mutual sharing of the risks and benefits attaching to the combined enterprise.

Minority interest is that part of the profits and net assets of a subsidiary not owned by the parent.

Fair value is the amount for which an asset could be exchanged between knowledgeable, willing parties in an arm's length transaction.

Monetary assets are money held and assets to be received in fixed amounts of money.

Goodwill is the difference between the cost of the acquisition and the acquirer's share of the fair value of the identifiable assets and liabilities.

Negative goodwill arises if the acquirer's share of the fair value of the identifiable assets and liabilities is greater than the cost of the acquisition.

A parent company should present consolidated financial statements. Intra-group balances and intra-group transactions and any unrealised profits should be eliminated in full. Consolidated financial statements should be prepared using uniform accounting policies. Minority interests should be presented in the consolidated balance sheet separately from liabilities and shareholders' equity. Minority interests in the consolidated income statement should also be shown separately.

In virtually all business combinations, one enterprise acquires control over another. Control is assumed when more than half of the voting rights are obtained, unless it can be shown otherwise. Control may exist even if less than half the voting rights are acquired. Other factors can be used to help identify an acquisition. These include for example if the fair value of one enterprise is significantly greater than that of the other, or if the combination involves an exchange of shares for cash, or if the management of one enterprise dominates the selection of the management of the combined enterprise.

Acquisitions should be accounted for by using the purchase method of accounting. This is similar to the purchase of other assets and uses cost as the basis for recording the acquisition. The acquirer should include the results of operations of the subsidiary in the income statement and recognise the assets and liabilities of the subsidiary and any goodwill arising on acquisition in the balance sheet. The cost of an acquisition should be the amount of cash paid or the fair value of any other purchase consideration. The identifiable assets and liabilities should be recognised at their cost or fair value. Any minority interest should be stated at the minority's proportion of the fair value of the identifiable assets and liabilities.

Goodwill should be shown at cost less accumulated amortisation or impairment losses. It should be amortised on a systematic basis over its useful life, which should not normally exceed twenty years. The amortisation should be treated as an expense. IAS 36 Impairment of Assets should be used to determine if goodwill has been impaired. Negative goodwill should be shown as a deduction from the assets of the reporting enterprise in the balance sheet classification for goodwill.

In exceptional circumstances, acquisition accounting may not be practical because it is difficult to identify an acquirer. The shareholders of each enterprise may join in an equal arrangement to share control. The management of both enterprises may participate in the management of the combined enterprise and the shareholders of both enterprises share in the risks and benefits of the combined enterprise. This is not possible without a mainly equal exchange of voting shares between the two enterprises. This uniting of interests should be accounted for using the pooling of interest method. The combined financial statements of both enterprises should assume they had been combined from the beginning of the earliest period presented. Any difference between the amounts recorded as share capital issued plus any other consideration and the amount recorded for the share capital acquired should be adjusted against equity.

comparison with FRS 2, FRS 6 and FRS 7 and FRS 10

FRS 6 and IAS 22 have similar definitions in regard to uniting of interests (merger accounting).

FRS 7 and IAS 22 have the same requirement for assets and liabilities to be valued at their fair value.

FRS 10 and IAS 22 have similar rules regarding the treatment of goodwill in that it should be amortised over a maximum of twenty years.

FRS 2 and IAS 27 have similar requirements for consolidating accounts.

IAS 28 – ACCOUNTING FOR INVESTMENTS IN ASSOCIATES

An associate is an enterprise where an investor has significant influence but it is not a subsidiary. Influence may be indicated by board representation or participation in decision making. Significant influence is the power to participate in the financial and operating policy decisions but not to have control. If an investor holds 20% or more of the voting power, it is presumed there is significant influence.

Associates should be accounted for in consolidated financial statements using the equity method. This is where the investment is recorded at cost and adjusted thereafter for post acquisition changes in the investor's share of the net assets. The income statement reflects the investor's share of the profit. Any difference between the cost of the acquisition and the investor's share of the fair value of the net identifiable assets is accounted for as goodwill as per IAS 22. The associate's financial statements should be adjusted where its accounting policies are different to those of the investor. Investments in associates are classified as long term assets and disclosed separately in the balance sheet.

If an investor holds less than 20% of the voting power, it is presumed there is not significant influence and it is treated as an investment. This is accounted for using the cost method where the investment is recorded at cost and the income statement only includes income received by way of dividends after the date of acquisition.

comparison with FRS 9 – associates and joint ventures

The requirements of FRS 9 and IAS 28 are broadly similar. Joint ventures are not assessable at Level 4 of NVQ Accounting.

OTHER STANDARDS

The final group of International Accounting Standards covered in this chapter relate to a variety of issues.

IAS 10 – EVENTS AFTER THE BALANCE SHEET DATE

Events after the balance sheet are those events that occur between the balance sheet date and the date when the financial statements are issued.

An **adjusting event** relates to conditions that existed at the balance sheet date. The accounts should be changed to reflect adjusting events.

A **non-adjusting event** relates to conditions that arose after the balance sheet date. Significant non-adjusting events should be disclosed in the accounts

comparison with SSAP 17 – post balance sheet events

There are no significant differences between IAS 10 and SSAP 17.

IAS 12 – INCOME TAXES

This standard sets out the treatment of current and deferred taxation.

Current taxation is the amount of income taxes payable in respect of the taxable profit for the year. Unpaid current taxation for the current period should be recognised as a liability.

Deferred tax liabilities are amounts payable in future periods in respect of taxable temporary differences. Temporary differences arise when the taxation due for a particular period is deferred because of the impact of capital allowances or other factors. A deferred tax liability should be recognised for all taxable temporary differences.

comparison with FRS 16 – current tax

There are no substantial differences between FRS 16 and IAS 12 in respect of current taxation.

comparison with FRS 19 – deferred tax

FRS 19 also requires full provision for all timing (temporary) differences so there is no substantial difference between FRS 19 and IAS 12 in respect of deferred taxation.

IAS 14 – SEGMENT REPORTING

Many enterprises provide a range of products or services in many parts of the world. These are called segments. Each may have different levels of profitability, growth or risk. Information about these segments is relevant to assessing the performance of an enterprise, but may not be available from the aggregated data in the financial statements. IAS 14 states that the following information should be disclosed for each segment:

*   revenue
*   results (net profit or loss)
*   assets
*   liabilities
*   capital expenditure
*   depreciation/amortisation

comparison with SSAP 25

The two are broadly similar except that SSAP 25 requires disclosure of turnover, operating profit and net assets for each segment.

IAS 21 – THE EFFECTS OF CHANGES IN FOREIGN EXCHANGE RATES

The principal issue in accounting for foreign exchange transactions and operations is to decide which exchange rate to use and how to show the financial effect of changes in exchange rates in the financial statements.

comparison with SSAP 20 – foreign currency translation

The basic definitions and explanation of the issues are the same in IAS 21 and SSAP 20.

IAS 24 – RELATED PARTY DISCLOSURES

Parties are **related** if one party has the ability to control the other party or exercise significant influence over the other party in making financial or operating decisions.

A **related party transaction** is a transfer of resources or obligations regardless of whether a price is charged.

Related party relationships where control exists should be disclosed irrespective of whether there have been transactions between the related parties. If there have been transactions between the related parties, they should be disclosed.

comparison with FRS 8

There are no significant differences between IAS 24 and FRS 8.

IAS 26 – ACCOUNTING AND REPORTING BY RETIREMENT BENEFIT PLANS

A defined contribution plan is where the benefits are determined by the amount paid into a fund and related investment returns.

A defined benefit plan is where benefits paid are based on employees' earnings and length of service.

Many retirement benefit plans have a separate fund into which contributions are paid and out of which benefits are paid.

comparison with FRS 17 – retirement benefits

Your studies require you to know the above definitions; there is no difference between FRS 17 and IAS 26.

Case Study

INTERBREW SA: FINANCIAL STATEMENTS, USING INTERNATIONAL ACCOUNTING STANDARDS

The following figures are taken from Interbrew's annual report for the year ending 31 December 2002. This brewing company is based in Belgium and reports in euros using international accounting standards. The financial statements have been modified for ease of illustration. Interbrew can be visited on www.interbrew.com

Consolidated income statement
for the year ended 31 December 2002

	euros (millions)
Net turnover	6,992
Cost of sales	(3,418)
Gross Profit	3,574
Distribution expenses	(758)
Sales and marketing expenses	(1,317)
Administrative expenses	(593)
Other operating expenses	(70)
Profit from operations, pre restructuring charges	836
Restructuring charges	(108)
Profit from operations	728
Net financing costs	(134)
Income from associates	71
Profit before tax	665
Income tax expense	(162)
Profit after tax	503
Minority interests	(36)
Net profit from ordinary activities	467
Extraordinary items	–
Net Profit	467

	euros
Basic earnings per share	1.08

Consolidated statement of recognised gains and losses
for the year ended 31 December 2002

	euros (millions)
Foreign exchange translation	(431)
Cash flow hedges	(1)
Net profit for the year	467
Total recognised gains and losses	35

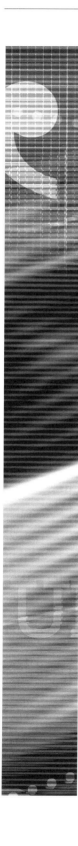

Consolidated balance sheet as at 31 December 2002

ASSETS	euros (millions)
Non current assets	
Property, plant and equipment	3,512
Goodwill	3,658
Intangible assets, other than goodwill	133
Interest bearing loans granted	10
Investments in associates	625
Investment securities	277
Deferred tax assets	199
Employee benefits	32
Long-term receivables	345
	8,791
Current assets	
Interest bearing loans granted	1
Investment securities	31
Inventories	444
Income tax receivable	92
Trade and other receivables	1,572
Cash and cash equivalents	215
	2,355
Total assets	11,146

EQUITY AND LIABILITIES	
Capital and reserves	
Issued capital	333
Share premium	3,212
Reserves	108
Retained earnings	1,041
	4,694
Minority interest	463
Non current liabilities	
Interest bearing loans and borrowings	1,433
Employee benefits	329
Trade and other payables	45
Provisions other than pensions	252
Deferred tax liabilities	242
	2,301
Current liabilities	
Bank overdrafts	122
Interest bearing loans and borrowings	1,320
Income tax payable	224
Trade and other payables	1,940
Provisions	82
	3,688
Total liabilities	11,146

Consolidated cash flow statement for the year ended 31 December 2002

	euros (millions)
Operating activities	
Net profit from ordinary activities	467
Depreciation and amortisation	641
Impairment losses (other than goodwill)	27
Net interest income and expense	116
Foreign exchange losses	15
Net investment income and expense	(1)
Gain on disposal of assets	(15)
Income tax expense	162
Income from associates	(71)
Minority interest	36
Operating profit before changes in working capital and provisions	1,377
Increase in trade receivables	88
Increase in inventories	(30)
Increase in trade payables	(243)
Decrease in provisions	33
Cash generated from operations	1,225
Interest paid	(145)
Interest received	31
Dividends received	25
Income tax paid	(91)
Cash flow from operating activities	1,045
Investing activities	
Proceeds from sale of assets	256
Proceeds from sale of subsidiary	1,846
Acquisition of subsidiary	(2,300)
Acquisition of assets	(788)
Net payment/repayment of loans	20
Cash flow from investing activities	(966)
Financing activities	
Proceeds from issue of share capital	3
Proceeds from other borrowings	5,680
Repayment of borrowings	(5,864)
Payment of finance lease liabilities	(7)
Dividends paid	(142)
Cash flow arising from financing activities	(330)
Net decrease in cash and cash equivalents	**(251)**
Cash and cash equivalents at beginning of year	344
Cash and cash equivalents at end of year	**93**

Chapter Summary

- International Accounting Standards are issued by the International Accounting Standards Board.

- Existing standards from the former International Accounting Standards Committee are called International Accounting Standards (IAS); new standards developed by the Board are designated as International Financial Reporting Standards (IFRS).

- The IASB 'Framework' sets out the concepts which underlie the preparation and presentation of financial statements.

- Users of accounts will be more able to compare accounts across national boundaries when the accounts are prepared using the same rules.

- A mandatory European Union regulation requires that all EU listed companies are required, from 1 January 2005 at the latest, to prepare their consolidated accounts in accordance with International Accounting Standards.

- All quoted companies in the UK must therefore use International Financial Reporting Standards from 1 January 2005.

- There is no requirement yet to extend this to all companies in the UK, but this will probably follow in time.

- Many of the IAS standards are similar to existing UK standards.

Key Terms

IAS	International Accounting Standard
IASC	International Accounting Standards Committee (now defunct) is the body that issued International Accounting Standards until 2001
IASB	International Accounting Standards Board is the body which is now responsible for issuing the Standards
IFRS	International Financial Reporting Standards are issued by the International Accounting Standards Board – consequently all new standards will now be IFRS's
SAC	The Standards Advisory Council forms a link between the national standard setters and the IASB.
IFRIC	International Financial Reporting Interpretations Committee (IFRIC is the body that interprets international standards).

ANSWERS TO STUDENT ACTIVITIES

CHAPTER 1: PURPOSE OF FINANCIAL STATEMENTS

1.1 (a) **1.2** (c)

1.3 Students should list any three of the following:

Existing and potential investors who are interested in:
- Profit
- Liquidity and cash flow
- Annual sales turnover

Lenders who are interested in:
- Profit
- Loan capital and risk
- Asset and balance sheet value
- Liquidity and cash flow

Suppliers and creditors who are interested in
- Cash flow and liquidity
- The value of assets and liabilities

Employees who are interested in
- Profit
- Liquidity and cash flow

Customers who are interested in
- Profit
- The value of assets and liabilities
- Liquidity and cash flow

The government which is interested in
- Profit
- Annual sales turnover

The general public which is interested in:
- Profit
- Liquidity and cash flow

1.4 Stewardship relates to the entity management and the ways in which it is accountable for the safekeeping of the organisation's resources and their proper efficient and profitable use.
Economic decisions are the management's strategy with regard to the business entity covering investment or potential investment decisions on a day-to-day basis.

1.5 (a) Going concern
This assumes that the business will continue to trade for the foreseeable future and there is no intention to downscale or sell off key operations of the business.

(b) Prudence
This concept stipulates that a business should not include in the accounts revenues that have not been realised, and that costs that are likely to be incurred should be included and charged to the profit and loss account.

(c) Business entity

All financial statements should report and record on its business activities only. Therefore personal transactions are not part of this reporting and recording process and should be kept separate.

(d) Matching/accruals

This means that revenues and costs are matched to the accounting period to which they relate. Thus revenues and costs incurred are shown in the profit and loss account rather than the amounts received and paid (which is referred to as cash accounting).

1.6 (a) Business entity concept

The private transactions of the managing director are his own affairs and nothing to with the business. Therefore the payment of his daughters' school fees should be charged to him and should not be an expense of the company.

(b) Materiality Concept

A box of pencils in the stationery cupboard is not a material amount and will not have any real significance in the preparation of the annual accounts. Therefore it should not be treated as part of closing stock but written off as an expense to profit and loss account.

(c) Going concern concept.

If HH Limited is not likely to continue in the near future then different accounting rules would need to be adopted to reflect this; for example, fixed assets would need to be recorded at their net realisable value rather than at their net book values. Such a 'gone concern' approach is in contrast to the going concern concept, which presumes that an entity will continue in the foreseeable future.

(d) Matching/Accruals concept

Here expenses and revenues must be matched so that they relate to the same goods and time period. Rent clearly overlaps two accounting periods, the year ending 20-2 and 20-3, part being paid in advance (£1,000) which is carried forward as an asset on the balance sheet.

(e) Prudence concept.

If the debt is irrecoverable then the £500 should be written off as a bad debt and charged against this year's profit. If there is any doubt to the liquidation question then the £500 should appear as part of the provision for bad debts.

(f) Consistency concept

The stock should continue to be valued on a FIFO basis unless there are any genuine reasons for adopting another method of valuation, which will give a more true and fair view of the company's accounts. The manipulation of tax payments does not fall within this category.

1.7 (a) There is a conflict here between the accruals or matching concept and the prudence concept. The accruals concept states that costs should be matched against revenue which they generate. Thus it might be argued that, since half the revenue expected to result from the advertising campaign will be achieved in 20-6, it might be appropriate to defer half the costs of the advertising campaign until 20-6. However, the concept of prudence states that profits (and revenue) should not be anticipated but that provision should be made for all known losses (and expenses). When prudence and accruals conflict, prudence prevails – subject to the overall objective of reliability for financial statements. The most likely accounting treatment is that all the cost of the advertising campaign should be written off as an expense in the 20-5 accounts.

(b) The managing director has taken stock for his own use; the cost of the stock should be charged to him, and the value of closing stock reduced accordingly.

(c) Under the business entity concept the company is separate from Jonathan Brown. As the loan was made to the company it should be disclosed in the financial statements.

1.8 **Task 1**

(a) The objective of financial statements is to 'provide information about the financial position, performance and financial adaptability of an enterprise that is useful to a wide range of users for assessing the stewardship of management and for making economic decisions'.

(b) In a limited company, financial statements provide information to shareholders to enable them to assess the performance of management, for example in generating profits for the period or in improving the financial position of the company. It may also assist them in deciding whether to continue holding their shares in the company, to acquire more shares or to dispose of all or part of their holding.

Task 2

(a) The elements of financial statements are:

- assets
- liabilities
- ownership interest
- income
- expenditure
- gains
- losses
- contributions from owners
- distributions to owners

(b) The accounting equation that underlies the balance sheet relates to the following elements:

Assets – Liabilities = Ownership interest

The change in ownership interest in the period is equal to the capital contributed from owners plus gains in the form of revenue and losses in the form of expenses. Revenue less expenses equals profit. Thus the profit and loss account explains how the change in ownership interest arising from sources other than contributions from owners came about (note that some gains or losses are reported only in the statement of total recognised gains and losses and not in the profit and loss account).

1.9 (a) *Assets* are rights or other access to future economic benefits controlled by an entity as a result of past transactions or events.

Liabilities are obligations of an entity to transfer economic benefits as a result of past transactions or events.

Ownership interest is the residual amount found by deducting all of the entity's liabilities from all of the entity's assets.

(b) In the ownership interest section of the balance sheet of a limited company capital balances would appear. These can include amounts of share capital paid in, plus reserves which are owed to shareholders (such as the balance of profit and loss account).

1.10   NOTES FOR THE DIRECTORS

(a)   The elements in a balance sheet and the balances in Machier Ltd which fall under those elements are as follows:

Elements	*Balances*
Assets	Fixed assets
	Current assets
Liabilities	Current liabilities
	Long-term liabilities
Ownership interest	Capital and reserves

(b)   The accounting equation is as follows:
      (figures in £000)

Assets	–	Liabilities	= Ownership interest
(£4,282 + £975)	–	(£749 + £2,800)	= £1,708
£5,257	–	£3,549	= £1,708

CHAPTER 2: INTRODUCTION TO LIMITED COMPANY ACCOUNTS

2.1   (b)

2.2   (c)

2.3   (a)

2.4   Preference shares have a fixed rate of return and this is the maximum dividend that any such shareholder can receive on their investment.

Preference shares rank above ordinary shares in the case of a winding up or liquidation order. This means that if there are any surplus funds left after paying all the creditors, preference shareholders will receive their money before the ordinary shareholder.

Ordinary shares are often referred to as equity shares as they are the primary risk takers who are rewarded with any surplus (equity) funds. The dividend payable tends to vary from year to year based upon the profits generated, the higher the net profit then the more likelihood of an increased dividend.

Ordinary shareholders are the only type of share normally to receive a vote at an AGM. Therefore as owners they can dictate and vote on company policy and the election of the directors.

2.5   – any four from:

- Directors salaries
- Debenture interest payable
- Corporation tax payable
- Dividends paid and proposed.
- Retained profit for the year

2.6 **Profit and Loss Account for Gretton plc for the Year to 31 March 20-2**

	£000	£000
Sales turnover		2,350
COST OF SALES		
Opening stock	140	
Purchases	960	
	1,100	
Closing stock	180	
Cost of Sales		920
GROSS PROFIT		1,430
Less Expenses:		
Administrative expenses	210	
Distribution costs	420	
Rent, rates and insurance	487	
Depreciation – plant and machinery	95	
		1,212
NET PROFIT BEFORE TAXATION		218
Taxation		32
NET PROFIT AFTER TAXATION		186
Dividends – ordinary dividend		60
RETAINED PROFIT FOR THE YEAR		126

Balance Sheet of Gretton plc as at 31 March 20-2

FIXED ASSETS	Cost	Dep'n	Net
	£000	£000	£000
Plant and machinery	950	315	635
CURRENT ASSETS			
Stock		180	
Debtors		670	
Cash at bank		15	
		865	
CURRENT LIABILITIES			
Creditors	260		
Corporation tax	32		
Dividends proposed	60		
		(352)	
NET CURRENT ASSETS			513
			1,148
Represented by:			
CAPITAL AND RESERVES			
Ordinary shares			600
Share premium account			240
Profit and loss account (182 + 126)			308
			1,148

Working notes:
Journal

		Dr £000	Cr £000
1	Stock – Balance Sheet	180	
	Stock – Trading Account		180
2	Taxation – Profit and Loss Account	32	
	Corporation Tax Payable		32
3.	Ordinary dividend Profit and Loss Account	60	
	Dividends proposed		60
4	Depreciation (Plant) – Profit and Loss Account	95	
	Accum Depreciation – Plant		95

2.7 **Profit and Loss Account of Hickson plc for the Year to 30 September 20-2**

	£	£
Sales turnover		280,000
COST OF SALES		
Opening stock	25,000	
Purchases	125,000	
	150,000	
Closing stock	49,000	
Cost of Sales		101,000
GROSS PROFIT		179,000
Less Expenses:		
Wages and salaries	40,000	
Directors fees	29,000	
Printing, telephone & stationery	7,000	
General expenses	6,000	
Rent, rates and insurance	11,000	
Loan interest payable	4,000	
Depreciation:		
– Equipment	14,000	
– Fixtures and fittings	6,000	
– Motor vehicles	12,500	
		129,500
NET PROFIT BEFORE TAXATION		49,500
Taxation		8,000
NET PROFIT AFTER TAXATION		41,500
Dividends		
– Preference dividend	3,000	
– Ordinary dividend	6,400	
		9,400
RETAINED PROFIT FOR THE YEAR		32,100

Balance Sheet of Hickson plc as at 30 September 20-2

FIXED ASSETS	Cost	Dep'n	Net
	£	£	£
Equipment	140,000	34,000	106,000
Fixtures and fittings	40,000	16,000	24,000
Motor vehicles	80,000	42,500	37,500
	260,000	92,500	167,500
CURRENT ASSETS			
Stock		49,000	
Debtors		26,000	
Cash at bank		5,000	
Cash In hand		1,000	
		81,000	
CURRENT LIABILITIES			
Creditors	14,000		
Corporation tax	8,000		
Dividends proposed	9,400		
Accruals	4,000		
		35,400	
NET CURRENT ASSETS			45,600
			213,100
LONG TERM LIABILITIES			
8% Debenture loan			50,000
			163,100
Represented by:			
CAPITAL AND RESERVES			
Ordinary shares			80,000
Preference shares			30,000
Share premium account			6,000
Profit and loss account (15,000 + 32,100)			47,100
			163,100

Working notes
Journal

		Dr	Cr
		£	£
1	Stock – Balance Sheet	49,000	
	Stock – Trading Account		49,000
2.	Interest payable	4,000	
	Accruals		4,000
3	Depreciation – Equipment P/L A/C	14,000	
	Accum Depreciation – Equip		14,000
	Depreciation – Fixtures P/L A/C	6,000	
	Accum Depreciation – Fixtures		6,000
	Depreciation – Motor Vehicles P/L A/C	12,500	
	Accum Depreciation – Vehicles		12,500
4	Preference Dividend –P/L A/C	3,000	
	Ordinary Dividend – P/L A/C	6,400	
	Dividends proposed		9,400

| 5 | Taxation – Profit and Loss Account | 8,000 | |
| | Corporation Tax Payable | | 8,000 |

2.8 **Profit and loss account of Grayson plc for the Year to 31 December 20-2**

	£	£
Sales turnover		2,640,300
COST OF SALES		
Opening stock	318,500	
Purchases	2,089,600	
	2,408,100	
Closing stock	340,600	
Cost of sales		2,067,500
GROSS PROFIT		572,800
Less Expenses:		
Administration expenses (120,180 – 12,200)	107,980	
Selling & distribution exp (116, 320 + 21,300)	137,620	
Wages and salaries	112,800	
Directors' salaries	87,200	
Loan stock interest payable (10,000 + 10,000)	20,000	
Postage and telephone	7,900	
Bad debts	8,900	
Motor expenses	12,280	
Bank charges and loan interest	7,720	
Increase in provision for bad debts	2,400	
		504,800
NET PROFIT BEFORE TAXATION		68,000
Taxation		45,000
NET PROFIT AFTER TAXATION		23,000
Dividends		60,000
RETAINED LOSS FOR THE YEAR		(37,000)

Balance Sheet of Grayson PLC as at 31 December 20-2

FIXED ASSETS	Cost	Dep'n	Net
	£	£	£
Office equipment			110,060
Motor vehicles			235,000
			345,060
CURRENT ASSETS			
Stock		340,600	
Debtors	415,800		
Less Provision for bad debts	12,474		
		403,326	
Prepayments		12,200	
Cash at bank		20,640	
		776,766	

CURRENT LIABILITIES

Creditors	428,250		
Corporation tax	45,000		
Dividends proposed	60,000		
Accruals (21,300 + 10,000)	31,300		
		564,550	
NET CURRENT ASSETS			212,216
			557,276
LONG TERM LIABILITIES			
10% Loan stock	200,000		
Bank loan account	50,000		
			250,000
			307,276
Represented by:			
CAPITAL AND RESERVES			
Ordinary shares			200,000
Reserves			
Profit and loss account (144,276 − 37,000)			107,276
			307,276

Working notes
Journal

		Dr £	Cr £
1	Interest payable − Profit & Loss	10,000	
	Accruals − Balance Sheet		10,000
2	Payments in advance − Balance Sheet	12,200	
	Administration expenses − Profit & Loss		12,200
	Selling and Distribution expenses − Profit & Loss	21,300	
	Accruals − Balance Sheet		21,300
3	Increase in provision Bad debts − Profit & Loss	2,400	
	Provision for Bad debts − Balance Sheet		2,400
4	Stock − Balance Sheet	340,600	
	Stock − Profit and Loss Account		340,600
5	Taxation − Profit and Loss Account	45,000	
	Corporation Tax Payable − Balance Sheet		45,000
6	Dividends − Profit and Loss Account	60,000	
	Dividends proposed − Balance Sheet		60,000

Increase in provision for bad debts − working

	£
New provision (3% x £415,800)	12,474
Less already provided	10,074
Net increase in provision	2,400

CHAPTER 3: PUBLISHED ACCOUNTS OF LIMITED COMPANIES

3.1   (d)

3.2   (c)

3.3   (b)

3.4   (a)

3.5   A statement of Total Recognised Gains and Losses as prescribed by FRS3 Reporting Financial Performance, acknowledges the fact that not all gains and losses pass through the profit and loss account.

Realised gains and losses are collected in the profit and loss account and these transactions are used to calculate net profit. However, unrealised gains and losses are not accountable here, and these tend to pass exclusively through the balance sheet. Eg the revaluation of tangible fixed assets will be adjusted against the value of tangible fixed assets and a special reserve, that of a revaluation reserve. Any movements in valuation will then be recorded between these two accounts.

3.6   Items that are included in a Directors Report include any four of the following:
- Directors names and their shareholdings
- Dividends proposed
- A review of the previous 12 months activities
- Future developments
- Significant differences between the book value and the market value of Land and Buildings
- Political and Charitable contributions
- Policy on the employment of disabled people
- Health and safety at work of employees
- Action taken on employee involvement and consultation
- Policy on the payment of creditors

3.7   **Task 1**

Journal

	Debit £000	Credit £000
Stock – Balance Sheet	180	
Stock – Trading Account		180
Taxation – Profit & Loss Account	65	
Creditors – CT payable – Balance Sheet		65
Dividends – Profit & Loss Account	280	
Creditors – Dividends payable – Balance Sheet		280

Task 2

Proudlock plc: Profit and Loss Account for the year ended 31 March 20-2

	£000
Turnover – continuing operations	2,295
Cost of Sales [1]	1,180
GROSS PROFIT	1,115
Distribution costs	500

Administrative expenses	240	
OPERATING PROFIT	375	
Income from fixed asset investments	75	
PROFIT ON ORDINARY ACTIVITIES BEFORE TAXATION	450	
Tax on profit on ordinary activities	65	
PROFIT ON ORDINARY ACTIVITIES AFTER TAXATION	385	
Dividends	280	
RETAINED PROFIT FOR THE FINANCIAL YEAR	105	

Proudlock plc:
Balance Sheet as at 31 March 20-2

	£000	£000
FIXED ASSETS		
Tangible assets (1,000–500)		500
Investments		600
		1,100
CURRENT ASSETS		
Stocks	180	
Debtors	600	
Cash at bank and in hand	75	
	855	
CREDITORS:Amounts falling due within one year **2**	740	
NET CURRENT ASSETS		115
		1,215
CAPITAL AND RESERVES		
Issued share capital		700
Share premium account		200
Profit and loss account (210 + 105)		315
		1,215

Working notes (see profit and loss account and balance sheet)

		£
1	Cost of sales	
	Opening stock	160
	Purchases	1,200
		1,360
	Closing stock	180
		1,180

2	Creditors: Amounts falling due within one Year	
	Trade creditors	300
	Accruals	15
	Other creditors	80
	Corporation tax payable	65
	Dividends payable	280
		740

3.8   **Task 1**

Journal	Debit £000	Credit £000
Stock – Balance Sheet – Profit and Loss Account	250	
Stock – Trading Account		250
Depreciation – Buildings (210–110 x 5%) – Profit and Loss Account	5	
Accum – Dep'n Buildings – Balance Sheet		5
Depreciation – Plant (125 x 20%)	25	
Accum – Dep'n Plant – Balance Sheet		25
Taxation – Profit & Loss Account	135	
Creditors – Cpn. Tax payable – Balance Sheet		135
Dividends – Profit & Loss Account	300	
Creditors – Dividends payable – Balance Sheet		300

Task 2

Broadfoot plc: Profit and Loss Account for the year ended 31 March 20-2

	£000
Turnover – continuing operations	1,300
Cost of Sales[1]	388
GROSS PROFIT	912
Distribution costs (240 + 6)	246
Administrative expenses (185 + 6)	191
PROFIT ON ORDINARY ACTIVITIES BEFORE TAXATION	475
Tax on profit on ordinary activities	135
PROFIT ON ORDINARY ACTIVITIES AFTER TAXATION	340
Dividends	300
RETAINED PROFIT FOR THE FINANCIAL YEAR	40

Broadfoot plc: Balance Sheet as at 31 March 20-2

	£000	£000
FIXED ASSETS		
Tangible Assets[3]		182
CURRENT ASSETS		
Stocks	250	
Debtors	728	
Cash at bank and in hand	15	
	993	
CREDITORS: Amounts falling due within one year[4]	585	
NET CURRENT ASSETS		408
		590

CAPITAL AND RESERVES

Issued share capital	200
Profit and loss account (350 + 40)	390
	590

Working notes to the profit and loss account and balance sheet

1   Cost of sales

	£
Opening stock	150
Depreciation[2] (see calculation in note 2 below)	18
Purchases	470
	638
Closing stock	250
	388

2   Depreciation

	Total	Cost of sales 60%	Dist'n 20%	Admin 20%
Buildings	5	3	1	1
Plant	25	15	5	5
Total	30	18	6	6

3   Tangible fixed assets

	Land and Buildings £000	Plant and Machinery £000	Total £000
At Cost	210	125	335
Dep'n b/f	48	75	123
Charges	5	25	30
Total	53	100	153
Net book value	157	25	182

4   Creditors: amounts falling due within one year

Trade Creditors	60
Accruals	90
Tax payable	135
Dividends payable	300
	585

3.9   Task 1: Journal

	Debit £	Credit £
Interest payable	10,000	
Accruals		10,000
Payments in Advance	12,200	
Administration		12,200
Distribution Costs	21,300	
Accruals		21,300

Increase in provision doubtful debts	2,400	
Provision for Doubtful debts		2,400
Stock – Balance Sheet	340,600	
Stock – Trading Account		340,600
Taxation – Profit & Loss Account	45,000	
Creditors – CT payable		45,000
Dividends – Profit & Loss Account	56,000	
Creditors – Dividends payable		56,000

Task 2: Grandware plc: Profit and Loss Account for the year ended 31 December 20-2

	£
Turnover – continuing operations	2,640,300
Cost of Sales[1]	2,067,500
GROSS PROFIT	572,800
Distribution costs[2]	237,620
Administrative expenses[2]	219,280
OPERATING PROFIT	115,900
Income from fixed asset investments	2,100
Profit on ordinary activities before interest	118,000
Interest payable and similar charges (10,000 +10,000)	20,000
PROFIT ON ORDINARY ACTIVITIES BEFORE TAXATION	98,000
Tax on profit on ordinary activities	45,000
PROFIT ON ORDINARY ACTIVITIES AFTER TAXATION	53,000
Dividends	56,000
RETAINED (LOSS) FOR THE FINANCIAL YEAR	(3,000)

Grandware plc: Balance Sheet as at 31 December 2002

	£	£
FIXED ASSETS		
Tangible Assets (110,060 + 235,000)		345,060
Investments		20,000
		365,060
CURRENT ASSETS		
Stocks	340,600	
Debtors[3]	415,526	
Cash at bank and in hand	20,640	
	776,766	
CREDITORS: Amounts falling due within one year[4]	560,550	

NET CURRENT ASSETS		216,216
		581,276
CREDITORS: Amounts falling due after more than one year		200,000
		381,276
CAPITAL AND RESERVES		
Issued share capital		200,000
Share premium account		40,000
Profit and loss account (144,276 – 3,000)		141,276
		381,276

Working notes to the profit and loss account and balance sheet

		£000
1	**Cost of sales**	
	Opening stock	318,500
	Purchases	2,089,600
		2,408,100
	Closing stock	340,600
		2,067,500
2	**Distribution costs**	
	Distribution	216,320
	Accruals	21,300
		237,620
	Administration	220,180
	Prepaid	(12,200)
	Bad debts	8,900
	Increase in provision for bad debts	2,400
		219,280
3	**Debtors**	
	Trade Debtors 415,800	
	Provision for bad debts	(12,474)
	Prepayments	12,200
		415,526
4	**Creditors: amounts falling due within one year**	
	Trade creditors	428,250
	Accruals (10,000 + 21,300)	31,300
	Corporation tax payable	45,000
	Dividends payable	56,000
		560,550

3.10

Task 1

			£	£
1	DR	Dividend	600	
	CR	Dividend proposed		600

2	DR Stock (balance sheet)	7,878	
	CR Stock (trading account)		7,878
3	DR Taxation	1,920	
	CR Taxation payable		1,920
4	DR Sales	204	
	CR Trade debtors		204
5	DR Interest	240	
	CR Interest payable		240
6	DR Land	500	
	CR Revaluation reserve		500

Workings:

Dividend: £4,000,000 x 15p = £600,000

Interest: £6,000,000 x 8% x $^1/_2$ = £240,000

Revaluation: £5,500,000 − £5,000,000 = £500,000

Task 2

Hightink Limited
Profit and loss account for the year ended 31 March 2002

	£000	£000
Turnover		
Continuing operations (W1)	31,506	
		31,506
Cost of sales (W2)		14,178
Gross profit		17,328
Distribution costs		6,852
Administrative expenses		3,378
Operating profit		
Continuing operations	7,098	
Profit on ordinary activities before interest		7,098
Interest paid and similar charges (W3)		480
Profit on ordinary activities before taxation		6,618
Tax on profit on ordinary activities		1,920
Profit on ordinary activities after taxation		4,698
Dividends (W4)		1,000
Retained profit for the financial year		3,698

Workings:

All figures in £000

W1 Turnover

Sales per TB	31,710
less Credit sales in wrong period	204
	31,506

W2 Cost of sales

Opening stock	6,531
Purchases	15,525
Closing stock	(7,878)
	14,178

W3 Interest paid

Interest per TB	240
Accrued interest	240
	480

W4 Dividends

Final dividend	600
Interim dividend	400
Total dividends	1,000

Hightink Limited
Balance Sheet as at 31 March 2002

	£	£
Fixed assets (W1)		14,105
Current assets		
Stock	7,878	
Debtors	5,251	
Cash	304	
	13,433	
Current liabilities		
Trade creditors	2,363	
Accruals	240	
Dividends	600	
Taxation	1,920	
	5,123	
Net current assets		8,310
Long-term loan		(6,000)
		16,415
CAPITAL AND RESERVES		
Issued share capital		4,000
Share premium		2,000
Revaluation reserve		500
Profit and loss account		9,915
		16,415

Workings:
All figures in £000

W1 Fixed assets

	Cost	Accumulated Depreciation	NBV
Land	5,500	–	*5,500
Buildings	3,832	564	3,268
Fixtures and fittings	2,057	726	1,331
Motor vehicles	3,524	1,283	2,241
Office equipment	2,228	463	1,765
	17,141	3,036	14,105

* Land: 5,000 + 500 = £5,500

3.11

WYVERN OFFICE PRODUCTS LIMITED

Profit and Loss Account for the year ended 31 December 2004

	£000
Turnover	
Continuing operations	10,576
Cost of sales	6,667
Gross profit	3,909
Distribution costs	1,700
Administration expenses	1,411
Operating profit	
Continuing operations	798
Interest payable and similar charges	160
Profit on ordinary activities before taxation	638
Tax on profit on ordinary activities	215
Profit on ordinary activities after taxation	423
Dividends	320
Retained profit for the financial year	103

Balance Sheet as at 31 December 2004

	£000	£000
Fixed assets		
Tangible assets		1,674
Investments		1,850
		3,524
Current assets		
Stock	2,533	
Debtors	1,536	
Cash at bank and in hand	44	
	4,113	
Creditors: amounts falling due within one year	(2,613)	
Net current assets		1,500
Total assets less current liabilities		5,024
Creditors: amounts falling due after more than one year		(1,600)
		3,424
Capital and reserves		
Called up share capital		2,000
Share premium		750
Profit and loss account		674
		3,424

working notes

(All figures £000)

1   Sales (turnover) 10,641 less returns inwards 65 = 10,576

2   Calculation of cost of sales:

Opening stock	2,220
Purchases	7,028
less Returns outwards	48
	9,200
less Closing stock	2,533
Cost of sales	6,667

3   Interest payable:

80 + 80 (half-year's interest on 10% debentures accrued) = 160

4   Dividends:

Interim dividend paid	120
Final dividend proposed	200
	320

5   Fixed Assets:

	Cost	Accumulated depreciation	Net book value
Land	510	–	510
Buildings	1,490	705	785
Fixtures and fittings	275	197	78
Vehicles	316	172	144
Office equipment	294	137	157
	2,885	1,211	1,674

6   Debtors:

Trade debtors	1,592
less Provision for doubtful debts	80
	1,512
Prepayments	24
	1,536

7   Creditors: amounts falling due within one year

Trade creditors	2,051
Corporation tax payable	215
Dividends proposed (see above)	200
Accruals (67 + interest 80)	147
	2,613

8   Profit and loss account:

at 1 Jan 2004	571
Retained profit for the year	103
at 31 Dec 2004	674

CHAPTER 4: ACCOUNTING FOR ASSETS

4.1   (a)

4.2   (b)

4.3   1   (a)   2   (c)

4.4   (b)

4.5   (c)

4.6   (c)

4.7   SSAP4 – *Accounting for Government Grants.*

Many different types of business grant have been obtainable from government departments. Where these relate to revenue expenditure, eg business rates subsidy, they should be credited to the expenses account in the period when it was incurred.

This is based on the fundamental concept of matching.

Where grants relating to capital expenditure are received, then this matching concept is once again observed by crediting the amount over the expected useful life of the asset. This may be achieved in one of two ways:

1   By treating the grant as a deferred credit, a proportion of which is credited to the profit and loss account each year over its anticipated life (in line with depreciation).

2   By crediting the whole of the grant against the actual purchase cost of the asset and then depreciating the net amount over its anticipated lifetime.

For most businesses either of the methods listed above is acceptable, however for Limited Company accounts it is recommended that the first method be used, in accordance with the concept of historic cost accounting whereby the asset is originally recorded at its full purchase cost.

If a company receives a conditional grant where there may be a liability to repay, if not all of the conditions are met, then a formal note to the accounts is required.

4.8   SSAP 13 – *Accounting for research and development.*

SSAP 13 looks at research and development from three perspectives:

- Pure or basic research is experimental or theoretical work undertaken primarily to acquire new scientific or technical knowledge. However, there is no clear commercial end in view and therefore it has no practical application.

- Applied Research is also experimental or theoretical work undertaken primarily to acquire new scientific or technical knowledge, but this has a specific aim and application (eg the effect of baking soda on toothpaste).

- Development expenditure is the use of existing scientific and technical knowledge to produce new or substantially improved products or systems, prior to the commencement of commercial production.

4.9   SSAP 21 – *Accounting for Leases and Hire Purchase contracts.*

SSAP 21 requires that a finance lease (and hire purchase agreement) should be accounted for by the lessee as if it were the purchaser of the asset outright (substance over form). Thus the asset would be capitalised on the balance sheet and then depreciated over its anticipated economic life. Any amounts outstanding on the agreement would be shown as a finance lease creditor, and any interest payments charged, will be transferred to the profit and loss account.

Under an operating lease only the rental will be taken into account by the lessee and these rental charges will be written off and charged to the profit and loss account only.

4.10 FRS 15 and SSAP 19

FRS 15 – *Tangible fixed assets* states that all assets (with the exception of land) have an economic life and are subject to the rigours of depreciation. FRS 15 requires that all tangibles should initially be recorded at cost and some systematic approach to depreciation applied. However the standard also recognises that alternative accounting rules such as revaluation can apply, and so long as revaluation policy is consistent, ie that one asset is revalued, then all assets within that class/category should also be similarly revalued.

If a property is deemed to be an investment property then it falls under the guidelines laid out in SSAP 19 – *Accounting for investment properties*, whereby the asset would not be depreciated each year. Instead the asset would need to be revalued on an annual basis and therefore included in the balance sheet at its current market valuation. Any changes in valuation would then pass to an investment revaluation reserve (or profit and loss account if losses are incurred).

4.11 **Task 1 – losses interpreted to be permanent**

Fixed Assets at cost

		£000			£000
20-0			20-0		
Jan 01	Cost – Castle Hamlets	400	Dec 31	Balance c/d	400
		400			400
20-1			20-1		
Jan 01	Balance b/d	400			
Dec 31	Revaluation	40	Dec 31	Balance c/d	440
		440			440
20-2			20-2		
Jan 01	Balance b/d	440			
Dec 31	Revaluation	20	Dec 31	Balance c/d	460
		460			460
20-3			20-3		
Jan 01	Balance b/d	460	Dec 31	Revaluation (40 + 20)	60
				Profit and loss Account	20
				Balance c/d	380
		460			460
20-4					
Jan 01	Balance b/d	380			

Investment Revaluation Reserve

		£000			£000
20-1			20-1		
Dec 31	Balance c/d	40	Dec 31	Investments	40
20-2			20-2		
			Jan 1	Balance b/d	40
Dec 31	Balance c/d	60	Dec 31	Investments	20
		60			60
			20-3		
Dec 31	Investments	60	Jan 01	Balance b/d	60

Makeshift Enterprises plc

Balance sheet extracts as at 31 December

FIXED ASSETS	20-0	20-1	20-2	20-3
	£000	£000	£000	£000
Investments	400	440	460	380
CAPITAL AND RESERVES				
Investment revaluation				
Reserve		40	60	

Makeshift Enterprises plc

Profit and loss Account for the year ended 31 December

	20-3
	£000
Loss on fixed asset investments	20

Task 2 – if losses interpreted to be temporary

Fixed Assets at cost

20-3		£000	20-3		£000
Jan 01	Balance b/d	460	Dec 31	Revaluation	80
		___	Dec 31	Balance c/d	380
		460			460
20-4					
Jan 01	Balance b/d	380			

Investment Revaluation Reserve

20-3		£000	20-3		£000
Dec 31	Investments	80	Jan 01	Balance b/d	60
		___	Dec 31	Balance c/d	20
		80			80
20-4					
Jan 01	Balance b/ d	20			

Makeshift Enterprises plc

Balance sheet extracts as at 31 December

CAPITAL AND RESERVES	20-1	20-2	20-3
	£000	£000	£000
Investment revaluation			
Reserve	40	60	(20)

4.12 (a) Project Xchem has all the attributes of being research expenditure, as laid down in SSAP 13 accounting for research and development. As a consequence, the costs incurred of £295,000 should be written off and charged to the profit and loss account accordingly.

Chemco Company

Profit and loss account (extract) for the year to 31 December 20-3

	£000
Expenses	
Research and development costs	295

(b) Project Zchem appears to meet all the deferral requirements of SSAP 13 and therefore should be carried forward on this years balance sheet as an intangible asset.

Chemco Company

Balance Sheet (extracts) as at 30 December 20-3

	£000
Fixed Assets	
Intangibles – development costs	435

According to SSAP 13 any deferred development should be written off over a reasonable period and the years 20-4 to 20-8 (five years) seem most appropriate as no competition can enter the market during that time. This means that with the straight line method of amortisation £87,000 (£435,000÷5) will be transferred to the profit and loss account each year, until it is totally written off the balance sheet altogether by the end of 20-8.

4.13 FRS10 – *Goodwill and intangible assets.*

Task 1

Definition of goodwill: the difference between the value of a business as a whole and the aggregate of the fair values of its separable net assets.

Task 2

There are many factors which make up goodwill. Examples include:
- Skilled management team
- Skilled workforce
- Good employer and employee working relations
- Contacts with customers
- Contacts with suppliers
- Strategic location
- Business reputation
- Technical know-how and experience
- Possession of favourable contracts
- Possession of patents, logo's etc.

Any five of the above (or similar) are acceptable.

Task 3

It is usual for the value of a business as a going concern to differ from the aggregate value of its separable net assets. The difference, which can be positive or negative, is described as goodwill. Therefore goodwill is an asset which cannot be realised separately from the business as a whole.

The factors which lead to goodwill, are said to be intangible and it is difficult to place a monetary value on them. For this reason it is not usual to show goodwill as an asset on the balance sheet, unless one business acquires another as a going concern. In such circumstances this is known as purchased goodwill as it has been evidenced by a purchase transaction. Where goodwill is presumed to exist, but no purchase transaction has been undertaken to effect this, it is called non-purchased or inherent goodwill.

Provisions of FRS10:

- Both positive purchased goodwill and purchased intangible assets should initially be capitalised and classed as an asset at cost.

- Inherent or non-purchased goodwill should not be capitalised.

- When intangible assets are acquired as part of a take-over they should be capitalised separately from goodwill if their fair value can be reliably measured. If this is not possible, then they should be subsumed into goodwill.

- If negative goodwill arises, this should be shown on the balance sheet separately and directly underneath any positive goodwill.

- Goodwill and intangible assets should be amortised on a systematic basis over their useful economic lives. If this is considered to be infinite then no amortisation is required.

- The standard presumes that intangibles and goodwill have a life of less than 20 years but accepts that this could be argued against. It is the responsibility of each reporting entity to review the anticipated economic life annually (annual impairment review).

4.14 (a) Development costs may be deferred to future periods if the following criteria given by SSAP 13 are met:
- there is a clearly defined project
- expenditure can be separately identified
- outcome of the project can be assessed with reasonable certainty
- costs will be more than covered by future revenue
- adequate resources exist to complete project

It appears as though the company has considered these criteria and that a case for deferral can be made. The costs will be carried forward in the balance sheet until the project commences commercial production. The costs will then be amortised over the life of the project.

(b) Although the selling of the stock is an event which happened after the year end, under SSAP 17 this is an example of an adjusting event. Adjusting events are 'post balance sheet events which provide additional evidence of conditions existing at the balance sheet date.' The sale of the stock provides evidence as the net realisable value of the stock reported in the financial statements for the year under review. Under SSAP 9, stock is to be valued at the lower of cost and net realisable value.

4.15 **1** (a) The Companies Act 1985 states that historical cost principles constitute the normal basis for preparing financial statements. However, alternative bases are allowed for revaluation of assets.

(b) If the alternative basis was used the land and buildings would be shown in the balance sheet at their valuation of land £641,000 and buildings £558,000. The difference between NRV and valuation would be credited to a 'revaluation reserve' which would form part of the capital and reserves of the company.

(c)   Revaluation would improve gearing. The lower gearing would make the company look less risky from the point of view of the bank and thus they may be more willing to lend the company the money to finance the acquisition. However, the fact that the gearing is already fairly low, it may not make too much difference to the bank's attitude.

(d)   Future results would be affected because depreciation on the buildings would be calculated on the revalued amount and not on the basis of the original cost.

2   The investment is a current asset, as it was purchased for resale, and, in accordance with the concept of prudence, should be shown at the lower purchase price and net realisable value. The prudence concept says that profits should not be anticipated but foreseeable losses provided for. As we can foresee a loss on the sale of the investment it should be shown at its realisable value of £56,000.

3   SSAP 9 states that stocks should be shown at the lower of cost and net realisable value (NRV). NRV is the expected selling price less any costs of getting them into a saleable condition and selling costs. If NRV is less than cost then, given the prudence concept that requires losses to be provided for as soon as they become probable, the stock should be reduced to NRV. The comparison of cost and NRV should be done for separate items of stock or groups of similar items and not on the total of all stocks. Applying this policy would lead us to value the undervalued items at cost of £340,000 and the overvalued items at the sales price of £15,000. The effect of this is to reduce the value of stock overall from the £365,000 in the accounts to £355,000.

CHAPTER 5: ACCOUNTING FOR LIABILITIES AND PROFIT AND LOSS ACCOUNT

5.1   (d)

5.2   (a)

5.3   (d)

5.4   (b)

5.5   (d)

5.6   Quite often there will be events occurring after the balance sheet date which will provide new evidence about the value of assets and liabilities at that time. Changes can be made to these valuations up until the time the board of directors formally approve the financial statements. After this time it becomes impossible to alter them.

SSAP17 – *Accounting for post balance sheet events*, identifies adjusting and non-adjusting events.

Adjusting events relate directly to something that existed at the balance sheet date. If material, changes should be made to the amounts shown in the financial statements. Examples of adjusting events include:

–   fixed assets – where the purchase price, or sale price, of assets bought or sold before the year-end is fixed after the year-end

–   property, where a subsequent valuation shows a permanent fall in value

Non-adjusting events arise after the balance sheet date and have no direct link with the conditions that existed at the balance sheet date. No adjustment is made to the financial statements; instead changes are disclosed by way of notes in order to ensure that the financial statements are not misleading. Examples of non-adjusting events include:

– mergers and acquisitions

– issue of shares and debentures

5.7 These are uncertainties that must be accounted for consistently in financial statements, if user groups are to achieve a full understanding. FRS 12 – *Provisions, Contingent liabilities and Contingent assets* aims to ensure that appropriate recognition and measurement is applied to provisions, contingent liabilities and contingent assets, and that sufficient information is disclosed in the notes to the accounts, to enable users to understand their nature, timing and amount.

FRS12 states that a **provision** should be recognised as a liability in the accounts when:

• an entity has an obligation as a result of a past event
• it is probable (more then 50% likely) that a transfer of economic benefits will be required to settle the obligation (eg cash)
• a reliable estimate can be made of the obligation

The amount of a provision is recorded as an overhead in profit and loss account, and a liability is shown on the balance sheet (under the heading 'provisions for liabilities and charges').

Disclosure in the notes to the financial statements requires:

• details of changes in the amount of provisions between the beginning and end of the year
• a description of the provision(s) and expected timings of any resulting transfers
• an indication of the uncertainties regarding the amount or timing of any resulting transfers

A **contingent liability** is a possible obligation, ie there less than 50% likelihood of its occurrence.

A contingent liability is not recorded in the financial statements but should be disclosed as a note which includes:

• a brief description of the nature of the contingent liability
• an estimate of its financial effect
• an indication of the uncertainties relating to the amount or timing of any outflow
• the possibility of any re-imbursement

Thus in summary:

Provision = Probable = more than 50% likely.

Contingent liability = Possible = less than 50% likely.

5.8 FRS 3 – *Reporting Financial performance*, introduced a new accounting statement, that of the statement of total recognised gains and losses to expand upon the financial information required in the published accounts.

The statement of recognised gains and losses brings together the realised profits of the business, as shown in the profit and loss account, together with other unrealised gains and losses, which tend to pass exclusively through the balance sheet.

A good example of this is the revaluation of land and property, which may increase the value of the fixed asset in the balance sheet which is recognised by the transfer to a revaluation reserve which appears as part of shareholders funds also in the balance sheet.

5.9   Segmental accounting requires that information relating to the accounts should be broken down (segmented) in two principal ways – by class of business and by geographical location.

SSAP 25 requires that, where a business has two or more classes of business, or operates in two or more geographical segments, it should disclose for each class of business and geographical segment:

- turnover
- profit
- net assets

5.10   FRS 17 – *Retirement benefits* identifies two schemes:

A **defined contribution scheme** – here the amount of pension payable to the employee cannot be guaranteed, as it will depend upon how wisely and effectively the pension fund has been invested.

A **defined benefit scheme** – here the amount of pension payable to the employee is guaranteed and predetermined and is usually based upon the employee's salary immediately prior to retirement and the number of years' service.

5.11   SSAP20 – *Foreign Currency translation* deals with the expression of foreign currency amounts in the accounts. There are two terms relating to the valuing of foreign currency amounts:

- **Conversion**, which is the process of exchanging amounts of one foreign currency for another.
- **Translation**, which is required at the end of an accounting period, when a company still holds assets and liabilities in its balance sheet which were obtained or incurred in a foreign currency.

    Two different methods of 'translation' valuation can be used:

    - a 'temporal' method based on historic cost.

    - a 'closing rate' method based on the exchange rate at the year-end

CHAPTER 6: CASH FLOW STATEMENTS

6.1   (c)

6.2   (d)

6.3   (b)

6.4   (a)

6.5   (d)

6.6 Advantages of producing a cash flow statement:

(a) Cash is said to be the life blood of any business, and the survival of a company will depend on its ability to generate sufficient cash in order to fund its activities and meet its day-to-day obligations.

(b) The level of cash is an important indicator of business performance.

(c) Users of financial statements can easily identify with cash (often more so than profit) and employees may look at the level of cash when negotiating the next pay award.

(d) Cash flow accounting can be used to compare business performance against previous periods or against other companies. Cash flow forecasting can also assume a role in the budgeting process, by reviewing past performance and as a planning tool for future growth.

6.7

CASHEDIN LIMITED

CASH FLOW STATEMENT FOR THE YEAR ENDED 30 SEPTEMBER 20-5

	£'000	£'000
Net cash inflow from operating activities		
Returns on investments and servicing of finance		104
Interest paid		(218)
Taxation		(75)
		(189)
Capital expenditure		
Payments to acquire tangible fixed assets	(358)	
Proceeds from sale of fixed assets	132	
		(226)
		(415)
Equity dividends paid		(280)
		(695)
Financing		
Loans	200	
Issue of ordinary share capital	150	
		350
Decrease in cash		(345)

Reconciliation of operating profit and net cash inflow from operating activities

	£'000
Operating profit	24
Depreciation	318
Increase in stock	(251)
Increase in debtors	(152)
Increase in creditors	165
Net cash inflow from operating activities	104

6.8 **Radion plc**

Reconciliation of operating profit to net cash flow from operating activities for the year ended 31 December 20-3

		£000
Operating profit		104
Depreciation		30
Increase in stock	(203–175)	(28)
Increase in debtors	(141–127)	(14)
Increase in creditors (142–118)		24
NET CASH FLOW FROM OPERATING ACTIVITIES		116

6.9 **Pratt plc**

Task 1: Reconciliation of operating profit to net cash flow from operating activities

	£000
Operating profit	2,520
Depreciation[1]	318
Loss on disposal of tangible fixed assets[2]	3
Increase in stock (84–69)	(15)
Decrease in debtors (270–255)	15
Increase in creditors (108–81)	27
Net cash flow from operating activities	2,868

Task 2: Cash Flow Statement: Pratt plc
Year ending 31 October 20-3.

		£000
Net cash flow from operating activities		2,868
Returns on investments and servicing of finance		
Interest paid		(168)
Taxation[3]		(429)
Capital expenditure		
Payments to acquire tangible fixed assets[4]	(629)	
Receipts from the sale of tangible fixed assets	8	(621)
		1,650
Equity dividends paid [5]		(459)
		1,191
Management of liquid resources		
Financing		
Issue of shares[6]	627	
Repayment of loans	(1,800)	(1,173)
Net increase/(decrease) in cash		18

Working notes

1

		Depreciation charges			
20-3		£000	20-2		£000
Oct 31	Disposal	18	Nov 01	Balance b/d	1,500
Oct 31	Balance c/d	1,800	20-3		
			Oct 31	P/L account (bal fig)	318
		1,818			1,818
			20-3		
			Nov 01	Balance b/d	1,800

2

		Vehicle disposals			
20-3		£000	20-3		£000
Oct 31	At cost	29	Oct 31	Accum depreciation	18
			Oct 31	Sale proceeds	8
			Oct 31	P/L account (bal fig)	3*
		29			29

* Denotes a loss on sale

3

		Taxation			
20-3		£000	20-2		£000
Oct 31	Paid (bal fig)	429	Nov 01	Balance b/d	285
Oct 31	Balance c/d	606	Oct 31	P/L account	750
		1,035			1,035
			20-3		
			Nov 01	Balance b/d	606

4

		Tangible Fixed Assets			
20-2		£000	20-3		£000
Nov 01	Balance b/d	8,400	Oct 31	Disposals	29
20-3					
Oct 31	Additions (bal fig)	629	Oct 31	Balance c/d	9,000
		9,029			9,029
20-3					
Nov 01	Balance b/d	9,000			

5

		Equity Dividends paid			
20-3		£000	20-2		£000
Oct 31	Paid (bal fig)	459	Nov 01	Balance b/d	144
			20-3		
Oct 31	Balance c/d	225	Oct 31	P/L account	540
		684			684
			20-3		
			Nov 01	Balance b/d	225

6

	£000
Issue of shares	
Issue of called up shares (3,000–2,550)	450
At a premium	177
Total sales proceeds from issue	627

6.10   Cash Flow Statement: Sadler plc
Year ended 30 June 20-3

		£000
Net cash flow from operating activities		2,880
Returns on investments and servicing of finance		
Interest paid		(100)
Taxation[3]		(300)
Capital expenditure		
Payments to acquire tangible fixed assets[4]	(4,300)	
Receipts from the sale of tangible fixed assets	1,400	(2,900)
		(420)
Equity dividends paid[5]		(600)
		(1,020)
Management of liquid resources		
Financing		
Issue of debenture stock		1,000
Net increase/(decrease) in cash		(20)

Sadler plc
Formal notes to cash flow statements
Note: these are not the working notes (which follow on the next page).

Note 1: Reconciliation of operating profit to net cash flow from operating activities

	£000
Operating profit	1,100
Depreciation[1]	1,900
Profit on disposal of tangible fixed assets[2]	(200)
Increase in stock (340–300)	(40)
Increase in debtors (1,300–1,200)	(100)
Increase in creditors (800–600)	140
Decrease in prepayments (100–80)	20
Increase in accruals (120–60)	60
Net cash flow from operating activities	2,880

Note 2: Reconciliation of net cash flow to movement in net debt

	£000
Net cash inflow (outflow) for the period	(20)
Cash received / paid from loans	(1,000)
Change in net debt	(1,020)
Net debt at start of year	40
Net debt at the end of the year	(980)

Note 3: Analysis of changes in net debt

	At start Of year £000	Cash Flow £000	At end of year £000
Cash in hand	40	(20)	20
Loans etc		(1,000)	(1,000)
Total	40	(1,020)	(980)

Working notes

1

Depreciation charges

20-3		£000	20-2		£000
Jun 30	Disposal	400	Jul 01	Balance b/d	8,160
Jun 30	Balance c/d	9,660	20-3		
			Jun 30	P/L account (bal fig)	1,900
		10,060			10,060
			20-3		
			Jul 01	Balance b/d	9,660

2

Machinery Disposals

20-3		£000	20-3		£000
Jun 30	At cost	1,600	Jun 30	Accum depreciation	400
			Jun 30	Sale proceeds	1,400
Jun 30	P/L account (bal fig)*	200			
		1,800			1,800

Denotes a Profit on sale

3

Taxation

20-3		£000	20-2		£000
Jun 30	Paid (bal fig)	300	Jul 01	Balance b/d	360
			20-3		
Jun 30	Balance c/d	260	Jun 30	P/L account	200
		560			560
			20-3		
			Jul 01	Balance b/d	260

4

Tangible Fixed Assets

20-2		£000	20-3		£000
Jul 01	Balance b/d	13,600	Jun 30	Disposals	1,600
20-3			Jun 30	Balance c/d	16,300
Jun 30	Additions (bal fig)	4,300			
		17,900			17,900
20-3					
Jul 01	Balance b/d	16,300			

5

Equity Dividends paid

20-3		£000	20-2		£000
Jun 30	Paid (bal fig)	600	Jul 01	Balance b/d	400
			20-3		
Jun 30	Balance c/d	200	Jun 30	P/L account	400
		800			800
			20-3		
			Jul 01	Balance b/d	200

6.11

GEORGE LIMITED

CASH FLOW STATEMENT FOR THE YEAR ENDED 31 MARCH 20-5

	£'000	£'000
Net cash inflow from operating activities		350
Returns on investment and servicing of finance		
Interest paid		(20)
Taxation		
Corporation tax paid (20-4)		(21)
Capital expenditure		
Purchase of fixed asset	(110)	
Receipts from sale of fixed asset[1]	7	
		(103)
		206
Equity dividends paid		(30)
		176
Financing		
Issue of ordinary share capital (40 – 25)	15	
Long term loan (200 – 100)	100	
Redemption of debentures	(500)	
Net cash outflow from financing		(385)
Decrease in cash		(209)

Reconciliation of operating profit to net cash flow from operating activities

	£'000
Operating profit	237
Depreciation	275
Profit on sales of fixed assets	(2)
Increase in stocks (210 – 200)	(10)
Increase in debtors (390 – 250)	(140)
Decrease in creditors (150 – 160)	(10)
Net cash inflow from operating activities	350

Working note

1   Receipts from sale of fixed assets

Disposals of fixed assets

	£		£
Fixed assets (cost)	10,000	Accumulated depreciation	5,000
Profit on sale	2,000	Proceeds (bal fig)	7,000
	12,000		12,000

CHAPTER 7: INTERPRETATION OF FINANCIAL STATEMENTS

7.1   (d)

7.2   (c)

7.3   (d)

7.4   (a)

7.5   1   (b)
        2   (d)
        3   (a)
        4   (a)
        5   (c)

7.6   Task 1

		Hanadi PLC	Abeer PLC
(a)	Gross Profit %		
	$\frac{\text{Gross Profit} \times 100}{\text{Sales}}$	$\frac{250}{350} \times 100 = 71\%$	$\frac{200}{300} \times 100 = 67\%$
(b)	Net Profit %		
	$\frac{\text{Net Profit before tax} \times 100}{\text{Sales}}$	$\frac{150}{350} \times 100 = 43\%$	$\frac{150}{300} \times 100 = 50\%$
(c)	ROCE		
	$\frac{\text{Net Profit before tax} \times 100}{\text{Capital Employed}}$	$\frac{150}{470} \times 100 = 32\%$	$\frac{150}{350} \times 100 = 43\%$
(d)	Current Ratio		
	$\frac{\text{Current Assets}}{\text{Current Liabilities}}$	$\frac{220}{215} = 1{:}1$	$\frac{160}{135} = 1.2{:}1$

(e)   Acid Test Ratio

$$\frac{\text{Current Assets} - \text{Stock}}{\text{Current Liabilities}} \qquad \frac{220 - 110}{215} = 0.5:1 \qquad \frac{160 - 70}{135} = 0.7:1$$

Task 2

	Hanadi PLC	**Abeer PLC**
Gross Profit	Better performance More sales at a higher margin	
Net Profit		Better performance More control over costs and expenses
ROCE		Both results are good but Abeer has a higher return; it is utilising its capital far more effectively than Hanadi.
Current Ratio		Both are on the low side but Abeer has a better margin from which to pay off debt.
Acid Test Ratio		Again both are on the low side but Abeer has more cash in the business to pay off short-term debt whereas Hanadi appears to have too much cash tied up in stock.

Conclusion: Abeer PLC is more attractive than Hanadi PLC from an investment point of view.

7.7   Accounting ratios need to be analysed and interpreted and not just listed as sets of numbers. Ideally they need to be compared with the previous year's figures and wherever possible, with similar companies to evaluate and highlight trends.

But there are dangers in relying on the numbers without first looking behind the figures:

1   Financial statements present only an overall picture of the company, and the balance sheet is only a snapshot of the company at a particular moment in time. The balance sheet may not actually be representative of the company as a whole, eg the accounting year-end of a business with seasonal trade is typically timed for when the business is least busy.

2   The problem with accounting policy is no more evident than with ratio analysis. Depreciation and stock valuation, for example, involve different methods of valuation and the choice of method can lead to distortion in comparative figures.

3   Larger businesses frequently aggregate operations and this can make comparison of individual areas of activity difficult.

4   Comparisons can be difficult between a company which finances fixed assets by renting them (thus showing the rental as an expense with no asset on the balance sheet) and a company which purchases its assets outright and then depreciates them over the anticipated working life.

5   Ratios should be open to interpretation, as what is good for one company may not be suitable for another. For example it is generally accepted than the ideal current ratio is 2:1. However retailers such as supermarkets can in fact work on a much lower margin because of rapid stock turnover and their predominantly cash sale base (ie few debtors).

6   Whilst in principle inter-firm comparisons are very worthwhile, there may be considerable differences between companies in the same industry. They may, for example, vary in size and in application of accounting policies.

In conclusion, ratios are a very useful way of investigating the performance of a company over a number of years or comparing one company with a similar one. However ratios cannot be relied upon as the absolute answer and should not be used as absolute standards of performance. Care and consideration needs to be given to points 1-6 above.

7.8

REPORT

To: Jake Matease

From: A Student

Subject: Interpretation of financial statements

Date: December 2001

This report has been prepared to assist in the interpretation of the financial statements of Fauve Limited. It considers the profitability and return on capital of the business for 2000 and 2001.

(a)   Calculation of the ratios

	2001		2000	
Return on capital employed	$\dfrac{1,251}{8,430}$ = 14.8%		$\dfrac{624}{5,405}$ = 11.5%	
Net profit percentage	$\dfrac{1,251}{4,315}$ = 29%		$\dfrac{624}{2,973}$ = 21%	
Gross profit percentage	$\dfrac{2,805}{4,315}$ = 65%		$\dfrac{1,784}{2,973}$ = 60%	
Asset turnover	$\dfrac{4,315}{8,430}$ = 0.51		$\dfrac{2,973}{5,405}$ = 0.55	

(b)   Explanation and comment

Return on capital employed

- This ratio shows in percentage terms how much profit is being generated by the capital employed in the company.

- The company is showing a higher return on capital employed in 2001 compared to 2000 and hence is generating more profit per £ of capital employed in the company.

Net profit percentage

- This ratio shows in percentage terms how much net profit is being generated from sales.

- The ratio has increased over the two years.
- This could be explained either by an increase in the sales margins or by a decrease in expenses, or both.
- It is also the case that the percentage of expenses to sales has decreased from 39% in 2000 to 36% in 2001.

Gross profit ratio

- This ratio shows in percentage terms how much gross profit is being generated by the sales of the company and thus indicates the gross profit margin on sales.
- The ratio has improved over the two years with an increase in the percentage from 60% to 65%.
- The company is increasing its sales without significantly cutting its margins.
- This may be due to increasing its sales price or reducing the cost of sales or both.

Asset turnover

- This ratio shows how efficient the company is in generating sales from the available capital employed/net assets.
- The ratio has deteriorated between the two years and less sales are generated from the available capital employed/net assets in 2001 than in 2000.
- Considerable new investment has been made in fixed assets and current assets in 2001 and it may be that the investment has yet to yield the expected results.

(c)   Overall

The ratios show that the return on capital employed has improved in 2001 and that the company is generating more profit from the capital employed/net assets. This is due to increased margins and to greater control over expenses, perhaps brought about by economies of scale. However, the efficiency in the use of assets has deteriorated in 2001 and this has reduced the increase in return on capital employed. It may be that the increased investment in assets that has taken place in 2001 has yet to yield benefits in terms of a proportionate increase in sales and that the situation will improve when the assets are used to their full potential.

Regards,

AAT Student

7.9

	Company A		*Company B*	
Return on capital employed	$\dfrac{200}{1000}$	= 20%	$\dfrac{420}{2800}$	= 15%
Net profit margin	$\dfrac{200}{800}$	= 25%	$\dfrac{420}{2100}$	= 20%
Asset turnover	$\dfrac{800}{600}$	= 1.33:1	$\dfrac{2100}{1700}$	= 1.24:1

Other possible ratios:

Gross profit margin $\quad \dfrac{360}{800} = 45\% \qquad\qquad \dfrac{1050}{2100} = 50\%$

Expenses: Sales $\quad \dfrac{160}{800} = 20\% \qquad\qquad \dfrac{630}{2100} = 30\%$

From the calculations we can see that Company A has both the highest return on capital employed and also the highest profit margin and asset turnover. It would, therefore, be the better company to target for takeover. However, the gross profit margin for Company B is, in fact, higher suggesting that the underlying business is more profitable. It is only because of the expenses of Company B in relation to sales that it has a lower net profit margin. If Company B could be made more efficient in terms of expenses and utilisation of assets by the introduction of a new management team on takeover, then, given the more profitably underlying business, it might be worth considering as a target for takeover.

7.10

REPORT

To: **Finance Director, Rowan Healthcare plc**
From: **AAT Student**
Date: **3 December 20-8**
Re: **Analysis of Patch Ltd's financial statements**

Introduction

The purpose of the report is to analyse the financial statements of Patch Ltd for 20-8 and 20-7 to determine whether to use the company as a supplier.

Calculation of Ratios

The following ratios for the company have been computed:

	20-8	Industry Average 20-8	20-7	Industry Average 20-7
Return on capital employed	$\dfrac{552}{5,334} = 10.3\%$	9.6%	$\dfrac{462}{5,790} = 8.0\%$	9.4%
Net profit percentage	$\dfrac{552}{2,300} = 24\%$	21.4%	$\dfrac{462}{2,100} = 22\%$	21.3%
Quick ratio/acid test	$\dfrac{523}{475} = 1.1{:}1$	1.0:1	$\dfrac{418}{465} = 0.9{:}1$	0.9:1
Gearing: Debt/Capital employed	$\dfrac{1,654}{5,334} = 31\%$	36%	$\dfrac{2,490}{5,790} = 43\%$	37%
or Debt/Equity	$\dfrac{1,654}{3,680} = 45\%$		$\dfrac{2,490}{3,300} = 75\%$	

Comment and Analysis

The overall profitability of the company has improved from 20-7 to 20-8. The return on capital employed has increased from 8% in 20-7 to 10.3% in 20-8. This means that the company is generating more profit from the available capital employed in 20-8 as compared with 20-7. The company was below average for the industry in 20-7, but has performed better than the average in 20-8. The net profit percentage has also improved. It increased from 22% in 20-7 to 24% in 20-8. This means that the company is generating more profit from sales in 20-8 than in the previous year. In both years the company had a higher than average net profit percentage when compared against the industry average. From these ratios it would seem that the company is relatively more profitable in 20-8 as compared with 20-7 and that it now performs better than the average of the industry. This suggests that its long-term prospects for success are higher than the average of the industry.

The liquidity of the company has also improved in the year. The quick ratio shows how many current assets, excluding stock, there are to meet the current liabilities and is often thought of as a better indicator of liquidity than the current ratio. The quick ratio in Patch Ltd has improved from 20-7 to 20-8. It has gone up from 0.9:1 to 1.1:1. This means that in 20-8 there were more than enough quick assets to meet current liabilities. Again, the quick ratio of Patch Ltd is better than the industry average in 20-8, and matched it in 20-7. We can conclude that Patch Ltd is more liquid than the average of the industry in 20-8.

There has been a considerable decline in the gearing of the company in 20-8 as compared with 20-7. In 20-7 the gearing ratio was 43% and this has fallen to 31% in 20-8. This means that the percentage of debt funding to equity funding has declined between the two years. High gearing ratios are often thought of as increasing the risk of the company in that, in times of profit decline, it becomes increasingly difficult for highly geared companies to meet interest payments on debt, and in extreme cases the company could be forced into liquidation. The gearing ratio of Patch Ltd was above the industry average in 20-7, making it relatively more risky, in this respect, than the average of companies in the industry. However, the ratio in 20-8 is considerably less than the industry average and hence may now be considered less risky than the average. There is thus less of a risk from gearing in doing business with the company than the average of companies in the sector.

Conclusions

Overall, based solely on the information provided in the financial statements of the company, it is recommended that Rowan Healthcare should use Patch Ltd as a supplier. The company has increasing profitability and liquidity and a lower level of gearing in 20-8 than in 20-7. It also compares favourably with other companies in the same industry and seems to present a lower risk than the average of the sector.

CHAPTER 8: CONSOLIDATED ACCOUNTS

8.1   (b)

8.2   (c)

8.3   (a)

8.4   (b)

8.5   (b)

8.6   (d)

8.7   (b)

8.8 According to FRS 2 the following conditions are required for a parent/subsidiary relationship:

- The parent undertaking holds a majority of the voting rights in the subsidiary company.

- The parent company is a member of the subsidiary and therefore has the right to have a vote to remove or appoint its directors.

- The parent company can exercise a dominant influence over the subsidiary company:
  - through the contents and provisions of the subsidiary company's memorandum and articles of association, *or*
  - by virtue of a control contract

- The parent undertaking is a member (shareholder) of the subsidiary undertaking and it is the sole controller of that company due to an agreement with all the other members, which constitutes it a majority holder of the voting rights in that company.

- The parent company has a participating interest in the subsidiary and therefore can:
  - exert a dominant influence *or*
  - the parent and subsidiary are managed on a unified basis

- A parent undertaking can be treated as a parent company if its subsidiary also has a subsidiary. By definition the third company (sub-subsidiary) is also a subsidiary of the original parent company.

8.9 Phantom plc

Calculation for Goodwill	Total Equity
	£000
Shares	800
Share Premium account	200
Revaluation reserve	700
Profit and Loss Account	1,750
	3,450
Group share 80% x £3,450	2,760
Total purchase consideration	2,900
Goodwill on acquisition	140
Minority interest 20% x £3,450	690

8.10 Ringer plc

Consolidated Balance Sheet as at 30 April 20-3.

	£000	£000
Fixed Assets		
Intangibles	620	
Tangibles (6,000 + 1,900)	7,900	
		8,520
Current Assets		
Stocks (1,900 + 800)	2,700	
Debtors (1,500 + 500)	2,000	

Cash at bank (600 + 100)	700	
	5,400	

Creditors: amounts falling due within one year.

Creditors (1,500 + 400)	1,900	
Taxation (400 + 100)	500	
Dividends	1,000	
	3,400	
Net Current Assets		2,000
		10,520

Creditors: amounts falling due within one year

Long-term loans		2,500
		8,020

Capital and reserves

Called up share capital		2,000
Share premium account		1,000
Profit and loss account		4,100
Shareholders funds		7,100
Minority interest (40% x 2,300)		920
		8,020

Working notes

Ringer holding in Sterling	=	$\dfrac{600,000}{1,000,000}$	x 100	=	60%
Minority interest	=	$\dfrac{400,000}{1,000,000}$	x 100	=	40%

Revaluation	Debit Fixed Assets	£300,000
	Credit Revaluation reserve	£300,000

Goodwill

	Total	*Group*	*Minority*
	100%	*60%*	*40%*
	£000	*£000*	*£000*
Shares	1,000	600	400
Share premium	500	300	200
Revaluation	300	180	120
P/L A/C	500	300	200
Total	2,300	1,380	920
Cost of investment		2,000	
Goodwill		620	

8.11 **Consolidated profit and Loss Account**

	£000
Profit before taxation (25% x £420K)	105
Taxation (25% x £120K)	30

Consolidated Balance Sheet

Share of net assets (25% x 1,000K)	250
Purchased goodwill	145
	395
Share of post acquisition profits (25% x 300)	75

Working Note: Purchased Goodwill

	£000
Share of net assets at acquisition (1,000K – 300K = 700K x 25%)	175
Cost of investment	320
Purchased goodwill	145

8.12 **Winston plc**

Consolidated Balance Sheet as at 30 November 20-3

Fixed Assets	£000	£000
Intangibles – Goodwill (495 – 99)	396	
Tangibles (5,000 + 600)	5,600	
		5,996
Current Assets		
Stocks (150 + 30 – 5)	175	
Debtors (80 + 35 – 10)	105	
Cash at bank (10 + 5)	15	
	295	
Creditors: Amounts falling due within one Year.		
Creditors (160 + 120 – 10)	270	
Net Current Assets		25
		6,021
Capital and reserves		
Called up share capital		4,000
Profit and loss account (1,980 + 90 – 5 – 396)		1,966
Shareholders funds		5,966
Minority interest (10% x 550)		55
		6,021

Working notes:

■ Winston **holding** in Churchill = $\frac{360,000 \times 100}{400,000}$ = 90%

■ **Minority interest** = $\frac{40,000 \times 100}{400,000}$ = 10%

■ **Goodwill**

	Total 100% £000	Group 90% £000	Minority 10% £000
Shares	400	360	40
Profit and Loss Account	50	45	5
Total	450	405	45

Cost of investment		900
Goodwill		495

Amortised 20-2 and 20-3, ie 2 years

£495,000÷10 years = £49,500 per annum

2 years x £49,500 = £99,000 written off

■ **Consolidated reserves**

Holding Co P/L Account	1,980	
Post acquisition profit	90	(£150,000 – £50,000 x 90%)
Unrealised stock	(5)	
Goodwill Amortised	(99)	
	1,966	

■ **Minority Interest**

Shares	40	(£400,000 x 10%)
Profit and Loss Account	15	(£150,000 x 10%)
	55	

8.13   **TOM LIMITED AND SUBSIDIARIES**

Consolidated Profit and Loss Account for the year ended 31 December 20-2

		£000
Group turnover	800 + 400 + 300 − 20 − 80	1,400
Cost of sales*		890
Gross profit		510
Distribution costs	80 + 50 + 20	150
Administrative expenses	100 + 30 + 20	150
Group operating profit		210
Interest receivable/payable		−
Profit on ordinary activities before tax		210
Tax on profit on ordinary activities		68
Profit on ordinary activities after tax		142
Minority interests	32 x 25%	8
Profit on ordinary activities after tax and minority interests		134
Dividends		100
Retained profit for group		34

			£000
*	cost of sales:		
	opening stock	200 + 150 + 100	450
	+ purchases	600 + 300 + 200 − 20 − 80	1,000
	− closing stock	300 + 200 + 80 − 20 (unrealised profit)	560
			890

8.14

PERRAN PLC

Consolidated Profit and Loss Account for the year ended 31 March 2004

	£000
Turnover	45,900
Cost of sales	23,090
Gross profit	22,810
Distribution costs	6,945
Administration expenses	4,745
Profit on ordinary activities before interest	11,120
Interest payable	2,020
Profit on ordinary activities before taxation	9,100
Tax on profit on ordinary activities	2,480
Profit on ordinary activities after taxation	6,620
Minority interests	520
Profit for the financial year	6,100
Dividends	2,500
Retained profit for the financial year	3,600

Workings

All figures £000

- Turnover:

	£
Perran sales	36,450
Porth sales	10,200
Less inter-company sale	(750)
	45,900

- Cost of sales:

Perran cost of sales	18,210
Porth cost of sales	5,630
Less inter-company purchase	(750)
	23,090

- Minority interests: 25% x £2,080   =   £520

Index of UK accounting standards

* note that, for *Drafting Financial Statements,* FRS 13 is not assessed

Index of international accounting standards

* please see www.iasb.org.uk for details of these standards

Text index